COUNTRYGOER IN THE DALES

By the same author
  Three Rivers
  Off to the Lakes
  Off to the Dales
  Lancashire Landscapes
  Lancashire's Fair Face
  Lancashire—Westmorland Highway
  The Curious Traveller Through Lakeland
  West Pennine Highway
  The Curious Traveller: Lancaster to Lakeland
  Lancashire Countrygoer
  Portrait of Lancashire
  Countrygoers' North
  North Wales for the Countrygoer
  Lancashire's Old Families

Countrygoer
in the Dales

JESSICA LOFTHOUSE

Illustrations by the Author

LONDON
ROBERT HALE & COMPANY

© Jessica Lofthouse 1964
First published in Great Britain April 1964
Reprinted April 1964
Reprinted (with revisions) August 1973
Reprinted September 1975

ISBN 0 7091 3955 1

Robert Hale & Company
Clerkenwell House
Clerkenwell Green
London EC1R oHT

PRINTED IN GREAT BRITAIN BY
CLARKE, DOBLE AND BRENDON LTD.
PLYMOUTH

Contents

CONTENTS

Illustrations

Fell crossing between Ure and Swale

Foreword

Rich Heritage

THIS BOOK LIKE its forerunner and companion *Lancashire Country-goer* is written for the 'walking motorist'—that is for the car owner who still possesses and uses his walking legs, and for walkers who use the local buses 'to get them there'.

I doubt if this book will arouse the queries from surprised non-northerners which its companion did. "Has Lancashire any country left to go into?" And: "If Lancashire has country worth going into, do Lancashire people ever go into it? Don't they all make a beeline for Blackpool?"

Surely everyone knows the dales—the Pennine dales, the Yorkshire dales—have superlative touring and walking country, the loveliest landscapes, the most beautiful villages, the nicest people?

Or do they? Yorkshire tourist boards are having their doubts. They feel that non-northerners think of a Yorkshire entirely taken up by woollen towns, woollen factories, woollen cloth—plus artificially 'mistified' wildernesses as seen in Brontë films. They want to replace this by a picture more persuasive. In fact a picture we of north-east Lancashire, west Yorkshire and south-west Durham have for generations known and enjoyed. It means, to those who know it, green valleys (unspoilt), winding rivers (unpolluted), miles of moors and fells, blue into infinity (free to the hill walker), welcoming villages (pleased to see strangers of the quiet appreciative kind—

which we trust we are). In the same picture are proud castles in dramatic ruin, ancient abbeys in quiet solitude, and many noble houses 'open to the public'.

This is not only my kind of country, but 'my own, my native' country. Being dalesbred on both sides—paternal grandparents of Nidd, Wharfe and Craven, and maternal wholly Ribblesdale—it was natural that any bias should be towards the dales. Long wanderings began when youth hostelling, and what a newfound freedom this proved. *Off to the Dales* was written as outcome of these many journeys dale to dale.

Later farms and cottages opened their doors to us, we stayed at friendly guest houses, at village inns, and in the homes of many new made friends.

I grew to love every corner of the Pennine dales so very close to Lancashire and so quickly reached by the Clitheroe-Hellifield-Ribblehead line—closed, alas, in part—or the Blackburn-Skipton railway. Roaming from dale to dale I began to 'go deeper'—not into the underground world of caves, for having claustrophobia and a dislike of leaving the light of day I would be sure to make a bad show—wondering why each had developed in its own special way though each has much in common, geologically and historically.

Especially historically. I hope the users of this book have a bias towards the history. Nature has wrought wonders in the Pennine country; flower and bird lovers, and those who watch wild life have their own paradises within the dales. But if history localized is your interest then you find the dales bring in every phase of it. Dalesfolk following the castle overlords helped to make not only north country but English history; quite a slice of Scottish history too.

The pattern of history is fascinating; the same threads appear in each dale's tapestry. Take the Ice Age(s). When glaciers scooped out and smoothed down Pennine watersheds and daleheads they made a line of communication for the first wayfarers and for the flow of history. Dales not opened up so conveniently remained cut off from history, which was, more often than not, a blessing. Where the limestone known as Great Scar gave suitable platforms and terraces for human habitation there men of prehistory threw up stockades, earth-works and defences. Iron Age Celts watched the first Roman invaders from formidable hill forts on the gritstone caps of the same hills.

The great military highways of the Romans—roughly coinciding with A1, the Great North Road, and another keeping west of the Pennines—were linked by roads through the same ice-smoothed passes prehistoric traders had travelled. Think of them on A65 in the Aire Gap and on A66 over Stainmore. They had minor roads too making for subsidiary forts; we walk them to Bainbridge, Grassington, Greta Bridge and Rey Cross.

The Romans went, the marauding Angles came. Later waves settled on the best farming land low in the dales; their Ton, Ley and Ham place-names are clues to where they lived.

Danish Vikings who raided the east coast later pushed inland and where they decided to stay the Bys, Thorpes and Wicks are plentiful. A later wave of invaders entered from the Irish Sea estuaries, penetrating from Morcambe Bay and Eden valley towards the high Pennines; many crossed the watershed and settled in the dale head 'outback' of wild fell country, rocky gills and mighty waterfalls; Norse Setts, Sides and Seats are many.

The mixed population suffered as one during the Harrying of the North—William's reprisal for non-co-operation of Yorkshire men after his Conquest. Those who survived had to endure the rule of new overlords, the Norman barons. Their castles remain in the throat of each dale.

In every dale a castle stands. Clitheroe of the De Lacys leads us from Lancashire into country of the Romillys of Skipton. The ancient highway of Blubberhouses takes us into the Barony of Knaresborough where, overlooking the Nidd gorge, was Serlo de Burgh's stronghold, an eagle's aerie of a castle. Where the Ure opens to the plains Middleham Castle stands; its builders were kinsmen of William of Normandy as were the first Lords of Richmond who erected their strongpoint above the Swale. Another leap over the intervening fells to Tees and there is the castle Bernard Ballieul built and which gave a name to the burgh which grew around it.

Norman barons mindful of the hereafter were lavish in gifts to the church. Sons and grandchildren of the friends of the Conqueror founded religious houses or were benefactors of abbeys in their own dales. Skipton lords were founders of Bolton Priory, Knaresborough's aided small abbeys and were benefactors of the monks at Fountains, Middleham's Breton lords and their family were responsible for Coverham Abbey and befriended Jervaulx, a close neighbour. Easby Abbey was hard by Richmond Castle; the great earls did much for Jervaulx and Egglestone Abbeys also. Close to Barnard Castle is Egglestone. The Clitheroe De Lacys founded Whalley Abbey which was a translation from Mersey side at Stanlaw; Henry de Lacy was devoted to good works and after an attempt to settle a band of Cistercians near Barnoldswick helped them to establish themselves on a permanent site at Kirkstall.

A castle and abbey in every dale; and not only those but ancient halls, towers or peles, and great houses which grew out of them.

Castle overlords and great earls who answered only to the king in turn raised to high office men who had loyally served them. These clingers to the third rung down the feudal ladder were often rewarded for service at home and abroad by grants of land. Soon they seized the chance to enlarge humble houses; with royal consent they embattled and crenellated their unprotected halls—extra defence against the Scots!—and as often gave their overlords second thoughts, so high and mighty did they become within their houses vying with the castles in strength and height.

Each dale has examples of such fortified halls. The families who built them sometimes rocketed into royal favour when their lords fell from power. Crucial times for many to rise or fall were after the Wars of the Roses when those who were for the Yorkists were rewarded and Lancastrian followers eclipsed; when Henry VII brought back supporters of the House of Lancaster and down went the men who fought for Edward IV and Richard III; when Henry VIII suitably repaid those who approved of his dissolution of the abbeys by letting them have rich pickings from monastic properties. When defenders of the old ways rose in the Pilgrimage of Grace they had suffered sorely, losing life and lands, and where sons were left to carry on many of them in participating in the Rising of the North, intended to throw down Elizabeth and the Reformed Church and put Mary Queen of Scots in her place and restore the Old Faith and the abbeys, put an end to their family fortunes. These and the Civil War deeply affected the landowning families in Yorkshire.

Each castle, hall, great mansion, has some part in this rich history. It is not difficult to discover on which side their owners fought. Look for their tombs and effigies in the parish churches.

Look also for the recurring surnames of old families, yeomen and farming families, whose history often goes back as far as, maybe farther than that of the barons and earls in their castles and fine mansions 'Open To The Public'.

NECESSARY MAPS

Small scale motoring and touring maps are good for planning routes in the dales, but only the one inch to the mile Ordnance Survey Maps give the countrygoer the freedom of byways, tracks and footpaths, and have the fascination of old names in farm and hamlet, of ancient sites, historic places.

The Dales National Park and areas in the Pennine country in this book are covered by the following sheets:

Sheet 96—for Skipton area and lower Airedale, and a little of lower Wharfe and Nidd.

Sheet 91—covers upper Nidderdale, lower parts of Ure and Swale.

Sheet 85—takes in most of Teesdale.

Sheet 84—covers the roof of England, the Pennine watershed from Tees head to the Eden.

Sheet 90—my particular favourite, my own map battered, taped and re-taped; this for Uredale, Swaledale and the mountain birth place of many rivers, Aire, Ribble, and Wharfe among them.

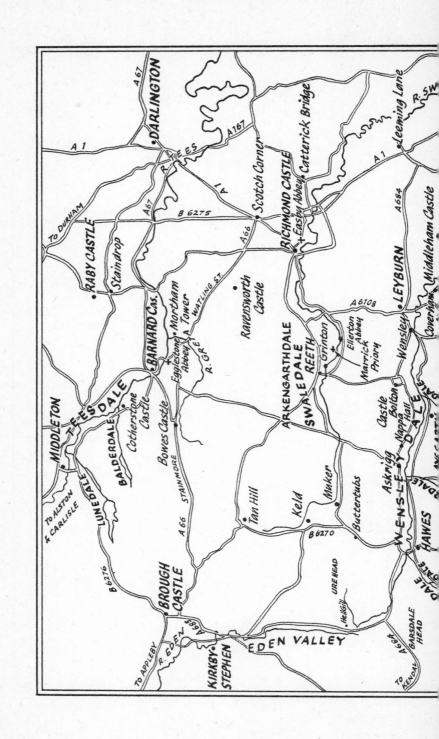

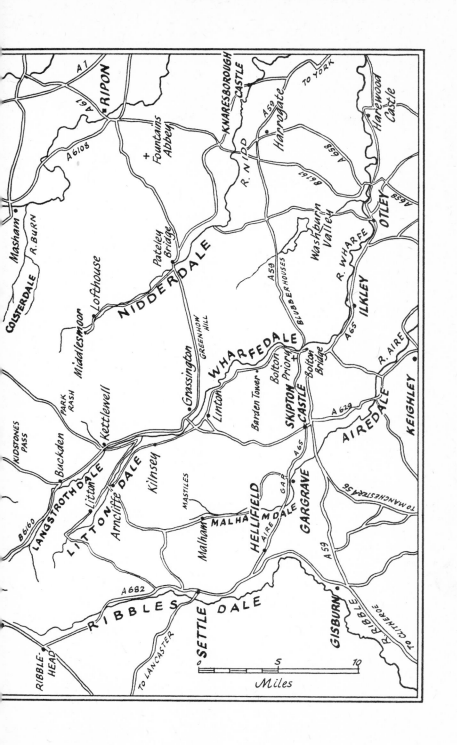

COLSTERDALE · Masham · R. BURN · R. BURN · RIPON · A1 · A61 · A6108 · A1 · KNARESBOROUGH CASTLE · TO YORK · A59 · Harrogate · A658 · TO YORK · Harewood Castle · A659 · + Fountains Abbey · Pateley Bridge · R. NIDD · A658 · Middlesmoor · Lofthouse · NIDDERDALE · Washburn Valley · OTLEY · A659 · BLUBBERHOUSES · A59 · R. WHARFE · R. AIRE · Greenhow Hill · WHARFEDALE · Grassington · Bolton Priory · ILKLEY · A65 · KEIGHLEY · PARK RASH · Kettlewell · Linton · Barden Tower · Bolton Bridge · + · R. AIRE · KIDSTONES PASS · Buckden · Kilnsey · + · SKIPTON CASTLE · A629 · AIREDALE · B6160 · LITTONDALE · Littondale · Arncliffe · MASTILES · A65 · TO MANCHESTER A56 · LANGSTROTHDALE · MALHAM · HELLIFIELD · GARGRAVE · GAR · Malham · AIREDALE · A59 · A682 · RIBBLESDALE · SETTLE DALE · GISBURN · RIBBLE · TO CLITHEROE · RIBBLE-HEAD · TO LANCASTER · TO LANCASTER · 0 · 5 · 10 · Miles

Clifford's barbican: Gateway, Skipton Castle

One

AIREDALE

1. Pattern of History

OF ALL THE rivers in this book the Aire has suffered most since industry used its waters. As a century ago in *Water Babies*, the black defiled river still passes between the factory walls of the large Yorkshire woollen towns whilst the clear and undefiled stream of Malhamdale is just as bright, dancing and glancing under the little bridges of Malham, Airton and Eshton. Only the second face of the Aire belongs to this book, from the moors about the Tarn and Cove to Skipton.

The pattern of history in Airedale is firmly linked with that of Wharfedale, for Skipton has the Norman and Edwardian Castle of early Romillys and later Cliffords, but Bolton by Wharfe is site of the noble priory which was foundation of the one and the burial place of the others. The lands of both families spanned the two dales, their hunting grounds extended over their watersheds and when the priory waxed rich with their land grants the Prior of Bolton owned granges for his herds, vast sheep walks for his flocks, breeding grounds for horses, corn mills, fisheries, mines and turbary rights, held manorial courts and sent his canons to serve parish churches in both dales.

Because of the Romillys and Cliffords, the influence of the Priory and also of the other great landowner, Fountains Abbey, the history of Airedale from the coming of the Norman barons to the Dissolution of the Monasteries is exceeding rich and varied.

Before 1066 the dale was already highly civilized and farmed by descendants of Anglian settlers who lived in the Hams and Tons—which are numerous from Skipton updale to Malham itself—and by families of Danish and Norse name who left their mark in the also numerous Bys and Bers and Laithes, in most of the farm names and field names, and those given to the becks, gills, waterfalls and natural features. A fascinating study the place names of Airedale!

And long before the first Anglian settlers reached the dale the green floor and the limestone slopes were patterned by the small field enclosures, the cattle 'corrals' and village sites of the Celts. In the Aire Gap hardly one knoll but has some sign of prehistoric occupation; on the heights above Malham Moor and dale head men were on watch, on guard, herding their stock, growing crops, looking out for raids of envious neighbours, centuries before the first Roman soldiers tramped through the Gap or battled against gales on Mastiles.

Ever since it was possible for men to make their way across country traders have known the Aire, keeping above river and swamp level. Great glaciers defined the route as they moved across the Pennines, grooved out the Gap, and as they pushed eastwards and the ice melted—a process covering many thousands of years—the water was held back in lakes by dams of moraine debris. When the water seeped through the dams and the left-overs of piled debris, boulders, sand and gravel were thickly smeared with clay deposits; these we now see as the numerous rounded hillocks, 'like eggs in a basket', about one hundred feet above the surrounding country, and almost all of them named. These are the drumlins on which early dwellers took their stand, around which the Scandinavian incomers carried on their agricultural pursuits, naming Bomber, Tosber, Cober, Smarber, Greenber and scores of others.

Whether we track down the route of Early or Late Bronze way-makers forging westwards in search of copper, lured to Ireland for gold, or Iron Age men who passed through in their wake, or follow the Roman Queens Way, the Craven Old Road, or trace the settlements of Angles east and west of the Gap, or recognize this as a highway used by Norsemen when Dublin and York were seats of rival kingdoms, we are never far from the march of early history in the Aire country.

The routes we travel are very near the ancient ways, whether we keep to the busiest modern cross-Pennine highroad—A65 or approach from Lancashire and the south by two highways, A59 direct link with Ribblesdale and Clitheroe, Preston and Liverpool, and A56 which by way of the Calder towns, Colne and Burnley, brings north roads from Manchester and its environs. The first is the middle stretch of the Lancaster-York cross road, later turnpiked—old mile stones tell you it is the Keighley-Kendal Turnpike—its history well recorded. The two roads from Lancashire converge upon Skipton with an Aire feeder, Earby Beck, and several minor streams watering the gentle pastoral countryside between, a very pleasant lead-in to a region which is soon to burst—with all the drama of rugged fells, towering cliffs and aweful gorges—upon the unsuspecting stranger.

Skipton which advertises itself as Gate to the Craven Dales is heart of this historic landscape.

2. Skipton in History—Town and Castle

In Skipton past and present jostle each other, and town and country meet. The medieval highway, the Keighley-Kendal Turnpike of stage and mail coaches, the modern A65—each in turn has used the High Street as thoroughfare, traffic manœuvring between market stalls and wares set out on cobblestones, dodging countryfolk from 'up dales'—you may recognized them by their ruddy faces and slow, deliberate movement—and townsfolk who weave in and out among them.

Behind the tall frontages of the High Street and Sheep Street shops used to be a rabbit warren of ancient, picturesque and insanitary back lanes, ginnels, alleys and courts which, we believed, were designed narrow, cramped and hide-away the better to keep out

Scots raiders. We felt like fugitives from justice making devious ways down tortuous ways emerging either at the canal side or coming between dark archways—which were so easily barricaded against enemies—into the busy main streets. Acres of cleared space and rubble are all you see now where old Skipton once lurked.

The Georgian Town Hall, the arcaded ground floor of which was a sheltered market and the cellars often used as lock-up, is islanded in mid-street. The eighteenth century has been adapted to the twentieth. Among the modern shops and cafés is a Chinese Restaurant, and near by in Sheep Street, where wealthier merchants and traders of the seventeenth century had their handsome houses, are intrusions tucked away down winding alleys which would make beaux, dandies and Coffee House frequenters of a bygone Skipton stand, amazed. New restaurants extend into old yards, cafés catering for teenagers, and there are more changes imminent in demolition areas behind Sheep Street and High Street.

I like shopping in Skipton. Especially do I appreciate what has been done in Craven Court. So many alleys like this have disappeared before bulldozers' onslaughts; here the many old dwellings flanking a narrow paved court have been used to display furniture, period and modern, in perfect and fitting setting. This is one of the pleasantest surprises tucked up Skipton's full sleeves.

There is no such state as 'a quiet time' in Skipton, except in the parish church where 'peace comes dropping slow.' The noisy world is shut out. On the greyest days there is colour and brilliance within. The church flower decorations are always lovely, banked against pillars, massed against sanctuary steps; especially beautiful the Easter Sepulchre and the harvest array. Against the dark roof timbers the gilded and brightly painted bosses enliven the darkest day. As for the tombs of the Cliffords, surely no one ever disputed Dr. Whittaker's opinion that no tombs of any noble families in England bore so many splendid bearings as these, blazoning alliances with daughters of Veteripont, Clare, Berkeleys, Nevilles, Percys—the greatest names in the land. What an exercise in heraldry!

These tombs are very near the impressive barbican gatehouse to the castle, with the Clifford challenge in the motto DESORMAIS meaning HEREAFTER, in letters of stone on the parapets. It is but a stone throw from church east end to castle gate.

The church steps descend to street level, and not far below is Mill Bridge, and a new paved garden by a fourteenth-century ford. Follow the path by Eller Bank to Skipton Woods now opened between May and September. The shallow beck is on the one hand, the still black Springs Canal on the other.
and their successors once had their pleasure gardens; it was a link with the new Leeds to Liverpool canal. Quays and loading shutes were constructed for taking away of stone from nearby quarries. It was possible to travel by water all the way to the North Sea via Leeds and the Humber, or to the Irish Sea by Liverpool and the Mersey once the whole cross-Pennine project was complete.

This is fairly recent history. We are more thrilled by the frowning rock which beetles dramatically over the water, black birds cawing raucously from battlements and twisted boughs. This formidable natural rampart was the reason for the castle being at Skipton. Small chance of success for any invader storming either Romilly's Norman fortress or the Clifford's Edwardian defences; west facing to the route from which most enemies approached, this was wellnigh impregnable.

Skipton Castle is in private hands and open to the public at all convenient hours. Exciting from without, there is also a wealth of interest within. We pay our money, buy our picture postcards in the Shell Room, the walls still decorated by many of the shells Lady Anne's buccaneering father brought home from foreign parts—note well the knight tilting on horseback as weather vane—reminder of his other role of Queen's Champion. On the right of the Shell Room, within the massive drum tower, a modern room, lounge for the castle agent who often acts as guide, has Tudor decor designed at the time of the third earl, whilst the kitchens on the left have windows splayed in six-feet-thick walls and on a piece of masonry lettering laboriously chipped out by Civil War prisoners.

Pass through the archway and the centuries unroll. The formidable inner defences, the first Clifford's drum towers and curtains, brought low by the Roundheads were only partially built up by the last Clifford, Lady Anne, for the authorities refused to allow her to raise the walls to original height. Within the inner gate is the enclosed, silent Conduit Court with leaden cisterns into which water was conveyed by a conduit from springs outside the castle, and which were emptied during the harrowing time of siege when the garrison depended solely on rainwater collected on the flat roofs of the drum towers. Note Lady Anne's cipher: A.P. The tall yew which shadows the court was possibly planted by her when she 'came into her own'.

Steps lead down into horrid dungeons beneath Romilly's Norman walls, and steps lead up into fine apartments west of the court, into the kitchens where cooks and scullions sweated with the seething, broiling and roastings, into the banquetting hall where Cliffords feasted, and the withdrawing room where the ladies retired for peace and quiet when men at their cups grew too boisterous and rowdy.

High windows opening to the west, towards the Aire Gap, framing the sunset sky—they gave watchers warning of impending danger, they were the windows where waited fair ladies 'their gold combs in their hands' for their true loves who so often they saw no more.

Far below in gardens along Eller Beck Cliffords walked and talked of sad partings imminent, of expected homecomings, of joyful reunions, of lover's meetings—and of peace, and too often, war.

ROMILLYS, LORDS AND LADIES

Who were the Romillys and Cliffords who between them ruled the Skipton roost for nigh on six hundred years?

The first Romillys came in with the Normans. Before 1066 a very high-ranking Anglo-Saxon, Earl Edwin, was Lord of Skipton. How noble he was one may guess for he was younger brother of Earl Leofric of Mercia, brother-in-law of Godiva, and his nephew Hereward the Wake carried out a resistance against the Conquerer that placed him among the heroes of history. Edwin and his Yorkshire neighbours had as small success against William and suffered for their uprising by forfeiture of all their lands. Skipton Fee and Harewood Barony were among the Romilly's gains, and remained in their hands for two centuries though names changed; Romillys ran to female heiresses time and time again.

Robert de Romilly rejected Edwin's rural manor house at Bolton, choosing the cliff top at the 'sheep town' for his strong point. He built a strong keep on the highest point on a natural mound; on the 'town' side he raised outer walls enclosing the bailey where his retainers mustered. They were soon tested by Scots attackers in those unsettled years when the borders were constantly changing and Scots felt north England 'home ground'.

1138: that was a memorable year. William Fitz Duncan and his marauding Scots swept into England, crossed the Bowland hills to the Ribble, won a battle on its banks at Edisford, turned north—driving cattle and prisoners before them, and reaching the Aire country attacked and took Skipton. His campaign on his uncle King David's behalf was aimed against King Stephen who had taken the throne from the unfortunate 'White Queen', his cousin, Matilda.

William during his first coming to Skipton saw the young Alice, Robert de Romilly's heiress. At his second visit some years later he won her for his bride. Their combined estates were to stretch from Craven through Yorkshire into Westmorland, Cumberland—where their heir was born at Egremont Castle—and over the border into Scotland. The alliance was not against the wishes of the Romillys. William like all his uncles—Malcolm and the English Margaret had many sons—had many friends north and south of the border, in royal families in both countries. That their hopeful son, Young Romilly, died young and maybe in tragic circumstances, has become subject for ballad and story. Again an heiress appears in the Romilly line, Cecilia.

Cecilia married one in whom flowed strongly the blood of the English lords of Skipton, William de Meschines, grand-nephew of Earl Edwin. For two hundred years heiresses were to pass vast honours and estates from one noble family to another, until the time of Isabel de Fortibus, heiress of the earls of Albemarle in the thirteenth century. A daughter and heiress married a Plantagenet prince; later the Skipton lands passed to the Crown and Edward I handed over to his son who finally, after a brief spell when his favourite Piers de Gaveston came on the Skipton scene, passed the estates to a great soldier who had stood high in the favour of both kings, and whose family had for generations been 'well in' with royalty. Enter the Cliffords.

The Romilly castle is no more; only one archway in the Conduit Court is to be seen. Their benefactions and good works live after the Romilly ladies. At Embsay where she founded a priory and at Bolton to which it was translated we remember the 'lady Adeliza'. The north chapel in Burnsall church was the gift of another. Other ladies of Romilly blood were lavish in bequest to the nunneries of Arthington, Appleton and Sinningthwaite into which daughters of theirs and other noble families retired to be shielded from the wickedness of the world. One gave much to Fountains Abbey. Many centuries later Cliffords, Lady Anne and her mother, are remembered above all others of their name for acts of charity and benevolence.

ENTER THE CLIFFORDS

The Cliffords hailed from the Welsh border. An ancestor, close kin of William the Conqueror, took his name from the place he acquired with his English bride. Through a very beautiful daughter who caught the roving eye of Henry II the Cliffords came close to the Plantagenets. Fair Rosamund's son, William Longspée, was created by a father who loved him dearly earl of Salisbury; at times Henry possibly wished he, not the rebellious Richard, John and the young Plantagenets, was to succeed him.

King John had granted rich north country estates, the Barony of Westmorland and the Sheriffwick of Appleby to a Veteripont. Roger Clifford, a front line soldier during Edward I's wars to subjugate the Welsh princes, married a Veteripont heiress, so making the family's first link with the north. But Roger had no thought of leaving the Welsh borders, not until the king granted him a life tenure of Skipton. Any plans to move north were prevented by his death during fighting in Anglesey. Cliffords rarely died at home in bed.

His two sons were involved in the rebellions of Edward II's reign, the elder losing his possessions which however the younger, Robert, took over. He was a great soldier like his father, vigorous against England's foes. He was made lord warden of the Marches. He planned to move his family to Skipton for he had gained a 'permanancy' here by an exchange for the Clifford borderland estates, the King being agreeable. He arrived at the castle in 1310, found it in poor shape and set about rebuilding.

His fortress was planned like those with which the Crusaders had become familiar and which we call 'Edwardian'. Romilly's keep and bailey castle disappeared within the massive drum towers and thick curtain walls which joined them; beyond these defences was raised an outer gatehouse, the barbican with the dry moat, a deep and wide ditch north and south of it.

How Robert hated the Scots! As lord warden of the Marches he had already crossed the border carrying war into the heart of Bruce's own country, devastating Annandale with such ferocity the victims of his raids remembered and settled the score with even more venom when they had the chance to retaliate. The chance was not long in coming. Clifford's body was one in the procession of the noble dead carried south from Bannockburn, his to lie in the priory at Bolton he intended to aid. Not long afterwards the Bruce and his army swept through the Clifford domains, leaving homes and villages,

churches and Bolton Priory in ruin and ashes, their cry for revenge
sounding through Craven and the dales.

In the years to come many funeral corteges with plumes and lights
were to wind over the hills to Bolton. They bore for burial remains
of Cliffords who died fighting the infidel, who were killed in the
campaigns with the Black Prince and Henry V. Later they died on
English ground, among the Yorkshire nobility who espoused the
Lancastrian cause.

The Wars of the Roses. The eighth lord was killed at St. Albans.
His son, the ninth lord, was only twenty-six when he met his end on
the eve of the blood bath of Towton Field. History and Shakespeare
blackened his name; Black Clifford, the Butcher they called him,
because he was said to have slain in cold blood the Duke of York's
young son, and to have struck off the duke's head and borne it to the
Queen on a pike. He left to the mercy of the Yorkists a young widow
and three children.

Lady Clifford fearing the Yorkists hid her family, the heir being
concealed in various remote estates. For twenty-four years his whereabouts were unknown, which was as well. Clifford's forfeited estates
were enjoyed by the Stanleys and later handed to Edward IV's brother
—which is why you see on the Black Horse Inn wall in the High Street
near Skipton Castle a tablet telling that here Richard of Gloucester
stabled his horses. He also gave handsome gifts towards church
repairs.

Henry, the tenth lord, came into his own when Richard III fell
and the Tudors took the crown. Opponents of the Yorkists were their
friends. So from the rural backwaters in Cumberland where the boy
had grown to manhood, knowing little of his rich inheritance and
caring less, he was drawn back into public life. Birth had destined
him for castle and royal palace, but upbringing had made him averse
to any pomp or ostentation. He preferred the quiet dales to the king's
court and the family hunting lodge at Barden, which he made into
his chief residence, to the great castle at Skipton. His pleasure was
in simple things and in the friendship and companionship of the canons
at the priory who shared his interests in the new sciences, astrology,
astronomy and alchemy.

His son thought little of his father's way of life and broke loose
at an early age. With similarly inclined young bloods he ran wild,
sowed many wild oats, turned outlaw, attacked religious houses and
—if a later gift to the priory was conscience money—made himself a
nuisance around Bolton. He was on the way to bring his father's
grey head 'with sorrow to the grave'! The Shepherd Lord sorrowed
to see his son apparelled in rich garb "adorned with goldsmith's
work"—he thought himself a 'poor man' and expected his son to cut
his cloth accordingly.

Not so. Young Henry was crony of Prince Henry (later the VIII)
and Charles Brandon, and friend of the Princess Mary who became
queen to the old king of France. The wild lad was to be created
first earl of Cumberland, to show his loyalty to his old friend by

defending his town and castle of Skipton against the Commons in
the Pilgrimage of Grace—when many of his own men deserted to
Aske—and not many years afterwards when the abbeys were dissolved he was able to purchase from Henry's Commissioners the
priory and its extensive lands in the dales.

Skipton had been interested spectator in the bringing home to the
castle of many Clifford brides—each nobly born or well-dowered—
among whom were Clares, Berkeleys and Nevilles, Beauchamps and
Roos, Percys—one was daughter of Harry Hotspur—Dacres and
Bromflet de Vescy—rich alliances which add such lustre to the array
of shields on the tombs in the parish church. Of these none was
more cause for pride than that of the first earl's son with the 'royal
lady', the Lady Eleanor Brandon's grace.

Lady Eleanor brought the blood royal of England—Plantagenet
and Tudor—undiluted into the Clifford strain, though it was destined
to pass through her only daughter, Margaret, to the Stanleys and
make of the Countess of Derby a possible claimant in later years to
Elizabeth's throne. As Henry VII's great granddaughter, the daughter
of the second earl and Lady Eleanor had as good a claim as any of
them, was the opinion of staunch northerners.

When Princess Mary, queen dowager of France, returned a young
widow to England she married her childhood sweetheart, Charles
Brandon. Lady Eleanor, their only child, they married to the first
Earl's son. The Tudor range built for the newly-weds, regal apart-
ments, gallery and tower, has been nobly restored during 1971–2 by
Mr. Fattorini; a western range crowning the rock ramparts.

When Lady Eleanor died the earl remarried, his wife Anne Dacre
giving him two sons who were to succeed as third and fourth earls.

George, the elder, was the dashing gallant, the Queen's Champion,
as Elizabethan buccaneer sailing the high seas in ships which devoured his revenues. Fleets of ships he fitted out, nine expeditions
in all—the queen willingly allowing this at no expense to herself—
but all his exploits in piracy and against the Spaniards on the Main
and in their ports ended in failure. At home he earned the reputation
of lady-killer, in spite of a warty visage! His offspring were scattered
in many lowly places—but he left no male heir to succeed him. His
young son lies within a small alabaster tomb near his parents' in
Skipton church. His one legitimate heir to survive him was a
daughter, Lady Anne, and she was debarred from her inheritance by
the breaking of the entail. His brother Francis, and his son after him,
came before Lady Anne. She had to wait for many years to 'come
into her own'.

IN THE STEPS OF LADY ANNE

Travelling through the dales we are constantly reminded of Lady
Anne Clifford, an intrepid traveller herself in spite of her advanced
years when she 'took to the road' for the purpose of visiting her
widespread estates, surveying her many castles assessing Civil War
damage, planning large scale rebuilding, calling on her numerous

relatives scattered through the north, keeping an eye on her depend-
ants from whom she demanded ancient feudal dues because it was
her right. A stickler for rights; benevolent too, devoted to the church,
mindful of the needs of the poor.

What a story! She saw it was permanently 'documented'. When
she rebuilt Barden Tower a tablet was carved at her behest; here her
mother stayed *en route* for Skipton where Anne was to be born. Little
Anne was to live in many castles and royal courts; Appleby she
loved and the great fortress of Brougham from which she set out one
sad day in spring clinging to her mother in a farewell which was to
be their last. The scene of their parting is marked by Countess Pillar
—suitably inscribed—and every third day of April for ever according
to her will a ceremony was to be enacted on the spot with the dis-
tribution of an annuity of £4 for the poor within the parish of
Brougham; the story of Lady Anne was to be told and the older folk
receive half a crown and each child sixpence 'to keep her memory
green'.

The young girl, a petted favourite at the court of James I's queen,
was soon happily married to the earl of Dorset. Widowed, her second
marriage to the earl of Pembroke and Montgomery proved a misery
for he was 'profligate and spendthrift'; his death came as the happiest
of releases for Ann, and well-timed too. For years she had pleaded
in vain that she should have her inheritance; kings and high officials
had deaf ears. But the cousin who had succeeded her uncle Francis
as fifth earl died soon after her widowhood—and all the Clifford
castles and estates were hers at last.

All her energies—in spite of being a very little woman, but 4 feet
10 inches tall, she was brimful of energy—were directed on restoring
her possessions to their ancient splendour. That she was sixty-one,
an age when most women of her time sat back and let children and
grandchildren take over, mattered not at all. Castles slighted by Cromwell's demolitions, battered by Civil War sieges, churches unroofed
and windowless after cannon fire, houses in decay—she set to work
to repair and rebuild them all. Cromwell was tolerant. Let the
countess spend her fortune in this way if it pleased her; it was a
harmless occupation and would keep her out of mischief!

When she passed through the dales, stoically enduring the jolting
and jars on execrable roads and the comparative comfort of the first
wheeled carriage ever seen in these parts, hospitality was a simple
matter. She stayed with tenants, or with families linked with hers
by kinship or friendship. Often she left souvenirs or a gift of a well-
made lock for the front door; one key she left with her host and a
duplicate she kept herself!

Going north she looked in at Barden Tower, then updale to Starbotton where she rested the night at 'Mr. Symondson's new house'—
still there, hugging the fell foot—continuing the next morning to
Buckden, up the broad Rake to Kidstones and over the rough fell
road we call The Stake to Semerwater side and Countersett. She lodged
at the hall, or a few miles away at the pleasant Ure side hall of the
Colbys. They gave her ready welcome, as did the Metcalfes at Nappa

Hall, kinsmen of the Cliffords for had not a daughter of the first earl married Sir Christopher Metcalfe, a love match obviously for he took her with a meagre dowry of 900 marks, her father having a graded scale when dowring his daughters according to the rank of their bridegrooms. Sir Christopher was 'low grade'.

The Stake was arduous going, but the crossing from Ure to Eden as bad, as anyone who has walked the old road from Cotter End to Hell Gill and so onto Mallerstang well knows. Her marks hereabouts are many. Lady's Pillar was erected high on the fell top. The small

Old Hall at Bank Newton

church low in the Eden valley was built by her, and that legend-haunted castle called Pendragon, across the river, she restored.

The Whartons of Wharton Hall welcomed her. Kirkby Stephen folk did her honour as she passed through and every Eden side hamlet and village where the people had been tenants—of Veteriponts and Cliffords—from Norman times.

I think we feel closest to Lady Anne in Appleby. Here she celebrated with the townsfolk in the open street the Restoration of Charles II. The tall High Cross carries her motto, which guided her through life: FEAR GOD, HONOR THE KING, PRESERVE YOUR RIGHTS. Near by, almswomen today enjoy the lovely almshouses which she founded, and live according to the rules, slightly modified as concession to modern life, which she drew up.

It was at Brougham Castle she lived a great deal in her last years. There is an exquisite turret oratory with fan vaulting, and trefoil headed windows through which are long views over lands where

Cliffords sported with kings, English and Scots, over rich and fair landscapes ending with the blue mountain wall of the Pennines, or westwards towards the Lakeland fells; here she came to pray, and to meditate over the past and the glory of the Cliffords.

When she died at Brougham on March 22nd, 1675, the Dowager Countess of Dorset, Montgomery and Pembroke, by a long and continuous descent from her father and his noble ancestors Barroness Clifford, Westmorland and Vescy, High Sheriffess of the County of Westmorland and lady of the Honor of Skipton left as heiresses two daughters, and thirteen grandchildren to carry on the blood—but not the .name of Clifford.

In her life she had caused to be erected those splendid tombs to her parents and grandparents in Skipton church; here at Appleby church where she lies beneath a black marble effigy, and next her beloved mother, is displayed all the pride of the Cliffords with shields blazoning their descent and alliances from the days of King John.

"She was last 'on 'em, and best of the lot !" was a local comment.

Lady Anne's route is still a splendid walker's way through Pennine country, Skipton to Brougham Castle.

3. Approaches from Lancashire and the South

Coming out of Lancashire—the county boundary passed just south of Sawley—A59 crosses country which is true English plainsong, mounting the Ribble-Aire watershed most inconspicuously 4 miles north of Gisburn.

The green and pleasant landscape of little hills, the many Bers which are Ice Age drumlins cultivated around their feet and grazed by cattle or sheep for over a thousand years, has many old farms and tiny hamlets tucked away in its folds. Leave the highroad, and in a matter of minutes you are far from the madding crowd, in a clean bright world where farm tracks wind across the greenest pastures to quiet farms where men gathered for worship in secret in the seventeenth century, or paths—where hares leap away almost from under your feet—trail away to breezy skylines and hilltop sites known to prehistoric men. This is curlew-haunted country, larksong shrill and clear in the silence, lapwing's screaming loud as they swoop down to scare the trespasser from their nesting ground.

TO HORTON—AND PARADISE, TO GLEDSTONE AND BANK NEWTON

From A59 turn off for Horton—in Craven—a hamlet climbing a steep brow, with manor and hall, pretty cottages, an early chapel—and enveloping peace. Leave roads for the tracks to Paradise and Swinden Moor Head the watershed, where the Craven highlands, the serried ridges and gleaming walls of limestone northwards, are spread out in a multi-coloured back drop. This is the country where Aire is born, the wide view a foretaste of what is in store.

The next left fork from the highway leads to Gledstone Hall, passing through the most delightful off-the-beaten-track country. A pheasant crosses the lane, or hares lollop ahead, birds fly out in alarm from the lane edge coverts. Curious travellers are enchanted, especially in early spring, and in June when many come to see the rhodos and azaleas. Before October strips the trees all is aglow, camouflage for proud cock pheasant. The eighteenth-century Hall (Carr of York the architect) has gone, except for the turreted stable block, but the splendid modern mansion designed between the wars by Sir Edmund Lutyens for Sir Amos Nelson can be seen beyond the ornate wrought-iron gates—made by a local smith—and above the garden walls.

Ingthorpe Grange

The curious traveller in not too much of a hurry to reach the deep dales and high fells will find untold delight in sauntering in the quiet land between Gledstone and Gargrave—between A59 and A65. Belonging to Gledstone Hall and a mile away by path across open pastures is Ingthorpe Hall, a many-gabled seventeenth century farmstead on the site of a monastic grange. You have heard of apples called American Baldwins? An emigrant, a son of the Baldwins of Ingthorpe, carried in his seed chest pips from appletrees in the home orchard, and well they grew in the alien soil of New England.

Other comely old farms, Pasture House not far from the unexpected bus diversion and away in the fields, and Marton Scar near the three roads end at Gledstone, are known in nonconformists annals. In the days when ministers were 'in the wilderness' these houses sheltered Oliver Heyward and men like him and secret worship was held here frequently between the years 1676 and 1700.

Take the Bank Newton-Gargrave road, an hither and thithering lane which when I last travelled it was walled in by 12-feet snow-drifts, in February '63. Serene among green knolls, above a sparkling stream, and blue sky and white clouds behind it, stands Bank Newton Hall. Banks were an old Craven family, here from the fourteenth century though this hall dates from Tudor times. Fascinating relics of a richer past are heraldic panelling over a fireplace, and a scrap of ancient, possibly medieval, carving never intended to make of a pig sty a swine palace, as it does today.

Walkers discover canal country very near these bylanes. In certain meditative moods nothing beats towpath walking. The Leeds and Liverpool canal makes its circuitous way round about the green drumlins. From A59 by East Marton we look down on the still waters from the road bridge, but leave the highway—the road has the warning: NOT FOR MOTOR TRAFFIC—by the 'Cross Keys' inn and wander by deserted tow path or on the accompanying lane, and hours of pleasant tranquillity I promise you. The same canal rides high level above the Bank Newton lanes.

In summer, leaving the charming flower-bedecked cottages by East Marton bridge all the way to Newton Grange, it is flowers, a procession of flowers. Yellow flags, purple loosestrife, dog daisies and purple vetch, pink and white clover on the verge, wild roses and honeysuckle trailing over the limestone boulder walls. A small girl waves from one gay pleasure craft; her hands are full of buttercups and marguerites which she is about to cram into a jam jar on the cabin roof.

The boat jugs on, a hay-cutter mows down swathes of grasses and flowers in a meadow alongside, haymakers call and wave, swallows and martins swoop and dive to meet their own reflections. How cool the splashings of canal water squirted through lock gates.

From the happy foreground we look up and there, northwards, in direct contrast to the tranquillity about us, is the theatrical backcloth of the exciting Craven highlands whither we are bound.

TO BRACEWELL, GILL CHURCH, THORNTON AND ELSLACK

The byways to Horton and Swinden Moor, Gledstone and Bank Newton are more than matched by others leaving A59 on the right (south) hand for Bracewell, and Gill church which is near Barnoldswick, for Elslack and Thornton, and for Broughton. A56 runs purposefully through the same region north of Thornton-in-Craven, tapping a countryside which has everything to delay historically-curious travellers.

Again, each green drumlin knoll now so peacefully grazed by sheep was used by our Celtic forefathers herding their flocks. Roman armies marched along the Ribchester to York military road which large scale maps show running direct from Pendle through Brogden Hall, passing Gill church, Thornton, to Elslack—their camp here was bisected by the railway—on, south of Broughton, to cross the Aire east of Skipton.

The Roman road brought later invaders across the Pennines into this green countryside, and along it came the first White Priests sent as missionaries to the folk of the north-west dales. Paulinus sent them forth from York if he did not himself come with them. After A.D. 627 a string of churches—groups of new Christians who worshipped together—followed the same route of the missionaries. It is interesting to link up the churches now lining or very near, that Roman way. Bracewell, St. Mary le Gill, Thornton and Broughton churches are all ancient foundations well worth finding.

First, to Bracewell. The venerable wayside church with massive tower and Norman round-headed south door had Lidulph as its first (known) priest in A.D. 1135. Within are tombs and effigies of Tempests whose badge, the stormcock, appears on stone and glass. This family lived for centuries at the nearby hall of which but one stone out-building remains, the so-called King Henry's Parlor. Tempests were always a warring lot and in the Wars of the Roses when relatives at Waddington near Clitheroe sheltered the fugitive king, or before he left his earlier hosts, the Pudsays of Bolton by Bowland, he was here entertained by one of them.

Tempests were in the thick of things during Scots raiding days, leading local billmen and bowmen to Skipton, there to join the lords of the castle. One was made guard of King David Bruce when prisoner of the English. One was knighted at Agincourt; others rode behind their leader Henry Clifford, banners with their stormcocks fluttering, to share in the victory of Flodden. In the Civil War the king had their loyalty, and how they suffered for it. Rupert's cavalry, they say, camped on the green knolls across the road from the church before the march on Skipton, the long besieged. A young Tempest was shot before his own door by Cromwell's troops, who later looted the hall so thoroughly nothing was left but an old helmet for the household to use in 'boiling the broth'. In the Commonwealth, the head of the family in exile, the house and parks neglected, timber felled, deer killed, Bracewell folk watched the demolition of the Hall. With the Restoration and the Tempests returned, they built a new hall on their estates near Broughton, on a lovely spot above the beck. This house in turn was replaced by the fine Palladian mansion, with ornamental gardens, terraces, statuary, and roadside lodges which are at the roadside, on A59. Tempests, unlike most northern families, have lived on into the present.

Romillys and Cliffords were not the only great names in local history. This region was also under the influence of De Lacys, Lords of Clitheroe and of Pontefract, who founded an abbey near Barnolds-wick and later translated the monks to Kirkstall on Aire banks. Eight centuries ago Kirkstall monks served Bracewell church and they owned properties—the gift of Norman barons—in the surrounding countryside.

A story of a death bed, a vow and its result links Gill and Kirkstall. In 1147 the powerful Henry de Lacy nigh unto death cried, "If I live a new abbey will I build to the Blessed Virgin." He recovered. The Abbot of Fountains gave him direction. "Found a daughter house on land near Barnolds Wick," he said, "and there Alexander will be new abbot and eleven brethren labour under him."

The band arrived, surveyed the land, decided to demolish the exist-ing parish church. But the natives proved unco-operative, hindering the monks on every hand and glad of 'the plague of rains' which put paid to their plans. They loved their old church; the incomers they hated. No wonder the abbot wrote of them as semi-barbarous dwellers in a savage country. Finally, Alexander pleaded with De

Lacy. Give us a new site, one near Aire banks where poor brothers have lived as hermits, for there we can build a great abbey to fulfill your vow.

So—Kirkstall! And at Gill the folk built up their church once more. There are fragments of the ancient fabric, a tower added in 1514 and later rebuildings which have made of this one of the most perfect churches in the North. The sprawling town to the south has a new parish church, but St. Mary le Gill still has the devotion of many. The nave is partitioned into many box pews all with initialled doors and array of knobs. The three-decker pulpit is intact, beautiful linenfold for its panels. Strong roof timbering of primitive style rests on carved crossplates and 'angel' corbels.

Church at Thornton-in-Craven

The church stands high above a deep gill shadowed by fine beeches. Stand by the farm called Rock, and looking on the road below think of Roman armies marching by, heading for Eboracum, and imagine the coming of the first missionary priests of Paulinus' time.

Some local passes on a scrap of information. "There were a battle fought on yon hill—across Gill. Something to do with monks. They say Julius Caesar hid among church bells. In't Wars of the Roses likely." From which we might infer there was some fighting near Gill once upon a time "but what they fought each other for?"

Not far north Thornton church, another ancient foundation, stands high by the same Roman highway. A fine upstanding tower, its erection by the parishioners was in 1510. Shields of arms are on the stones. The key is worth 'going for'.

Thornton-in-Craven, with A56 as its main street, has an atmosphere of age. Imagine it as a hot spot, galloping Cavaliers careering up and down the hill, Cromwellian troops fighting their way into the village, Parliamentary troops entrenched around the Hall, their local H.Q., captains directing the campaigns for holding the Aire Gap, essential in cross-Pennine strategy. 1643: Skipton, still beleaguered, saw a party of Royalists sally forth to Thornton; their assault party was very successful, for they took the Hall and held on for a month. Then enemy troops returned, recaptured it and, according to church records, thirteen soldiers were killed, one of them young Captain Bradyll of Portfield near Whalley.

Walkers: follow the Roman way, a grass-grown track, to Elslack. By road, turn right by a cheerful lane edge inn 'Tempest Arms', of the typical eighteenth century coaching type. Elslack hides away at the Pennine foot, Pinhaw, the highest point above it, often flaring with beacons in dangerous days. Roman Burwens comes first, on the right near the railway, a raised platform grazed by sheep and lambs. The grey farm, hoary with age and far older than it looks, is Elslack Hall which Godfrey de Altaripa was empowered to embattle and crenellate in Edward III's days. From it the farmer tells me "a secret passage went from the deep dungeon cellars to Skipton Castle". Secret routes certainly, for Elslack men were with Cliffords whenever Scots needed repelling. Rolt Benson built the newer hall in 1672.

The village is a delightful surprise, charming, unassuming and very cosy after the wild moors and lonely crossings from Kildwick and Glusburn, or from Lothersdale and Colne. A century ago old Enoch Hall tended his garden and gave fruit to passing children; a well-loved character. As a youth he went soldiering under Wellington. He was one of Napoleon's guard on the voyage to St. Helena—and he returned to be schoolmaster to the young of Elslack. When he died, aged ninety, old scholars mourned him and raised the memorial you may read in Broughton churchyard.

From Elslack climb the winding hill road to sky-line cross roads, there taking the old Colne road as far as Lothersdale, a pieceful hamlet long drawn out by brook and millstream, and dreaming mill pond. The mill is an early one; Wilsons here produced fine worsteds in the eighteenth century, a giant among waterwheels turning for power.

At the hill foot is a Friends' Meeting House, lost in memories. We pass on the left as we drop down the brow the house called Stone Gappe, also a place with memories. Here for three unhappy months in 1839 Charlotte Brontë was governess to the 'unmanageable, perverse, riotous cubs', the Sedgwick children. Bedtime brought no relief, for their mother piled on Miss Brontë heaps of mending. She might have grown to love the valley had she been allowed 'the divine woods, winding white paths, green lanes', but only once did her prison gates open. Mr. Sedgwick wishing to exercise his Newfoundland dogs deigned to allow Miss Brontë to follow—at a discreet distance!

Emily would have found the moor tops congenial; how the winds 'wuther' up there!

Back to A56, the wide highroad, and on a green ridge, Broughton church silhouetted against the sky, as it also appears from A59. Paths lead to church over pleasant pastures from both highways, and from the churchyard wide Airedale prospects extend for mile upon mile. The church—like many we see in Craven—has a long nave unbroken by chancel arch, and in its arcade pillars curiously carved, empty niches. The Tempests had a chapel here with medieval oak screens about it; there is an ancient stone font, a mutilated statue of great age—the Virgin and Child—and a little gem of alabaster carving.

Below, the land slopes to the park of Broughton Hall, well timbered, wrapped in quiet. Beyond the humming highway, and traffic Skipton bound.

4. Western Approaches to Airedale (A65 and the Aire Gap)

The Aire Gap; the easiest Pennine crossing, therefore richest in history and busiest today. Bronze Age traders dealing in gold from Ireland, copper and tin, and smiths and craftsmen learned in the mysteries of metal work used it as a direct cross-Britain route. They left many a mark of their passing in lost palstaves, swords and flat bronze axes. On the rounded knolls are barrows for their dead and on Rombalds Moor stones bearing marks of their sun worship. Each succeeding wave of newcomers swept through the Gap: Romans, Anglian warriors and later, on their heels, the first Danish rovers with a desire to settle down. Danes from the eastern dales, and Norsemen from the western shores and Ireland, mingled in the tenth century when a Scandinavian kingdom was established and communications through the Aire Gap linked the capitals at York and Dublin; how well used was this land route then, far shorter and less dangerous than the sea ways round Britain.

No doubt about its soaking in history, and in blood of fighting men who in the Gap either battled to win it or defend it. Sometimes dalesmen held back the Scots here, or were forced back to Skipton. Yorkists and Lancastrians fought along the Gap and in the Civil War both armies made good use of the easy route from Aire to Ribble.

Eight miles of highroad link Hellifield, where Hammertons erected a fourteenth century Peel to ward off Scots, and Skipton where the castle served the same purpose. It is a road with constant passing traffic; therefore the more quiet-loving countrygoers leave it as soon as maybe.

BYWAYS OFF A65. FROM HELLIFIELD, CONISTON COLD AND GARGRAVE

Points of departure occur just east of Hellifield, a bylane to Airton passing through Otterburn, a lost, forgotten spot formerly land of Gamelbar in the domesday survey, later a centre for Fountains Abbey sheepwalks and a meeting place for packways in pre-Turnpike days.

We cross a one-arch bridge with clear mason's marks. Follow the beck upstream and we walk for 2½ miles a short cut, Kirk Path, to Kirkby Malham. Stray to any of the hilltops and the chances are we find the stone-walled fold foundations of prehistoric shepherds who provided this protection against wolves. The farmer at Park House will tell you the scourge of today is foxes; hundreds of cockerels had been their victims before my last visit.

The Otterburn to Airton lane; how it twists, turns, sinks below moss-encrusted walls and flower-covered banks, and sidles into secret nooks. I like the hollows about Brocka Laithe.

The second route is from Coniston Cold, a village strung out along the highroad just where it comes down to Aire valley levels—wild bleak miles left behind. We turn off to Bell Busk, a travellers' halt in packhorse days, and starting off place for picnic parties in Victorian wagonettes when all trippers to Malhamdale booked on the train to Bell Busk station, long closed down, alas! Prehistory is written on the green hills above the road going north to Eel Ark bridge—where the monk's servants trapped the wrigglers. From Coniston Cold to Airton—just over 3 miles.

The third road from A65 to Malham is none the worse for being the bus route. Leaving Gargrave it passes through such beautiful parkland with splendid old trees and avenues of beeches we wonder are we in private ground. Eshton Hall, a school, formerly mansion to Sir Matthew Wilson is heart of this pleasance. Early spring is lovely—white drifts of snowdrops; autumn catches at the heartstrings when sun bursts turn bare boughs to silver filigree and the last leaves to pure gold, all brilliant against the deep purple background of Flasby Fell.

Here is good fell walking for breezy days, miles of it on heathery heights, where an old path from Flasby works its way between the rough hummocks called Sharp Haw and Rough Haw and drops by Skyrakes, ancient hunting chase of the Cliffords, to Skipton. To find these fell ways—and many bits of bonny scenery—take the road forking right 1¼ miles out of Gargrave, just south of Eshton parkland.

A second lane leaves the Malham highway at Eshton House, a seventeenth century farmstead with handsome porch you cannot possibly overlook. This right turn also heads for Hetton and Wharfedale, but within the first mile are two pockets of the past, each fascinating. The first surprise might easily be passed without recognition; look for a stone trough on the left hand, brimming with a copious supply of crystal water coming from behind the wall. Here is St. Helen's Well —a circular basin with medieval carving at the finials of the sill, filled with water from many bubbling springs. Once there was a chapel for wayfarers near by. Later the holy well became a wishing well but that too is forgotten.

Not far ahead, on a sunny rise above Eshton Beck, is Friars Head, surely the comeliest house in Craven, a farmhouse now, once monastic grange and business centre, used by abbey officers and agents when on their travels. Legends—such a house has many—tell of the ghost of a monk howling in the windowless room called The Dungeon, and of bones of monks dug up in their former burial ground in the orchard.

5. Enter Malhamdale

Malhamdale has an atmosphere all its own, cradling peace. We can think of it as unchanged down the centuries, sheep country in the beginning, for Norsemen, for the monks, and for the farmers of today; pure pastoral landscape wherever you turn.

Peace—but not on summer week-ends, or during 'end of term' when half the schools in Lancashire and Yorkshire organize expeditions. One day in early July a farmer warned me: "You'll be able to walk across Malham roof to roof on them coaches likely." Seventeen were packed like sardines on the small green. The passengers—nowhere to be seen.

Malhamdale hills are large scale and can swallow up large numbers so the invasion (at least six hundred) made little effect. But I saw parties, juniors scrambling over rocks and having fun just where poor little Tom bathed in the clear waters and became 'sea-changed', seniors with note books and maps silhouetted above The Cove, grammar school groups in numerous high places surveying limestone and gritstone, the mark of the Celt and the Norseman.

As all sightseeers head updale for the greater sights few halt to see Airton, or even turn left for Kirkby Malham and its gentler beauties. They are haunts of ancient peace in a dale at times jammed with traffic.

AT AIRTON

Airton, the first sizeable nucleus, brings the discerning to a halt. They stray beyond the green down to the bridge. Here, what a ring of bright water, Aire crystal clear and dancing. Herons haunt its bank, dippers bob there and kingfishers dart by. Note well; the finger post by a stile reads PENNINE WAY.

The old mill overhanging the river; once a Bolton Priory mill and highly valued, it now bottles Dettol. The old houses round the green; all comely, all in harmony and mostly three centuries old.

Each looks to have a story, especially William Ellis's house recognized by plentiful supply of pigeon holes and the date stone:

E

W   A

1696

When half Airton folk were linen weavers Ellis who plied the same trade became a zealous Friend. He preached as far from home as America. To establish a meeting in his village he left house and land, with a proviso that "whosoever rented the premises should willingly entertain such teachers as might be called of God and by Him sent abroad to preach the Gospel in the free dispensation thereof". Free hospitality!

Malhamdale has often let me down. The days wild weather has

chased us to shelter; the hours we have watched the rain lash down !
Last November an Airton Friend invited us into the shelter of the
Meeting House and I was reminded of Ellis's concern for travelling
Friends. He provided 'six large coats and six women's hoods' for any
caught in foul weather. They must have been constantly 'loaned out'.

THE KIRK IN MALGHDALE

Kirkby Malham church has provided welcome shelter too. I have
dozens of interior sketches made while black clouds rolled by. I never
mind being marooned here for an hour or two, it is so crammed
with interest. They say pagan dalesmen had a site here, that the
Danish settlers raised their first Christian church on the same spot
and fifteenth century rebuilders
saw no reason to use any other.
Now it is a very large building
caught in a very narrow cleft
of the fells.

When I look at the ancient
preaching cross outside the
south door, and the round stone
font inside it, I try to imagine
not only the infant Gudrids
and Gudruns brought here for
baptism but the adult settlers
too who had thrown down
their images of Thor and Wodin
and accepted the White Christ.
They shared their church with
the Anglian settlers too, many
already long established at
Malham, Airton and Calton

Danish font, Kirkby Malham

and nearby homesteads.

In sunshine the masonry has
a warm golden tinge. The
spacious nave and arcading was the work of two abbeys, Fountains and
Bolton both being local landowners sharing the responsibility. From
King John's reign a Norfolk abbey, West Dereham, had charge of the
chancel. Of the stonework I find the canopied niches intriguing. We
know one held a statue of St. Nicholas and he looked down on the
lads taught by the chantry priest near his pillar; but which saints
occupied the others?

Time is needed to appreciate the woodwork. The elaborate cage-
like pews in the north aisle were apportioned and partitioned by
Wards, and Kings and Rimingtons who owned land in the parish:
good Jacobean design all of them. The sanctuary rails are 'home
made' according to the vicar, they were 'turned' by many hands and
no two turned out quite alike.

Malhamdale, though much of it was under monastic ownership,
had several families of long standing and none older than the

Lamberts of Calton Hall. Read the epitaph in their south aisle chapel telling of the death of the last male heir in 1701, last of an ancient family 'in line from William the Conqueror and related to him by marriage'. The dale is proud of Major General Lambert, 'Cromwell's Understudy' and husband of a favourite daughter. He was outstanding in his leadership of northern armies in many campaigns in the Civil War. In the vestry Cromwell's signature is on civil marriage contracts which date from his visits to Calton.

If sermons in stones and books 'the church yard tomb' are to your liking you will find good reading here. A curiosity against the north wall of the churchyard is where 'a stream of living water' flows between two graves, side by side.

West of the church the comely Vicarage was once the Old Hall, restored in 1620; its various roles have included workhouse and cotton factory! East of the church—the three seater stocks, and the inn which in early days was kept by the churchwardens who dispensed their home-brewed to thirsty bellringers and parishioners. It is a cheerful corner where the renamed 'Victoria' watches the world go by.

Walkers only; come to the church by the kirk path from Otterburn, and leave it by the lane to the bridge and follow the young Aire by the quiet millpond, then stile to stile by crystal springs—some say the true source of Aire—into Malham village.

The road updale climbs up—it is poised to give a staggering 'surprise view' of that great horseshoe of gleaming white cliffs, the Cove; then down it drops into Malham.

MALHAM OF THE MONKS: 'MALGHDALE' HISTORIC

Malham village lies below, grey houses about the green. The sun shines and over the limestone pastures behind it a fascinating pattern

By Priory sheepfolds, Prior Moon's bridges

is drawn, white and shadowed blue. "The walls", we exclaim, "look at the walls!" They wriggle over the slopes dividing the green into scores of irregular pieces and plots, just as though a giant among fishermen had cast a net over the dale and let it lie.

When all memories fade we remember the walls. Some mark enclosures of monastic times, some appeared after eighteenth century enclosure awards, some are mere stone piles—walltops 'broad enough for a horse and cart to drive over'—reared laboriously by the same husbandmen endeavouring to clear their stony acres. Still older walls recognized only by a seeing eye divide up the dale floor below the Cove and peter out under the hillside turf; they belong to pre-Roman days when Celtic farmers peopled Malhamdale.

Malham's antiquity is less obvious than Kirkby's. Names are clues. Malham east side was Bolton Priory's with Priors Hall—sited near the modern Youth Hostel—as business centre, and sheepfolds where flocks converged in their thousands at clipping time, near Beck Hall. Somewhere near were the milking stands where priory dairy maids—only old and ill-favoured employed—milked the ewes and made cheese in great quantities for the canons' tables. The first bridge was work of the canons, and soon before Dissolution their last prior, Moon, gave his name to the succession of clapper bridges spanning islet to islet over swift runnels hard by the sheepfold, one of the most beautiful bits of old Malham to my thinking, a place of tangled flowers, scent of crushed watermint, and small song from warblers.

Porch and pigeon loft: Hill Top, Malham

Fountains Abbey organized its interests in the dale from the 'estate office' near Beck Hall. Their sheep walks stretched upwards and beyond Malham Moor, the milking ewes only being kept near the village, away to Fountains Fell and Parsons Pulpit. They ran sheep also in the Winterburn valley and there bred horses near Bordley. The Tarn kept them copiously supplied with fish. Near the village the young Aire turned their watermill at Pan Holes falls.

Four centuries of benign monastic rule shaped this landscape. All changed after 1536.

Wealthy nominees of Thomas Cromwell and Henry's commissioners usually had first choice of monastic lands, but in Malhamdale many tenants whose forbears had worked granges and outlying farms for prior and abbot jumped at the chance to buy freeholds, and labour for themselves. They knew all about sheep and wool, still the pillars of prosperity; they prospered. The old, crudely-built booths and cotes soon disappeared. The newly-styled yeoman farmers spread their chests, surveyed their estates, and called in builders to erect substantial houses in stone. They built to endure and these farms and small halls are a feature of the landscape.

Apart from packmen and rovers Malhamdale was little known to the outside world until the eighteenth century. Then the windy acres of Malham Moor with their unexcelled limestone pastureland were taken over by graziers, like Mr. Bertwistle; before the autumn beef sales thousands of Scots cattle were driven in from over the border, and Great Close and moor enclosures were turned into a cattle market which would have put Smithfield's Christmas sales into shade.

MALHAMDALE SCENIC: THE COVE, GORDALE SCAR AND THE TARN

Next arrived the first tourists and topographers, some returning from the Tour of the Lakes; all were suitably impressed. They listed the Cove, Gordale Scar—and one or two, the Tarn—as not to be missed Wonders of the North. Most of them stayed at the 'Lister Arms' in Malham, named from the Gisburn family who owned the hunting lodge by the Tarn; by day they saw the sights; and after dinner—unless it was moonlight and romantic—they wrote up their impressions.

Here are some comments from the past. A traveller returning from the Lakes did not think Malham would merit a visit for he was surfeited with wonders already, but he came. No complaints! 'Great and terrible' were the sights he saw. He looked at the Cove, at the rocks lying stratum upon stratum, 'so that a person of great spirit and agility, but of small and slender body, might almost walk round'. The brook issuing from the Cove foot, he was told, "in flood when a small subterranean passage is not able to give vent to all the water . . . pours down in a stupendous cataract, in height almost double that of Niagara. This is the highest perpendicular rock I have ever seen and I think not enough known and admired by travellers. . . ." The actual height—240 feet.

Hurtley in 1786 wrote of great floods where the 'Rugg', or over-spill, too much for waterholes on the tops near the Tarn to swallow, swept down the dry watercourse to plunge in 'a magnificent cascade' over the face of the Cove. Victorian journalists even suggested that it would be a good thing to help Nature in reproducing this display by 'blocking the swallow holes and forcing the stream to run over ground to produce falls everyone agreed would better Niagara's'.

Thomas Gray must not have visited the Cove when in Malham in 1769. Wordsworth wrote of the scenery at second hand. Dr. Whittaker knew the dale but concentrated his great guns not on extolling the scenery but deprecating the intrusion of industry. The abbots' mill site had become a cotton factory, much to the doctor's disgust.

'Confine industry to valleys which man can neither mend nor spoil,' he wrote, but 'who that has either taste or eyes can endure it when combined with such scenery as the environs of Malham. . . .'

John Ruskin and Charles Kingsley as guests of Mr. Morrison of Tarn House wrote of their appreciation. Ruskin in *Proserpina* detailed the smaller beauties of the Cove, 'the stones of the brook softer with moss than any silken pillow, the crowded oxalis leaves—the herb robert and robed clusters of its companion overflowing every rent in the rude crags with living balm—scarcely a place where one might not lay down ones forehead on their warm softness and sleep'.

Kingsley's far better-known picture of the Cove is in *The Water Babies*, Tom's headlong flight was into a 'deep, deep, green and rocky valley very narrow and filled with trees'. He dropped down 'three hundred feet of steep heather mixed up with loose brown gritstone as rough as a file—down three hundred feet of limestone terraces one below the other as straight as if a carpenter had ruled them with his ruler and then cut them out with his chisel,' and slipped down slopes where grew basil, rockrose, thyme, saxifrage and all sweet herbs, very much as they are today.

Gordale received rather more notice from travel writers. Thomas Gray's poet's eye seized upon the full drama of the gorge. He followed his guide from the village and after a mile drew near cliffs in which 'hung a few goats: one danced and scratched an ear with his right foot, in a place where I would not have stood stock still'. When he came into the gorge below that 'great rock on the right under which we stand to see the fall' the horror struck him, as it does modern tourists, especially if they have the place to themselves, and their mood is in tune. 'I stood there,' wrote Gray, 'not without shuddering, a quarter of an hour and thought my trouble richly repaid for the impression will last for life'.

Another eighteenth century writer came upon Gordale from its upper end. After viewing the 'most stupendous of precipices' from the western bank he was 'tempted to descend with care and circumspection down the steep bank which being interspersed with trees and shrubs gave hand holds where we could find no sure foot hold'. Standing beneath the high overhanging crag the 'idea of personal safety excited some awful sensations accompanied by a tremor. . . . We stood too far under its margin to be affected by any crumbling descending fragment, and a small one would have crushed us to atoms. . . . Nothing fell upon us but a few huge drops which sweat from its horrid front'.

About the same time Hurtley with his usual zeal wrote of Gordale as a 'Stupendous Pavilion of Sable Rock apparently rent asunder by some dreadful although inscrutable elementary convulsion'. Others recognised it for what it is, a chasm in which you might imagine yourself in 'a great roofless cave!'

'The Cove always seems to look down on us with a good natured, honest face; but the Scar seems to say, "What feeble grasshoppers you are, and what if I were to close in and crush you".'

The stream issuing from the Cove and the rock-pent torrent coming through the walls of the Scar—both rise in the bare plateau of Malham Moor, between the Mid and North Craven Faults. The Tarn and its surroundings, acres of swampy ground with reeds and bog plants, was once a puzzle; how was the water held in by porous limestone? An outlying area of impervious slate, the green Silurian, crops up here between the two faults giving Yorkshire one of its rare lakes.

'The most significant fact about the Tarn is the fact that it exists at all.' It is the 'lone tarn' of the poem, encompassed by uplands unutterably desolate, bleak, bare and inhospitable when the wild north-easters blow. Anglers long ago were alone in appreciating it. Malghwater provided Fountains' monks with 'inexhaustible store of trout and perch'. Charles Kingsley, after good sport, declared it to be 'the best fishing in the whole earth'.

Skaters knew it for early frozen waters, 'ideal ground, where on sound pure ice the skater can rejoice in his glorious liberty through a bracing winter's day or in the silence and weirdness of the moonlit winter's night.'

At Gisburn in Ribblesdale is a painting of wild white cattle which once roamed in Gisburne Park. The artist has shown his mighty bull against a Tarn background. The Listers' hunting lodge occupied the site north east of the Tarn which the millionaire Mr. Walter Morrison used for his mansion, now the Tarn House centre for the Council for Promotion of Field Studies. Happy hunting ground for all interested in wild life, flora, fauna, geology, local history, it stands in splendid isolation. The grounds along the Tarn brink are a sanctuary for birds and rare plants. The drive is free to be walked on, and the grounds open for those who can appreciate them.

I enjoy all three places. The Cove is best in summer when brilliantly-winged dragon flies shimmer over the pools where the clear stream issues into light of day, and deep blue cloud shadows move over the pastures, picking out the white walls; and when very few folk are about. Gordale Scar is best visited after the crowds have rejoined cars and coaches and are homeward bound; evening, dusk approaching, or a sombre winter day, are right for the gorge adding mystery and gloom to recesses already awe-inspiring. The stream running hither and thither over the green floor near the farm flows over watercress beds.

As for the Tarn, I have been most delighted, not near water level, but looking down on its blue, sky reflecting waters from Nappa Gate, where the old Malham to Settle track comes to the watershed. Once we sheltered against the top wall watching a curtain of sleet and hail drawn over the Tarn and the Moor; all was white. Then out came the sun and miraculously soon all was grey and green and blue once more.

Said some friends of mine about to show off Malham to an American visitor: "Today we'll show you our Yorkshire Grand Canyon."

She scrambled gamely into Gordale and looked up. "My," was her comment, "how cute!" Seeing the Grand Canyon in 1971 I understood.

6. *Three Byways out of Malhamdale*

To leave the dale head every road must climb. Fierce gradients, hairpin bends, and long stretches of snowscreens are the order of the day. Cove Road climbs, west side, and Prior Rakes, east side of the valley, to Malham Moor and the Tarn cupped in a hollow of the plateau. Both meet a surfaced stretch of the ancient Mastiles road.

TO LITTONDALE

West of the Tarn a fell road, signposted Arncliffe 5¼ miles, strikes north from High Trenhouse to Water Houses. This lonely road to Littondale crosses Fountains Abbey country. The grey whale-back ridge on the west, to which the Pennine Way strides, is Fountains Fell. All about were the sheep walks of medieval times when the monks held 'sheepgates for wetherflocks and yowe flocks'. Look for the small folds and fields of Celtic herders outlined in the sun against the steep ledges overlooking Darnbrook. Little activity on this route nowadays; mild-eyed cows wait to see you through the gates or over the cattle grids, or lambs make a great show of alarm. Curlews shriek their shrill defiance. Redshanks uttering sweet warning notes rise as you near their nesting places. Friendly wheatears flit on walltops.

TO HALTON GILL

The Stainforth road runs due west from the Tarn as though heading for Penighent. Keep on without turning, an hilarious switchback way, the final drop sending you up by your own momentum to Sannet Hall. Here you go left for Stainforth, or right turn along a fine fell way. This begins as Goat Lane, comes to Peter Castle—prehistoric—leaves Dale Head farm on the left, passes Rainscar 'ranch' with its pedigree herd of galloways, reaches Giant's Graves—there to begin the steep descent into Penighent Gill. The scenery is as dramatic as the place names; Pennine landscape at its wildest. Halton Gill says welcome to Littondale. It is from this road, near the beck above Penighent House farm, that the easiest climbs to the mountain's hoary head begin.

TO RIBBLE

For magnificent Craven Fault scenery no road is more exciting than one turning south a mile west of Capon Hall. This Langcliffe and Settle route has not one or two but a whole series of scenic titbits to coax curious travellers to roam around on foot. Take the first low bridge over Cowside beck; the stream wanders away innocently enough, and not a hint that a mile below it is about to be hurled into a deep gill as Catterick Foss, one of the most enchanting and— after heavy rain—exciting 'sights' in Craven. Back to the road for a mile; turn right along the stony farm track to Winskills. This is a breezy limestone platform on which Samson's Toe, a dark boulder of Silurian rock, has been poised since an ice flow dropped it there. Turn around, back to the road and keep forward; the pastures give way to limestone screes and high ramparts of rock, the outer defences of Attermire. Scramble along the scar foot and on the left you come to a yawning hole, the mouth of Victoria Cave, which every north country archaeologist knows as one of the best bone caves in the country. Excavation proved that it had been a hyena den in pre-glacial times, with bones of hippo, straight tusked elephant and woolly rhino strewn about. Stone Age people used it, Bronze Age men sheltered here and Iron fugitives from Roman invaders.

This road drops dangerously into Langcliffe, then sedately down the Ribble to Settle.

Motorists, take care; Malham exits are all hazardous.

7. Walkers Only: Ways out to Other Dales

These are many; paths up limestone slopes to avoid the Cove road and Tarn road, old ways over into the Winterburn Valley, ancient tracks to Wharfedale, fell ways into Littondale and Ribblesdale.

TO WHARFEDALE

From the up and down lane beyond Gordale House two paths strike east, the first coming down to Bordley Hall, the second rounding Kealcup Hill—with traces of Iron Age settlement—and dropping in at Bordley's highest farm. The Winterburn runs down a green, enclosed dale of infinite beauty, passing pastures with old farms which were Fountains Abbey property with horse breeding as well as sheep walks. Lovely paths, some rarely used, run through flower-filled fields down dale, to Lainger House and up to the surfaced road which comes in from Hetton and Rylstone. A stony farm road climbs out of Bordley Head to the Malham Moor tracks near Lantren Holes Field; here three stones are left of a Bronze Age circle originally 150 feet round. Right turn to Hard Gate and Skyrethornes, or ahead to join the untouched sections of Mastiles and so down to Kilnsey. These have always been my choice of walking to Wharfedale.

TO LITTONDALE

Two perfect fell crossings strike north, from east of the Tarn, to Littondale. Both are clearly marked on the one-inch map though they are sometimes vague underfoot. From Malham to Arncliffe, by Great Close, Middle Barn and Middle House and over the unfenced cow pasture under Parsons Pulpit and Arncliffe Clowder, is 7½ miles. The walk forking north-east from this in Great Close crosses the 'slack' of High Mark then, between the Clowders of Arncliffe and Hawkswick, enters into vast solitudes before dropping by a deep gill to the Skirfare opposite Hawkswick village; this is 8 miles.

We tread historic and prehistoric ground. The great 'closes' the eighteenth century graziers used for fattening beef cattle are today gisted by cattle from less favoured farmlands. Fountains Abbey stock ranged the same upland acres, and a thousand years before them Norse herders and, going back in time, Iron Age hillmen had village sites, stockaded enclosures—against predatory wolves—and tiny 'corn-fields' on the Clowder slopes.

No fear of wild beasts today but, after May 12th, keep your eyes open for a solitary bull somewhere on the outer edge of a group of heifers; you may have a long way to run to the nearest wall—maybe miles and that broken-down—in vain attempt to escape him. We had an alarming meeting with one on the open fell north of Middle House one June day. Gazing enraptured on acres of Alpine flowers, cowslips and purple orchises, mountain pansies and mealy primroses, rockroses and heartsease, our delight was shattered by the bellowings of Taurus bearing down upon us. Broken clints—fissured and fractured limestone pavements—at the edge of a sheer wall of rock proved our salvation. We scrambled over the broken slabs where he did not choose to follow, and breathed again.

TO RIBBLESDALE

From Malham, west of the Cove, the 'Old Settle Road' by Stockdale is under 6 miles. A green path climbs to the watershed at Nappa Gate near old calamine workings, strikes due west over sheep-nibbled turf on the line of a minor Roman road. Far ahead are the Bowland fells, Ribblesdale hidden behind miles of brown inarable moorland; north lie the gleaming scars and broken skyline of the mid Craven Fault. Only one lonely homestead appears in the landscape. An oasis of green and precious intaken land surrounds Stockdale farm where Sawley Abbey tenants cared for the monks' estate. The babbling beck not far below does a disappearing act, hurled over rocks as Scaleber Foss. Near the three lane ends look for Roman camp and dewpond. Look towards the rock ramparts of Attermire; a path works around to Settle. Follow the downhill road and in 2½ miles you will be in the old town.

What improvements Airedale and Wharfedale roads have seen since 1964! Highways widened and straightened but byways little changed. Footpaths as pleasant as ever with the added bonus of new Nature Trails. A particularly rewarding one goes from Crookrise farm, between Skipton and Rylstone, through forestry and over the fells. Through Grass Woods overlooking the Wharfe north of Grassington, a Nature Trail with variants, something for everyone, all the year round attraction

Clifford hunting lodge, Barden Tower

Two

WHARFEDALE

1. *Pattern of History*

BECAUSE WHARFEDALE IS so near the largest Yorkshire towns, and as easily accessible to Lancashire townsfolk, it would head any popularity poll of Pennine dales. It is the nearest 'real country', unspoilt, the river unpolluted; the dale—and the fells above—offer days of untrammelled wandering.

The pattern of history? Its lords from early times surveyed Wharfedale estates from Skipton; their castle was the centre of local government—after Norman barons had taken the place of the English earls. Airedale and Wharfedale ran together, Romillys, Cliffords and the priors of Bolton ignoring the watersheds as division between the two rivers.

The 'home park' of Skipton—with its pale enclosing six miles by four—was neighbour to the Manor and Chase of Barden and a deer park taking in the empurpled heights overlooking Wharfe, Earl's and Simon's Seats. When out hunting from Skipton the lords and earls ranged from Aire, across Wharfe to the Cross of Greenhow— where lords of Nidderdale and Knaresborough Forest, the Mowbrays and Abbots of Fountains, held their forest bounds. Higher updale, Skipton hunting preserves joined with Littondale and Langstrothdale Chases enjoyed by the Percys, and beyond the watershed in Bishopsdale and beyond Park Rash in Coverdale, with the lords of Wensleydale's own forest lands.

Romillys, to ensure a safe passage into eternity, founded Embsay Priory, translated the canons to Bolton, and into the prior's hands passed many estates. Look east of Wharfe, beyond Possford—the Valley of Desolation—to 'Spectebeck and Walchesburn', that is from this green dale over the moors to the Washburn valley, and all between was the priory's, theirs to enjoy for sport and for pasture.

As in Malhamdale, Fountains Abbey rivalled and outstripped the priory in its land holdings with firm stake in the hills above Malham Moor, above Littondale, on Fountains Fell; their cotes are many by Skirfare. Their chief business centre was at Kilnsey where sheepfolds, clipping stands and dipping dubs were. Mastiles road to Ribble and Greenhow road to Nidderdale were constantly busy with abbey trade and traffic.

The highway updale, to Kettlewell and over Park Rash to Middleham was as busy as any in the middle ages, and a London-Richmond-Scotland highroad well into the eighteenth century. Nobles and kings found it well supplied with free hospitality at castles and abbeys at convenient intervals. Armies rode this route to the Border to repel

Scots invasion; Clifford led his dalesmen this way *en route* for Flodden.

Cliffords, and the priors, held so much power in their hands few others reached their level. Among families of some importance were Mauleverers and Claphams of Beamsley near Bolton, and Nortons of Rylstone Hall who so often came to blows with Cliffords over hunting rights on those rugged fells of Flasby and Crookrise; when one felt aggrieved at the other poaching deer he walled in his preserves, in vain hoping to end further trouble. They each erected towers—one named for each side—and Nortons and Cliffords glowered at each other. But the Nortons who kept firm to the Old Faith lost their hold after the Pilgrimage of Grace and were eclipsed after the Rising of the North—by which time the Cliffords were high in royal favour, purchasers of abbey and priory lands, married to royalty, and created earls of Cumberland.

Lesser families were the Yorkes, out of Nidderdale, and the Prestons who lived at Appletreewick's High and Low Halls. The humble Cravens from this same village rose in the world, one becoming Lord Mayor of London and his son earl of Craven, a loyal Royalist, friend, helpmeet—and some believe, husband of the royal princess, Elizabeth, the unfortunate widowed queen of Bohemia.

None of these great and less-great families remain. But there are still descendants of men who were foresters of the Cliffords, who followed the Clifford banner to Flodden, who continued farming ancestral acres when their lords were forgotten. They were the Listers of Barden, Blands of Woodhouse—a daughter was mother of Nelson—Knowles of Foxup, and Gills, and Fawcetts.

To the curious wanderer Wharfedale before 1066 is particularly interesting. Travelling through the dale we shall find marks of the Celts thick on the limestone scars. Their herders watched their flocks where abbey shepherds followed centuries later. Their fields were ploughed over by Anglian farmers; strip lynchets lie in bands across squared plots. What a palimpsest, this Wharfedale landscape!

Then there were the Romans against whom local Iron Age men raised their hilltop earthworks. Wharfedale watched them all.

2. History at Bolton Priory

The Cistercians knew a delectable site when they saw one, and the Augustinian canons were not far behind them in snapping up pleasant spots when they offered. The Romillys in 1120 founded a priory at Embsay very near their castle at Skipton, but when they gave the canons a chance of translation to the Wharfe banks in their manor of Bolton, a gift of Alice Romilly in 1154, the prior ordered the move almost before the signatures on the title deeds were dry.

A blessed spot! We have walked in the cloisters on a February day when the sun was kind as summer, all cold winds held at bay by the protecting walls. The high fells were as sheltering walls to the priory. They offered good hunting too, and the river the best of fishing.

Here are a few notes for the countrygoer who does more than a brief, ten minutes walk around the priory ruins during an afternoon's idling by the river.

In the beginning, before the Conquest, Earl Edwin, brother of the powerful earl of Mercia, owned Bodelton Manor, covering all Skipton parish and much of the upper Aire into Malhamdale and over the Gap to Hellifield. His hall was here on a green bank above Wharfe, a small chapel adjoining. After losing his lands in 1070 the Romillys as new lords much preferred the rock-edge site at Skipton for a stronghold to protect their honour. Eighty years later the canons of Embsay were to make use of the site of Edwin's manor house; it is quite likely that within the chancel north wall are stones of the Anglian chapel.

The prior and fifteen canons settled in with a large and growing number of workmen, indoor scullions, outdoor gardeners, skilled craftsmen, to undertake building projects, and thirty or so lay brothers who performed tasks the canons—who were priests—did not do. Later, when life was sorely upset by fear of Scots attacks, to the large 'personnel' was added a band of armed guards, sons of noble houses ready to repel enemies. The prior waxed rich as the largest landowner between Wharfe and Aire with desmesne farms, extensive sheep walks, dairy granges, horse breeding 'ranches', lead and iron mines, peat pits, salt pans, corn mills. As lord of many more manors—where courts had to be held as if he were a lay owner—he needed a large staff of lay officials to act as agents, overseers and bailiffs on his behalf.

According to the strict rule of St. Augustine the Canons Regular had to devote their lives to Prayer, Almsgiving and Hospitality; they were not bound within their priory walls but travelled to churches where they served as priests, took the chair at manorial courts and dealt with business for which minor officials were not competent. The prior was wool merchant, trader with foreign countries and, on occasion, money-lender. He entertained on a lavish scale, and went forth hunting over his own grounds when sporting prelates were his guests.

Outsiders were often critical of the wealthy canons. They noted outstanding cases of laxity. Canons went gadding about, grossly neglecting the poor at their gates, while cellarers waxed fat on stores in their care. But the canons had their worries following bad seasons when crops failed, when floods carried away stock, when murrain decimated their cattle. Also there was constant apprehension about the Scots.

Scots raids, from the Conquest onwards, came thicker and faster in the fourteenth century, with extra ferocity after Bannockburn. How Craven suffered, and all abbey properties. The priory was left in ruins, crops fired, stock stolen, and the prior and canons sought shelter in other houses farther from the danger belt. The archbishop offered payment for their upkeep—4 marks each for a year's board and lodging.

Setbacks regardless, the priory continued to grow. Cliffords took the place of early Romilly descendants as benefactors after 1310.

Many periods and building styles are obvious. 1155 to the 1530's saw destruction, rebuilding, enlarging. Before walking round the ruins take a good look at the model of the priory as it once was; it is in the north aisle of the parish church.

Start with the church which includes some of the earliest building and which remains intact and whole for it has served for centuries as place of worship for Bolton folk—for three hundred years when the canons were priests, for four centuries since the rest of the priory was dismantled. Look for the fine thirteenth century work on the high south wall—which sheltered the cloisters—and at the splendid west front which is partly screened by tower walls never completed. When the prior decided on widening the nave nothing was possible on the cloister side so the north wall was breached, massive pillars and arcading took its place, and the new north aisle was added with its very beautiful decorated windows.

Archway: Bolton Priory

The choir and chancel were built about 1170, but Scots damage was great and rebuilding was carried out with timely gifts of the new benefactors, the first Cliffords.

When the canons had come together again after the worst raids—so little was left no more raiders considered it worth a visit—money flowed into the prior's coffers, enough to consider better rebuilding and additions than ever before. Look up at the east end window, at the chancel and presbytery upper walls; turn round to admire the transepts. From the south transept southwards stretch foundations of other fourteenth century buildings: a chapter house, the long range covering the canons' day room which had their dormitory above, a rere dorter, and beyond, the prior's fine new lodgings. What is left of church walls and arches is impressive. How much more so it must have looked before Henry VIII decided on putting an end to the monastic system.

Only a few years before the Dissolution the last prior, Moon, had seen the first stage in building of a splendid west tower; it remains, as he left it, incomplete.

The end of the canons? All received pensions, some became parish priests. The priory? It was bought by the descendant of the Cliffords, its benefactors, for £2,490; this included buildings and lands—excluding Malham and Appletreewick. The first earl turned the gateway of the old prior's dwelling into a hunting lodge, and his successors centuries later turned it into a shooting lodge—as it is today. The canons' infirmary remains were incorporated into a new rectory—'the dream house of every young miss who ever hopes to marry a curate', enthused an early Victorian Guide, whilst the buttressed walls of ruins adjoining became a boarding school, the rector as master.

Few of us see the priory for the first time as unfamiliar. We must have seen reproductions of the landscapes of Turner, Landseer, Cox and Girton. Possibly we have read Wordsworth's 'White Doe' and the 'Force of Prayer'. Ruskin wrote of a visit here; the black crows cawing above the broken walls, said he, were the spirits of the black canons!

3.   Highways into Wharfedale

FROM LANCASHIRE AND RIBBLESDALE

Routes from Lancashire and Ribblesdale:

Follow A59 from Clitheroe, Gisburn and Skipton to Bolton Bridge, where the dales 'through road' turns north as B6160 to upper Wharfedale. Alternatives from Skipton are high level from Embsay over the fell—superb views and miles of August heather—to Barden Tower, and low level bylanes out of Embsay to Easby and Halton East where unfenced the way runs gently down the sloping pastures to the priory. Distance: 6 miles.

The main highway and bus route—B6265—leaves Skipton by excitingly named places, Craven Heifer (the original), None-go-by, to pleasant villages like Rylstone and Cracoe where the untroubled low land is in such stark contrast to the dark fells above, where Cliffords and Nortons in their generations glowered at each other from their respective hunting towers. Continue north through Threshfield, or turn off to Linton and Grassington.

FROM THE WEST RIDING TOWNS

From the large woollen towns highroads come to Wharfe by many routes. To use the above approaches take A629 from Keighley to Skipton. To strike into Wharfedale from Steeton cross the flanks of Rombalds Moor by A6034 arriving over scenic heights to the green dale at Bolton Bridge. Or, from Ilkley and middle Wharfe cut over the foot of Beamsley Beacon by winding lanes to Beamsley village not far from Bolton Bridge.

FROM YORK, RIPON AND HARROGATE

The highway from the north east is most historic of all. A59 is the Blubberhouses route, as undulating, switchback and exciting in spite of modern improvements as in bygone times. It is still at the mercy of winter storms as when Romans, medieval travellers and armies marching or riding to war, battled over. Note well the ranks of snow screens. Distance: Harrogate to Skipton, 22 miles.

FROM PATELEY BRIDGE

B6265 goes west over hill and dale through gale-swept country, hurled down to Pateley, forced up to Greenhow Hill and on to Hebden and Wharfedale, the route of Roman pack trains laden with lead, abbey flocks, and centuries of wayfarers. Distance: Ripon to Grassington, 21 miles. From the north west only one classified road, B6160, comes in from Aysgarth by Kidstones Pass. The fell roads are many.

4. Up Wharfedale—Slowly

Wharfedale is a most handy valley, good roads east and west of the river giving unlimited variations on the one theme, twenty miles and hardly a dull moment. The west side route (B6160) is the better for through travellers from Bolton Bridge to Burnsall, Threshfield, under Kilnsey's frowning crag, to Kettlewell and Buckden. The east side byway tends to wriggle alarmingly, crawls round awkward bends, squeezes between farm and barn so that hazards, in the form of the school bus, cows in leisurely procession to the milking shed, dogs herding sheep and happy wanderers disporting themselves, are to be anticipated to avoid trouble.

Imagine the delight of setting out to explore the banks of Wharfe knowing that but for a few stretches—between Grass Woods and Conistone—there is no need to leave the riverside from Bolton Bridge to the headsprings, if you are so minded. It is 'jog on, jog on the footpath way, and merrily hent the stile-a', and if the sad heart is not 'tired in a mile-a', it ought to be.

HISTORY AT BOLTON BRIDGE AND BEAMSLEY

Now for high spots and beauty spots, starting from Bolton Bridge, a good place for preliminary meditation. Join the watchers on the bridge; the Wharfe, smooth flowing, sets the mood for contemplation.

Walter White set out from Skipton one hot summer day in 1858 taking the whole morning to cover the first seven miles. Reaching the 'Devonshire Arms' and seeing a large number of vehicles drawn up he decided, rightly 'the numerous visitors betokened something unusually attractive'. Parked cars and crowds always do, but this is a place where folk have long congregated.

Over Blubberhouses from York and Knaresborough came an important highroad, travellers in early days crossing the river by ferry. The heavy-walled cottages at the bridge end have in their masonry stones of an ancient ferry house, and maybe of the Chantry where priests prayed for the wellbeing of wayfarers. Later was built the first Bolton Bridge.

In June 1644 Prince Rupert and his cavaliers, after camping the night in a cornfield, crossed the river, and away towards York. There was a tree known as Prince Rupert's Elm in the field and a story persisted of a fulfilled prophesy uttered by a local Puritan. As the king's men trampled the corn ripe for harvest so would they soon be laid low. The defeat on Marston Moor awaited them.

In 1838 a young traveller called Frederick Montagu penned in his *Gleanings in Craven* some amusing reactions to a halt at Bolton Bridge. He called at the Guide's House near the 'Devonshire Arms'— all strangers required a guide in this 'dangerous country'—and there was highly diverted to discover that 'pieces of dried washleather on wooden frames pendant from the ceiling' were the dalesman's staple diet—oatcakes. He watched the oatcake baking and carried away the recipe. He also noted the 'unmusical dialect, the uncouth, almost primitive simplicity and honest bluntness' of the farmers met there.

From the Yorkshire dalesfolk he had seen he had already gathered that they were most cleanly and to find that they 'whitewashed their cellars' would not have surprised him.

East of Bolton Bridge, high above the river yet low beneath the fell and beacon which it names, is Beamsley. Only a sorely diminished Beamsley according to local lore for a grander place was swallowed up long ago because of the evil doings of its people.

In quiet courtyard, Beamsley Hospital

At the roadside, behind a low-arched gatehouse, is a quiet garden place, peaceful as a nunnery. I have seen cars stop to visit the antique-seller's cottage adjoining, but few are aware of the Beamsley Hospital, unless they are interested in Lady Anne Clifford and her mother who endowed it.

Pass through the archway—the inscription was Lady Anne's doing —and old women at their doors come to see if they can help. Left and right of the archway are small dwellings. A paved path, between snowdrops and crocuses, daffodils and old-fashioned border flowers, goes direct to a turretted octagonal building. Half way was a stone house, alone, but a tree crashed in the February gales of '62 and I saw the walls demolished where it fell. The octagonal edifice holds bedsitters for almswomen. One section of the octagon is entrance passage, one a bathroom complete with immersion heater, another the visiting minister's vestry, leaving five sections for occupation. They surround a most complete little chapel which once kept all Lady Margaret's and Lady Anne's rules. Now, since Skipton Castle passed into other hands, rules are relaxed, so I am informed.

'This almshouse founded in 1593—God's name be praised', is the inscription over the entrance archway.

BEAUTY IN BOLTON WOODS

'I recommend to all lovers of beautiful scenery Bolton Abbey and its neighbourhood', wrote Wordsworth in 1807. 'This enchanting spot belongs to the duke of Devonshire; the superintendence of it has been entrusted to the Rev. William Carr who has most skilfully opened out its features; and whatever he has added has done justice to the place by working with the invisible hand of art in the very spirit of Nature'.

A man of many parts, Mr. Carr, excavating the ruins, opening out the woods, bridging watercourses, placing seats 'at every high spot for the view'—and dairy farming. He bred the famed Craven Heifer, a Smithfield beauty queen after which so many northcountry inns were named.

Victorian tourists knew the highspots and seats in the woods. They have attractive names: Skiphouse Wheel Seat, Cascade Bridge, Ungain Terrace, Cat Crag, Priors Stone and Friars Stone (near which ancient graves were found), Noscow Gill, Burlington and St. Briget's seats. The romantic used to sit and read the 'White Doe of Rylstone', musing on the past. The picnic parties more interested in the dramatic made their hilarious way, two miles of up and down paths, to the Strid. For them, and the foolhardy, guides of the time uttered warnings.

There are several 'little Strids' but the great Strid is unmistakable: 'the Wharfe rushing through swift, deep, ungovernable boiling and eddying in never ceasing tumult. . . . The rock worn smooth by the many who have stridden across caring nothing for tales of terrible accidents from a slip of the foot or giddiness'. The 'jumping off' rock is as slimy and treacherous in the 1960s as in the 1860s; death lurks in the same imprisoned waters, though they are not bottomless, frogmen have now proved.

Dalesfolk used to believe that every May morning a 'white horse with foaming mane' rose from the Strid, spelling doom to any who beheld it. Was this a cautionary tale to warn away young folk out 'a-maying'? My grandfather often saw it—always about dusk.

There is no reason to doubt that the Boy of Egremond, son of Alice Romilly and William FitzDuncan, the hope of two powerful lines, did leap the Strid when returning from the chase. Perhaps he did meet his death as legend says, pulled back by his hound when making the jump. But that his bereft mother founded the priory in his memory is disproved for he added his signature to deeds handing Bolton to the canons. It is too good a story to be forgotten, true or not.

Paths through the woods are many: water edge for scramblers, climbing paths for the 'surprise' and farflung views. Old carriage roads designed for Victorian tourists are now inroads for the modern motorist. Wanderers find themselves striking out along half lost paths, lose them, pick up the threads discovering enchanting gills like Possford, alias the Valley of Desolation—a cloudburst uprooted its trees in 1826 but Nature has covered up the traces—and chancing upon unsuspected cottages, like Laund House once a keeper's lodge when Cliffords were at their hunting tower of Barden. Outside the wood, at a higher level and parallel with the valley, are Hazelwood and Storriths and the vast deer park where the priors of Bolton entertained guests, nobles and clerics too, like the Archbishop Melton who brought his own pack of hounds when here on priory business knowing there would be plenty of time for sport. The same grouse moors today offer good shooting for the Duke of Devonshire's guests.

Whichever way you take from the priory to Barden you will pay for admission. If no money was extracted there would be no upkeep for paths and bridges; without made paths and safe crossings wanderings through the woods would never have been possible. From the priory and the Cavendish Memorial—tenants raised money for this fountain in memory of Lord Frederick so foully murdered by the Feinians in Phoenix Park, Dublin—cars may drive through the park to the Pavilion and the Wooden Bridge. The Strid is ahead, all on the grand scale, full of drama, and farther upriver Barden, Bridge and Tower. Between, some of the best walking in the dales; chose left or right bank.

AT BARDEN—BRIDGE AND HUNTING TOWER

At Barden Bridge and Tower history is gathered up; the scenes are surpassingly beautiful. Tearing floods partly destroyed the original structure over which Henry Clifford passed in 1513 leading

> 'A thousand warriors to the field
> Stout sons of Craven who would never yield'

billmen and bowmen, Sylvester Lister from the Tower among them. The field was Flodden where dalesmen with long memories of Scots depredations worked out old scores. Weapons used at the battle were brought back to show to their children. Some lie along the beams at Barden farm. The damaged bridge was made good in 1676 at the expense of 'the whole West Riding,' and a good job they made of it. It is just wide enough for modern traffic; a bus inches its way over, whilst pedestrians breathe in within the deep embrasures long ago designed for them.

The Tower, a dramatic ruin, stands high above the river. Cliffords built it as a hunting lodge; Henry Clifford, the shepherd lord who much preferred this remote spot to his castle halls, enlarged it into his most used residence. Four generations later Lady Anne Clifford, in 1658, rebuilt the Tower, then ruinous, a labour in vain for her daughter's descendants to whom the family estates passed planned demolition, a project too thoroughly completed in the 1770s.

Birds nest in the wall crannies, wind whistles through the broken window slits. Only the farmhouse in its shadow, once the home of the Clifford's chaplain and now a chapel of ease—a notice board gives times of services—remains intact.

You may have tea at the Barden farmhouse in a low raftered room with views out of the mullioned windows upon orchard and old walls. The Lister pikes are there on the rafters, mightily interesting to any who remember Flodden—with reservations.

Once I dropped a clanger at the farm gate. I thought the kilted Scot with sketch stool and easel would be pleased to know that if he took tea here he could examine weapons wielded by stalwart dalesman on that battlefield which we do know was an English victory, though many of us are a bit hazy about the outcome of other English v. Scots fights. He looked hard at me, drew himself to his full height, and said in all seriousness. "I happen to be a Scot. I do not wish to see them."

TO APPLETREEWICK

My own favourite walk by Wharfe; water-edge from Barden Bridge on right bank, smiling pastures to Drebley stepping stones, crossing a minor beck by Howgill Bridge, and back to the the river again. Now comes pure enchantment, for not only does the path thread open glades floored with May bluebells, and sunny clearings full of twinkling light and dappled shade, but hanging woods make the water green as bottle glass often sinister in its depths, and rocky, peninsulas out-thrust make the Wharfe twist and turn, frolic in falls, and swirl in trouty pools.

A field from the river is Appletreewick which would be my favourite village even were it not my father's birthplace. The Norsemen named it 'dairy farm among the apple trees'.

Village history? Norse settlers, Bolton Priory as Lords of the Manor from 1300, and after the Dissolution many local families take over. The Youngs who built High Hall, the Prestons of Low Hall, the Blands of Woodhouse, dominate the local scene, and the Yorkes who came over from Gowthwaite by Nidd, and the Cravens who from such humble beginnings as poor tenants of the priors became powerful far beyond the limits of this dale.

High Hall is the first large farm behind walls at the brow top. APPLETREEWICK name is on its barn. It is a house which looks to have a history, and more so before the giant of an elm, the ancient Gallows Tree at its gate, had to be felled. Youngs built the older parts, the Cravens the rest, the finer touches internally being the work of the William Craven who founded the family fortunes.

William, tradition says, went off to London in a carrier's cart and like Dick Whittington found his fortune and became alderman, then Lord Mayor in due time. The village took great pride in his rise, the more so since he remembered the needs of the parish, as we shall see at Burnsall in bridge, church and grammar school.

One November day I made many drawings inside the hall, having ample time to ponder on the Cravens and their work. Mellow sun poured through the diamond panes of the high, three-tiered transom and mullioned windows, throwing smaller diamonds of gold on the diamond set, stone pavings of the floor in the Great Hall. The same view outside of green dale and far fells they saw, and held their heads high. Family pride showed in the arms shaped in plaster above a parlor fireplace. Fine craftsmanship shows in the Great Hall gallery.

In the second generation his son, the earl of Craven, rose still higher in society and in royal circles, close intimate of Charles I's sister, Prince Rupert's widowed mother, once queen of Bohemia. If they married—as it has been thought, it was kept quiet.

High Hall stands highest. The one long street tumbles downhill to Low Hall. Between—go as slow as maybe, the better to peep down dark passages, to glimpse picture book cottages, a village post office and store tucked away behind the front row of houses. What a fascinating pattern varied chimneys make, how thick encrusted with velvetty mosses all the stepped roofs are.

Half way downhill—the Monk's Hall; think of the canons' or prior's officer doing manorial business here.

Beyond, where the street levels out, are the two inns, the 'New' and the 'Craven Arms', the superannuated stocks, and Onion Lane going down to the river pastures, and scenery lovely as Bolton Woods. 'Aptrick' was always a great place for markets and fairs, and the autumn onion fairs were held in this particular byway. Onions still grow well in the dale as the bunches hanging to dry in October on all the farmhouse walls—and in porches of greater houses like High Hall—indicate.

The outside walls of Low Hall flank the highway like the outer defences of a fortress; note well the massive water-trough hewn from a single stone. This is a spooky place after dark; less so than formerly when the most notorious of the Prestons, Thomas, evil in life and troublesome after death, haunted his old home, uttering bloodcurdling screams, groaning, howling. He had to be 'laid'; his last resting place is reputed to be a well called after him in Dibb Gill.

Dibb Gill can be eerie, but for chilling gloom seek out Trollers Gill haunted 'they say' by a flaming saucer-eyed barguest and howled over by rock-rolling trolls. Just south of Appletreewick the highway forks to Skyreholm, Greenhow and Pateley Bridge; a downhill fork goes off to Parcival Hall, a Bradford Diocesan Retreat, a gracious old house with superb rock gardens which are open to the public at the hours given on a road-edge notice. The timorous may stay enjoying the flowers but the stout-hearted carry on into the nearby Gill. Watch out for the spectre hound with eyeballs flaming. Best time to meet him is after dark. Once he pounced upon and struck dead a dalesman, unfortunate witness of hobgoblin midnight revels; his remains were buried in Burnsall churchyard!

Once we were caught in the Gill in a thunderstorm. How the peals echoed and reverberated, setting all the imprisoned underworld demons of our Norse ancestors raging and roaring. A nearby cave is called, aptly, Hell Hole.

The lovely gardens of Parcival Hall could not provide a greater contrast to the haunted gill or the wild bare moors above. Across these we follow old tracks first used by lead miners. Everyone knows of Dick Turpin but fewer have heard of a highwayman as daring who used to seek refuge at Parcival Hall after his more dangerous exploits. Will Nevison was Yorkshire's own schoolboy hero of a hundred escape stories. Even King Charles II appreciated his exploits and dubbed him 'Swift Nicks'.

TO BURNSALL VILLAGE

The road from Appletreewick to Burnsall passes near, on the levels, Woodhouse fields. The Blands of Woodhouse were great dealers in Scots cattle and traders in ponies. Their old homestead looks part of the landscape with its deep mullions, heavy stone roof, and tall wind-

Burnsall: church and Sir William Craven's school

break of trees cutting against the background of Thorpe Fells. A fieldpath goes through the farmyard where young Oates, the 'gallant gentleman' gave a hand as a lad on holiday, and pretty Mary, a daughter of the farm, carried a milking pail, little thinking her husband was to be a Lincolnshire clergyman and her son England's hero, Horatio Nelson.

Burnsall spread out on Wharfe side welcomes loiterers. The water edge green is a car park.

Angles named Brineshale and erected a church dedicated to Wilfred of York, of Ripon and Hexham, a true north-country saint. Norsemen must have designed the font—still used—carving on the bowl legendary sea beasts from pagan mythology. Anglian artists designed tall crosses with flowing interlacing patterns on the shafts; see fragments in the north aisle. The mortal remains of Norse dalesmen were

covered by stone hog-backed grave lids, like tiled roofs their pattern-
ing; you will find them near the font on entering the church. The
Normans came and their rebuilding left nothing of the early church;
but the font, an aged and valued object, was retained and with a
new base, diaper-edged, continued to serve for infant baptism. The
Norman lords of Skipton had lands at Burnsall; Lady Adeliza was
living when the Romilly chapel was added—all that now remains
from the second church.

Some great lord returning from wars in Europe saw an exquisite
piece of Italian work in alabaster, and returning to Wharfedale gave
it to Burnsall. It was lost and found again; you will find it in the
north-east chapel, a small panel of the Nativity, delicately wrought,
with faint vestiges of colour in the fold of Mary's robe.

Sir William Craven was justifiably proud of the benefits his riches
were able to confer on Burnsall; he left tablets perchance they were
forgotten. He gave the village the picture-book grammar school so
beautifully set by church and riverbank, and in 1612 'butified' the
church at his own expense.

Here are useful talking points if you chance to meet a villager
with time on his hands.

Though two centuries have passed since a particularly revolting
murder at Grassington no one in Burnsall has forgotten that it was
a local loiterer on Wharfe banks who was a horrified witness of the
attempt to dispose of the body. The moon shining from behind a
cloud lit up Tom Lee and his wife, high on Loup Scar top, and the
body—in a sack—as it was pushed over the rock to fall into a deep
pool.

Refer to Burnsall Sports, the Fell Race and inter-village rivalry of
past generations; all rewarding topics.

THORPE IN THE HOLLOW

It is recorded that Burnsall erected a maypole on the green in 1862,
but surely it was an earlier one the young men of Thorpe lifted
and carried off in triumph to their own hamlet, unbeknown. Burn-
sal's sleuth finally tracked it down, returned home for reinforcements,
and after a fierce fight overcame the 'cobblers' and bore home the
pole with shouts of victory.

You may follow the poles—telegraph poles—across the fields to
Thorpe, such a secluded spot we want to believe every tale and
tradition associated with it, even though many are debunked. It lies
in the arms of the hills, rather like some small Cotswold community
in the oolitic belt. Each knoll is named; Thorpe Kail, Elbolton (with
fairy caves which historian Dr. Whitaker thought of as dens of
banditti but which excavations proved to be homes of Neolithic
hunters and herders), Stebden, Butterhaw. In prehistoric times wild
cattle roamed these limestone slopes, goats too, and the fox and
wolf which preyed on them. Later Celtic dalesmen had settlements
here and grazing for flocks and herds.

At Thorpe-sub-Montem all periods come together. Traditions told

Fairy hills: road to Thorpe

of its use as a secure hiding place for local families and their stock when Scots came raiding. Tales are told of its shoemakers who made and repaired the footwear of Fountains monks. The best story of a meeting with Old Nick in Wharfedale concerns a certain Thorpe cobbler, Calvert, who coming over Greenhow from the abbey with a load of shoes to mend fell into conversation with the Old Lad, had a wrestling bout with him and won a promise for a new bridge over the Dibble. That was how Devil's or Dibbles Bridge was built!

There is very little to Thorpe: a stream, a grass strip, a few old houses and barns with many a weathervane on gables, a snow plough at the ready, and all outlets so narrow and high-walled snow must surely lie long between them in deep drifts.

Two lanes come in from the highroad, their signs so inconspicuous it seems Thorpe is not over eager to attract notice. Another lane follows the lower slopes of the limestone knolls above Linton Holms to the Skipton highway near Cracoe; SINGLE LINE TRAFFIC ONLY is the warning at each end.

Between Thorpe and Linton are breezy pastures with long broad turf-clad terraces, the strip lynchets of bygone centuries. Sheep feed in elysian fields and when they feel the need to rub themselves they use the same scattered boulders which flocks of a thousand years have so polished that their undersides are like black marble. The path starts by an outbarn on the Cracoe lane.

TO LINTON, THRESHFIELD AND GRASSINGTON

Burnsall to Grassington: 3 miles' walk along the Wharfe banks, but farther by road. A succession of high spots; Loup Scar is a dramatic crag overhanging dark pool, pleasant lingering to Hebden footbridge, bonny bits on the way to Linton stepping stones, and a mighty roar and thunder of foaming waters at the mill weir, especially after spate.

From the highway—which rides high and gives promise in the far views of good things ahead—we are tempted first towards Linton village, then to the church at the river edge, so passing the wayside school, seventeenth century and haunted by a jolly ghost, a fiddling elf called Pam! One of Halliwell Sutcliffe's pretty inventions!

The busy highway from Skipton passes through Linton; B6265 was the former stage and mail coach route. The village flanks the road and sits pretty round a green with a babbling beck flowing across it. Here is everything to make the perfect village, and this Linton is, an unassuming beauty queen voted first in a national newspaper competition. For first prize it was presented with a trophy, an astrolabe with which it does not quite know what to do.

At the road verge is the seventeenth century hall of Linton, the fine house flanked by a barn more than a hundred feet long. The old house nearby with drifts of snowdrops on its lawns in February and garden gate opening on to stepping stones and beck, is Troutbeck, where Halliwell Sutcliffe wrote many of his dales romances. Across the highway stands the Manor House, for generations home of the Deanes.

How I would like to turn back the clock for a look at eighteenth century Linton. Dr. Whitaker, an old boy of Threshfield Grammar School, left a full picture of village life as he knew it. Then it was almost self-supporting and had no use for money or tradesmen from outside. Every cottager had a vegetable patch, a pig in the sty, a cow on the common. Some grew oats which were parched at a communal kiln. Surplus milk was pooled for cheese making. The gossip on washing days when clothes were washed in the beck and beaten on the one batting stone, the wagging tongues as they were put to dry in the communal drying ground!

I wonder what they talked about? About the splendid town-size building going up, the like of which none had ever seen? The hospital for six poor men and women was provided for in the will of Richard Fountaine in 1721. He had left Linton a poor young man who made his money, tradition says, as a timber merchant who saw that wealthy citizens of London who died during a dread plague had coffins and decent burial; danger money! The hospital is certainly fine, and so were the 'blue cloaks or gowns lined with green' he stipulated the almsmen and women should wear. Now the 'residents' are being supplied with luxuries the first never dreamed of: electricity and hot water, baths, £25 a year pension and money for heating.

The new rector in 1733 set the village talking, and kept them agog peeping, reporting and commenting on the strange goings-on at the Rectory—now the Youth Hostel. They had heard of hunting and shooting and drinking parsons, but one whose ambition was to be the most elegant dancer was quite new. Peepers saw rector practising

steps before a full length mirror, and the fiddler who played for the
dancing with his back turned! And he paid a scholar to read to him
in bed—Greek and Latin! Although the Rev. Benjamin Smith, Sir
Isaac Newton's nephew, arrived with a chip on his shoulder and looked
down his nose at a mere 'half share in this benighted living in the
savage north, condemned to live among folk no more than baptised
brutes', he stayed over thirty years. He came to be considered not a
bad sort after all.

Light relief in 'the daily round, the common task' were mummings
and play-acting, revels after clipping, haytime and harvest, merry
nights in winter, and the Michaelmas Feast. All have lapsed—except

Linton village

village sports on the green, a shadow of the Feast, which I have
watched on a Saturday in October.

How well supplied is Linton with bridges. The County Bridge of
1892 replaced the shallow ford through which all Skipton traffic had
to splash, sending the ducks quacking in panic. Below this the step-
ing stones led to White Abbey, so named by Halliwell Sutcliffe.
The most venerable bridge by the ford was rebuilt near the Fountaine
Hospital; a clapper bridge with boulder piers and huge slabs, it is
now concreted and provided with handrails, safe for the most frail
almswoman to cross. Madam Redmayne repaired the most handsome
bridge in the eighteenth century, graceful, arched, and quite
wide enough to cope with packhorses, pedestrians and funeral
corteges; now it is the best place to stand and survey the Linton
scene.

Many townsfolk hankering after a country cottage see a barn in a likely spot and think its owner must be quite ready to sell. Farmers need their barns, however isolated and derelict they may appear to a townsman's eyes. But occasionally barns in decay do find new owners and what can be done to transform them into delightful modern dwellings may be seen in Linton; turn down the side lane near the post office. Threshfield, Linton's neighbour bestrides B6265 from Skipton but path and road link them. In spite of the highway it is a tranquil spot, inviting seats on a green, its Old Hall turned inn, its manor house, gabled end to road, having a most unusual wheel window with stone tracery. The buildings grouped at the bridge end include Ling House, and a stable with an odd assortment of horse, pony and two-piece cow shoes on the door.

Centuries ago Ibbotsons, said to have been border reivers, came to Ling House, settled, and became dealers in horses, owners of trains of packponies which carried the commerce of the dales. They took to besom-making using the raw material at hand, ling and heather from the moors! They travelled the dales with wagon loads of new brooms to sweep clean farmyards and cowsheds.

There is good walking around Threshfield. A beck-side path crosses Monksholm to Linton. I often hear my first curlew hereabouts, one lone advance guard sweeping effortlessly across the sky, curved beak and pointed wings clear cut against the clouds; the poignancy of that first cry, a steam of pure liquid, bubbling notes unlocking the gates of spring! A fell track climbs to the heather tops of Boss Moor— white violets at the lane side—where old coal pits are, and where long ago fairs were held for black cattle, galloways ponies and sheep; this is exhilarating all the way to the Winterburn. A third route: to Malham from Skirethorns, up Hard Gate passing Heights Cave, to the open moors and joining Mastiles Road near the 'Druid Circle'.

Linton church was sited to be roughly equidistant from the four communities which made up the parish, Linton, Grassington, Thresh-field and Hebden. Wharfe stepping stones were supplied for folk coming to service from the east side. We are more likely to approach from the highroad to Grassington, by a short cul-de-sac. Church Yett House was once an inn, conveniently placed for a quick one before men hurried after womenfolk who had been their pillion passengers.

St. Michael's is simple, lowly and lowlying near the Wharfe. It has some stones and a font from Norman times, a twelfth century bell turret on the west end and an atmosphere of settled calm. The versified epitaphs on the graves are interesting; Thomas Hammond's memorial in a wallplate on the south aisle is often referred to, for the dates have puzzled many. He died on the '24th day of March A.D. 1685 and was buried the 27th of the said March 1686'. The body was not kept from burial for a year and three days, nor is the date a 'misprint'. We forget that Lady Day, March 25th, was once New Year's Day—and a good day for it too. How much better to welcome a new year with the first stirrings of spring rather than in bleak mid-winter.

Dreaming of blue days and messing about by rivers? Think of hot stepping stones under bare feet, the cool splashings at the weir, children's voices in play, happy families picnicking on the greensward between Little Emily's—the small arched packhorse bridge—and the high Wharfe bridge.

Grassington spreads out high above the river, the place for you if you like old towns with plenty of atmosphere. You will enjoy the market place and poking into narrow ways leading off the main street. There is Jacobs Fold, Town Head—where cobbles are giving way to surfacing kinder to cars—and Gars Lane reminding one that Grassington had the early name of 'Gersintune'.

An old building off the main street, any villager will point out, was the famous theatre of the stage-struck Tom Airey. Edmund Kean trod its boards and Harriet Mellon, a later Duchess of St. Alban's; as well as the redoubtable Tom Airey.

On the main street a bright little fruit shop was two centuries ago the smithy of the murderer of a local doctor. The sorry tale is well remembered. Tom Lee, a violent and ill-tempered man, refused to listen to Dr. Petty's well-intentioned warnings when they met one evening at the 'Anglers', Kilnsey. Moreover he waylaid him at the north end of the Grass Woods and left him for dead. At his smithy he told his wife, and Jack Sharp his apprentice, overhearing, was silenced by implication. They took the youth with them to where the doctor lay, and finding life still flickering made him deal the death blow. How the three hid the body in this place and that and finally were seen hurling a sack into the Wharfe above Burnsall, is told with relish. Strangely, though guilt seemed conclusive, Lee after trial was acquitted and for years walked a free man. He had many enemies and one, angered at a cockfight in Litton, swore to 'see Tom Lee hanged'. Chance offered when both men were in York. With Lee was the apprentice Jack Sharp. At last the young man, who could no longer bear Lee's treatment of him, made known his secret and turned King's Evidence. They hanged Lee all right, on a gibbet they suspended his body in chains, to terrify all who walked near the scene of the crime at Grass Woods gate.

Looking above Grassington to the bare green hills do not be amused if some local oldster declares, "Owd Grassington were up yon!" It was—and prehistoric communities which must remain nameless. Go up the street and up beyond Town Head towards Yarnbury with its derelict lead mines; turn across any of the wide pastures on the left and you strike prehistory. The great enclosures were walled in the eighteenth and nineteenth centuries but look for turf-grown ridges, rows of grey boulders almost grassed over enclosing square and rectangular grassy places nibbled close by sheep. These were fields cultivated by Iron Age Celts and the terraced lynchets on the slopes were strips laboriously ploughed by their primitive tools. Archaeologists look at the so-called 'Druid Circle' in High Close. This, they say, surveying the oval area defined by boundary banks containing courses of ancient wall stones, was probably a community centre, a parliament where men from the village site in Grass Woods could foregather. Winds blew their words about as they do ours, moorbirds cried over them, and curlews objected to their presence too.

Bronze Age Celts buried their dead in the mound I find such a good viewpoint; it dates from about 1600 B.C. The Iron Age settlers who came later took over earlier sites including burial places; these they respected. In turn the Romans took over what Iron Age men had claimed for their own, building a road across their field systems, a camp upon a venerated site; the 'natives' raised defences against the invaders above Grass Woods, but no avail. Many must have been drafted into forced labour gangs to work the rich lead mines at hand.

The grey hills gave up their lead for nigh on two thousand years. In 1830 a curious traveller after visiting the thriving Duke of Devonshire's mines wrote of the miners, 'hard working, industrious and sober, putting earnings in the savings bank'. He had heard all about the way the labour was settled by contract on the last Saturday night each month, called Setting Day. Parcels of ground were auctioned, the miners bidding, beginning with the highest price and reduced by the bidders, the 'last one the taker and his name registered in the setting book'.

Thirty years later he would have told a different story; prosperity was over. A hundred years later—Yarnbury, a sad place of derelict buildings, broken walls, tottering shafts and gaunt chimneys, and scattered over miles of moorland, the litter of abandoned workings.

UPDALE—TO KILNSEY CRAG AND INTO LITTONDALE

Upriver, a choice of two roads to Kettlewell, and always attractive prospects ahead. Along B6160—ten miles to Buckden.

Over the bridge the main road—and bus route—turns by Long Ashes and Netherside to Kilnsey. This grey hamlet with steep pastures and the Crag bastions for background is in perfect harmony with all about it. Here was a busy place when medieval traffic crossed the river at Conistone and headed west over the monastic Mastiles road, when a Fountains Abbey grange (Kilnsey Hall occupies its site) brought streams of travellers, great and humble, to its hospitable door. Much of the woollen trade so important to the monks was centred here. Enormous flocks of sheep were herded along the green lanes above Kilnsey, some bound for summering pastures in Cumberland, some brought in for dippings at the Wharfe dubs, for clipping in the Kilnsey folds.

The abbots' grange has gone, the fine house Christopher Wade built in 1648 is derelict, but Kilnsey itself is by no means dead. Come on Show day in the first week in September when every field is so crammed with cars you could walk across-country on their roofs; or pass through when the ram and sheep sales are held. It has its finger on dales affairs now as always. Local industry? Limestone here is so pure—99·5% calcium—that the impact of Kilnsey Limes is small compared with vast, nightmarish Threshfield/Swinden lime works.

The Crag has always been a great showpiece. Like a sea cliff undercut by pounding waves its profile was indeed shaped by the Wharfedale glacier in the final phase of the Ice Age; what a spectacular
flourish it makes frowning down upon the tranquil valley! Crystal
springs run from the base of the rock, watering erstwhile green banks
where saddleback pigs root and grunt, then sprawl in sleep, flanks
heaving. Queues of cars slow down—not to survey the fine porkers.
They gaze upwards, fascinated.

The 'fly men' are crawling under the overhang, singing lustily as
they flirt with death; or so it appears. This is new style sport, hardly
rock climbing, which involves the use of a sort of bosun's chair with
stirrups, nylon ropes and lifelines. One man clinging to the rockface

Kilnsey under its Crag

by toetips and finger nails plays out his rope to the man dangling
in the 'chair' who 'pegs away', chiselling holes, inserting pegs and
ringscrews for threading his rope. It is slow progress, slow as the
climbers on Pavey Ark or Napes Needle, and watched from below
with the same fascinated intensity; here the police call a 'move on'.

The same glacier which undercut the Crag and smoothed the
contours of Wharfedale was joined by an ice flow from the long,
hollowed-out trough we called Littondale. It is a perfect U-shaped,
cradling valley with sweet peace in its arms. Content to let the world
pass by at the dale foot and over Dead Man's Hill, the folk think of
theirs as The Dale and Wharfe as a mere tributary. If you want
atmosphere turn off north of the Crag and find out what it has been
guarding for so long. You needs must find your own transport.
The market-day bus has been 'axed'.

Arncliffe road end is where friends with cars pick up visitors

arriving on the Buckden bus. Over Skirfare Bridge a second road runs
from Dead Man's Hill to Hawkswick and updale. Take your choice;
from each you look along a dale which is a ready-made picture for
a chapter on the glaciated valleys. The Skirfare, a river so bright it
seems to have had an extra polish, wimples and glances over a stony
bed, when it does not disappear altogether in dry season; it takes
possession of the wide flat valley floor, with meadows and trees on
either hand. The two roads run sometimes against the fell foot, sometimes at river edge, walled by piled river boulders; they are 'life lines'
for Arncliffe 'where eagles nested', for Hawkswick where a hawk-
eyed Viking became dairy farmer, for Litton, an Anglian community
which names the dale, and for the remoter dale head hamlets of
Halton Gill and Foxup where the road ends.

There is history and prehistory written not only on the raking
hills but in the ground beneath them. Caves riddle the limestone,
the best known being Dowkerbottom away behind Kilnsey Crag, in
its time a robbers' den, a shelter for hunted Celts, for Iron Age folk
and never without tenants throughout the Roman period. Some
bereaved soul scooped out a tiny infant's grave in the stalagmite of
its floor and maybe for its mother too. Someone left treasure to be
called for, dragon head brooches and Romano-British enamel work.

> In Craven hills is many a cave,
> Where men may lie as in a grave.
> In Craven rocks is many a den
> To shelter persecuted men.

Especially in Littondale's limestone.

Opposite Hawkswick, Blue Scar makes as good a showing as Kilnsey, a frowning monster towering above Hawkswick and Arncliffe
Cotes—all the many 'cotes' were monastic sheep farms—with Celtic
fields clearly outlined on the limestone pastures below it, and Iron
Age village sites above. If you are interested in Iron Age peoples,
and if you love the dales and find your element, as I do, on the limestone terraces, 'high level' Arncliffe is for you. Looking up to the
scar edges you notice many a standing stone and piled cairn. Local
farmers will tell you they are gathering stones, landmarks for shepherds rounding in their flocks past and present, with old sheep folds
near them. Such 'marks' stand boldly above each of the dale communities as though pointing to each its own gathering and meeting
place. "Of course hikers have piled some of 'em," we are told, "but
one of 'em, one of the Men above Arncliffe, now that is set to be a
sort of sundial."

Climbing above Arncliffe or Cowside up the sheep pastures, and
higher still to the windswept terraces below the Clowder, you find
six watching 'Men', holding silent council. These stone 'maen'—the
word is Celtic for rock or stone—are the permanent present population. Two thousand years ago many hillmen lived up here. You
may trace beehive huts, and rectangular dwelling foundations, with
nearby outer walls which surrounded square courts or stockyards.

Follow sunken tracks from these 'villages' and you come to the tiny fields which they cultivated; again the lower drystone foundations remain. Shallow depressions in the pastures were once their saucer-shaped dewponds where stock was watered. Other fantastic boulders and rock strangely shaped may be naturally eroded, or were they part of primitive ritual, or waymarks on recognized routes?

Arncliffe folk of modern times sun themselves low by the Skirfare. A bonny village, it surrounds a green; three young sycamores are valiantly attempting to take the place of a group of noble trees felled in '48. Summer days see grandfathers mowing the grass and children helping to make hay on the green.

The pleasant houses all look inwards, all grey and stone roofed,

Littondale farmhouses

except the dazzling white-walled post office cottage; many have seventeenth century datestones.

The main dale road sweeps in through an avenue of splendid syca-mores, turns and is away over the bridge to romp upriver to Litton. The church girdled by trees looks on, remembering the day when lads—very like those careering by on motor bikes—mustered here: Calvert boys, Bulcocks and Wederheads, Tenants, Langstraths and Wilsons, Fawcetts and Atkinsons, sons of Percy tenants or of the abbots, and the many Knowles brothers from up Halton and Foxup way. Their names are recorded inside the church on the Muster Roll for Flodden, telling which wielded bill or bow, or went forth proudly, 'able, horsed and harnished'.

Across the bridge where the Skirfare is pale amber with darting trout in its pools, and snowdrops, crocuses, daffodils and a whole procession of the season's flowers adorn a garden verge at water edge—that is Bridge End. Charles Kingsley knew this house, wrote of it in the Vendale chapter of *Water Babies* and so they tell you locally enjoyed a smoke sitting on a rock by the road which took him back to Malham. All views backwards and down on Arncliffe are very fair. We should all do far more sitting and musing on them.

Litton, two miles upriver, 'seems more barns than houses', which is what the most genuine villages always are. Its string of houses all face the sun. The oldest, Elbeck, turns its back to the highway; it is similar to Owlcotes, or Old Cotes, the comely farm with the 1660 datestone, on the roadside near Arncliffe. Like all the Litton houses its walls are hidden behind flowering creepers; flowers are banked under the walls and massed in gardens and crofts beyond them.

In summer I take a secret way between the villages, walking on the dry pavements of the Skirfare bed in a silent, strange world. On either hand cows ruminate in flowery meadows. Ruined barns and derelict farms brood darkly. One darkened by old trees was a tavern, unlicenced, which gave ale freely to any who bought parkin! Another, even more gloomy, mullioned windows eyeless, walls broken, is Spital Garth, a name denoting a monastic hospice. As a shelter it was well placed for the green road from Penighent Gill, where abbey sheep walks were, drops here to valley level. Colliers from Fountains Fell pits also used Spital Garth smithy centuries ago.

East Garth has tumbling waters roaring about its ears, waterfalls cascading down its hillside. Litton is a great place for water music.

Halton Gill, being so high above sea level, came to terms with the elements long ago. It offered welcome to wayfarers struggling over Horse Head Pass which stumbles in at its back doors. It has a friendly look we think when battling through the north-easters over Penighent side. Packhorse trains came along both routes, this being a main high-level route between Lancashire and Scotland.

Coming up the gentle dale you can have no idea what wild days can do on the tops—rain which turns to stinging sleet on Old Cote Moor, breezes which become howling gales on Horse Head. Halton Gill folk were tough types, like their parson, Thomas Lindley, who for sixty years hardly ever missed taking service at his two churches though to reach Hubberholm it meant six miles each crossing of fells, reaching to almost two thousand feet and often the tracks hidden under snow. He lived to be ninety-three; they buried him in Arncliffe churchyard.

The small grey church at Halton Gill has seen its parishioners dwindle. Halton has dwindled, so has Foxup which once had fifteen families and all its empty outbuildings were occupied houses, whilst the remotest community at Cosh is abandoned.

Foxup, where the made road ends, is girdled by protecting trees. One house dated 1686 was home of the Knowles family. We pass the farms when making towards Plover Hill and the under Penighent track to Hull Pot and Horton-in-Ribblesdale. On the Berghs—the shoulder of Plover Hill—stirks are let out in summer, and a bull with the heifers: beware!

Few find Cosh. It is in deepest solitude. Follow a stony track with a peat brown beck alongside, and as it dwindles the nearer you are to this old Norse shepherd's bothy. When folk lived at Cosh, doctor or district nurse had to be transported by jeep. Pawky Littondale humour gets to work on Cosh: 'Where they eat folk' and where 'they salted down t'old man in '47 eight weeks snow'.

Littondale men tendered this advise on how to cope with approaching bulls in lonely places. (a) Climb nearest wall. (b) Pick up three stones, wait until he is near enough to see whites of his eyes—then throw 'em. (c) Turn your back to him, bend down, put your head between your knees and shout "Boo".

Where the road ends: Foxup, Littondale Head

Having escaped from one on Parson's Pulpit we were not sure if these were meant to be funny. Method (c) never failed, said they.

Characters: Littondale has always had them. There was a parson over two centuries ago who wrote space fiction; his *Man in the Moon* was an aeronaut called Israel Jobson who took off into space from Penighent summit and had extraordinary adventures whizzing around sun, moon, and stars. Arncliffe had its witch who helped the lovelorn; they were told to gaze long into the Skirfare beneath the bridge—and doubtless their trueloves would look over their shoulders. Kilnsey at the dale end had a witch called Nan to match Arncliffe's Bertha. Her stock-in-trade was a guinea pig, divining rod and a pack of cards!

The dalesfolk nowadays are down to earth, even the infants. A teacher new to the dale was taking the children for a 'nature walk'. "How many sheep in that field?" she asked, whereat the four-year-old holding her hand commented, "Them's no sheep. They're b—

tups." They shoot badgers when sighted, organize shoots against foxes, and hunted down the goats which used to roam Old Cote Moor, the last survivor of patriarchal Billy, victim of the war years.

I once met Moudy Billy Lund, the dale's mole catcher; more about him I have heard from others. He kept down the moles in the dale, each farmer paying him so much an acre. Little about wild life he did not know.

If they say Hawkswick's full of queer folk, I am sure it is being confused with Austwick near Settle, the true home of 'daft' tales. Being on a narrower and less-used road updale this village has learnt how to keep itself to itself. It lines up by the road, the river flows near its doors, and the south-facing windows all open to the sun and the fairest scenes. From their back garden walls rise the fells, green turf sheep-nibbled, then brackens, screes and walls of rock. Old Cote Moor is miles of heather and cotton grass across which paths from Arncliffe bridge end and Hawkswick coming together make for upper Wharfedale villages. On these heights Nature is everything. Man has never had much of a look-in.

We still say, "There are great possibilities of quietude in England, thank God!" when we are in Littondale.

AT CONISTONE AND KETTLEWELL

What is the common conception of typical Wharfedale landscape? Mine is fulfilled north of Kilnsey, Skirfare bridge and Dead Man's Hill. The fells draw nearer, their grey scar edges break away in boulders which need no trolls to send them rolling. The dribbles of scree merge with pastures patterned with wriggling walls like a child's chalk scribblings, and these dip down steeply to the dale floor, green, very green, and threaded by the Wharfe flowing with trees on either hand.

North of Grassington where the byway east of the river passes between the old oaks and beech glades of Bastow and Grass Woods, the dale is wider, shallowed by ice sheets and more deeply grooved by the river action; glorious rock and woodland scenery. Leave the village by Wood Lane and you will be tempted into the woods, or down to the river, at many a gate.

From the gate at the bridge end the field path follows the river edge to Ghaistrills where bright water flows over smooth 'pavements' or is caught in deep rock sluices, like many minor Strids. The turf on the banks is sprinkled with small flowers, the pavements are full of flowers in crannies. In fact, it would be hard to find more lovely rock gardens of Nature's designing—and hers only—than these.

In June, feet tread patches of birds-foot trefoil or crush out heavenly scent from cushions of wild thyme. There are fluttering bright gold rock roses, masses of cranesbill, and on inaccessible rock ledges overhanging deep water, rock roses with petals deep cerise like those in the best Alpine or 'moraine' gardens in the dale. Birds? I listen for the sweet sandpipers calling and the small clear note of the dipper. Under the Netherside banks water wagtails have a favourite haunt, and so has that lone fisher, the stilted heron.

Much of Grass Woods, including plantations of the 1890s have been thinned or felled, letting sunlight into dim recesses, flooding clearings with flowers. New forestry has introduced conifers, but native hardwoods and stands of young larches are happily interspersed. One large section is a protected bird sanctuary. And of course there are the Nature Trails, and a procession of flowers: Easter primroses and violets, Whitsun bluebells and bird cherry. And October fire in the beech aisles nothing can dim.

In spite of felling there are many dark places easy to lose the path within, where the past seems very near. We can well believe that early dalesmen of prehistory chose to live here; sometimes we feel they are lurking still. We stumble upon their hut circles and are entangled in briars and cleavers; nettles grow luxuriantly around the walls.

One bright day a primeval dread sent me running out into the sunshine, unknown fear at my heels. I knew nothing of the murder at the spot where the horrors struck me, nor that for generations Grassington folk who passed along Wood Lane 'heard the rattle of bones and creak of chains', long after Tom Lee's remains had been buried!

Villages with distinguished names like Conistone—conyng's or king's tune—usually have a long history. This village looks good from the start. There is very satisfying architecture on all hands from the first farms with seventeenth century dates on their walls, beyond the maypole to the 'town head' houses. The church is possibly the most ancient foundation in the dale. What a fine and inspired restoration was completed here; the simple strength and austerity of Norman arches and pillars remain unimpaired. As I made my drawing of the west end, song of birds came in on the sunshine spilling through the south door, and with it sounds and scents from nearby hayfields; unwonted activity.

Conistone is usually 'asleep on its feet'. It retired from active participation in Wharfedale affairs with the end of Fountains Abbey in the 1530s. Formerly it was kept busy with monastic corn milling, with passing of all the trade and transport

Norman work in Conistone church

which crossed the river from Kilnsey, the abbey's most important grange.

Sweet and low round the village, there is plenty of the stern and wild just above. Climb east, up one of those 'dry-bones' limestone gorges with subterranean secrets, until the boisterous winds meet you on the tops. The gorge is Gurling Trough which with such a name should be peopled by trolls or like malevolent spirits. High above climb Conistone Pie—non edible!—for comprehensive landscapes, or follow the little Dibb and tracks which reach out to Bar House and Yarnbury where the utter loneliness is broken only by occasional mine shop relics.

After seeing Conistone church with a foundation back in Anglian times, take a good look at the very latest in ecclesiastical architecture at Scargill, just south of Kettlewell.

Ketil and his Norse followers arrived at the point where Kettlewell lies, almost throttled by fells, by one of many routes crossing from dale to dale. The Normans found it a good centre and so did the three monasteries which were granted local estates. Fountains received land grants, so did Bolton Priory, and Coverham Abbey too, which lies north over the watershed of Park Rash.

No village is planned more haphazardly: streets, back lanes, paths to bridge and stepping stones all tangled up and delightfully confused. With familiarity you discover they are not so impossible. They sort themselves into thoroughfares, four roads in fact, and tracks and paths which take to fell ways.

Two roads bring us updale from Grassington, and combined continue updale to Buckden. The fourth was the ancient monastic highway from Wharfe to Cover and Ure which later became the through coach route from London to Richmond and the north; strange but true.

So Kettlewell developed as a traveller's rest on the castle to castle, abbey to abbey route. It exchanged local news with foresters and herdsmen out of Langstrothdale and Littondale chases, and Coverham Abbey servants who herded large flocks on Scale Park Pastures. How history was being written over a larger field they gathered from agents of abbot and prior, and armed men riding to and from fighting with the Scots.

The Romans must have eyed with interest the same Park Rash pass. That was why Iron Age Celts raised horse-shoe earthworks at the gill head, prepared to make a backs-to-the-wall last stand.

History and prehistory are met with on all Kettlewell's fell slopes. Wander by the old straight track behind the village to Cam Head and the line of fortifications; snow lies deep within them well into spring. Look into the sunset dying in scarlet and gold along the sky line above the Old Cote Moor. We watch blue dusk growing deeper in the dale below; they watched for approaching enemies.

To get away from it all, follow the beck through the village to almost Alpine pastures tilted alarmingly to the deep, dark gill. Lads bound uphill to the Scouting Field Centre at Hag Dike and call as they pass; silence returns. The rocky crown of Great Whernside breaks against the eastern skyline. Cuckoos call, curlews wail overhead; then we hear hawks mewing and watch a great winged buzzard taking in both Great and Little Whernside with one mighty sweep. Along the high ridge strides the best walk—north to Coverdale, or over to the Nidd.

To Littondale: climb from the Wharfe bridge to Moor End House on the skyline, up again through the rock break called The Slit in the second limestone terrace. The line of the path is vague on the tops but eventually you find yourself with a bird's eye view over either Hawkswick or Arncliffe where people look like midgets moving among toy houses. The odds are you will lose your path but, mist being absent, you will find it—or one like it!

Come into Kettlewell by bus and it sweeps you in, over bridge, around acute corners and whisks you out before you have more than glimpsed a pretty cottage, a patch of flowers, an attractive nook.

Better stay; three inns of undoubted age, several houses and a youth hostel 'cater'. I find the church clock telling the hours of the night disconcerting. The church itself possesses a tub-shaped font of Norman design, proof of the community's antiquity.

STARBOTTON, BUCKDEN AND HUBBERHOLM

Updale to Starbotton and Buckden, road on east side, footpath on the west where as the Wharfe loops you have the feeling of treading a vast dried-up lake floor. Walkers with time to spare take a green track to Cam Head—from which the valley looks like a cradle about to rock, or a flat-bottomed boat with stone walls for ribs. The way runs across open fells for a while then between wriggling walls zigzags down to Starbotton's back garden walls. This Cam track is my choice.

My first stay in Starbotton was at the middle one of three Well House cottages, with 1663 over the door. This was 'John Symondson's house', a survivor of a disastrous waterquake which swept away houses and bridges before it in a mighty flood, leaving in its wake enough rocks, boulders and stone to rebuild what was destroyed. Look at the massive walls of crofts and intakes, built of the leavings, and of river-worn stones. Help to rebuild the devastated village was raised in far away churches, by means of briefs or Sunday collections.

Its name fits. Norse men called the innermost part of a valley a 'botn' or botton; this was a stony one.

When we come to Buckden, last village in the dale, we recognize it as an outpost. The two roads beyond cross high watersheds. One makes north by a new highway, replacing the Rakes up which the Romans strode and which is reverting to Nature; the hard highway is B6160, over Kidstones to Aysgarth.

The other follows the Wharfe linking a string of gill foot Norse settlements which later became hunting lodges of barons, or keepers' booths; this passed through 'the wildest part of Yorkshire', the Langstrothdale Chase route to Fleet Moss and over to Sleddale and Hawes.

Bucks and wild game abounded when Buckden was most important of dale head forest lodges. Langstrothdale's chief officer lived here and supervised from Buckden his underkeepers; he accounted for their doing to the Percys, and from Tudor days to the Cliffords. The last bucks, local folk will tell you, roamed the deer park in Frith Woods.

Buckden has always had to watch out for 'swift Wharfe's' moods. It is an unpredictable river, soon up, quickly down. Sudden spates had to be reckoned with, like one in the eighteenth century which swept away the nearest bridge, near Hubberholm. Money was collected for rebuilding but after a change of plan it was decided to build the handsome arched bridge at Buckden. Hubberholm had to make do with a temporary one—and the straight new road was made across the meadows to church.

Hubberholm was the retired spot where Hubba the warring Viking came to rest; it became centre of local Norse settlers who chose sites along the upper dale, where the present farming communities of Deepdale, Raisgill and Yockenthwaite are clustered.

The inn at the Hubberholm bridge-end might be mistaken for a farmhouse; its front door opens into a back yard. Once the parson lived here; it is still a 'church house', and there is nothing of the modern roadhouse about it. I remember shelter here during foul weather, hot coffee by blazing fires, and, as welcome, the cool parlour and cold shandy on hot days. Always farmers lounged on the benches saying little, waiting for what I could never find out. Their dogs waited patiently outside.

Highlights in Buckden's year rarely hit the headlines—the Feast with 'tatie pie supper' in October, Plot Night when a bonfire on the grass wedge, high as the houses, lights up the dale—but since a B.B.C. team recorded the New Year's Day land letting at the 'George', Hubberholm, the outside world has taken annual interest. Long ago a rough pasture—the fourth, I think, on the left as you go updale— was given to the parish, to be let and the rent to help the poor. Each first day in the year Vicar and Churchwardens—the Lords—and farmers as the Commons hold Parliament at the inn. After prayers auctioning of the Poor Pasture begins, the field falling to the highest bidder. A 'reet good do' follows.

No church is like Hubberholm's which has long and short masonry in the squat tower pre-dating the Conquest, Norman work in the upper part of the tower, a splendid Norman font—pure art, whereas the fabric as a whole is 'rough-hewn, nowise polished,' laboriously built up by local craftsmen with only simple tools and good intentions to guide their hands. Unique features: a post Reformation rood screen complete with its cross made by William Jake in 1558, during Mary's reign, preserved in this remote spot in Elizabeth's days when all others were destroyed. Possibly the Percys who held to the Old Faith—and how they suffered for it—sent it here for safe keeping. Another rarity; a lead roof, untouched during war years when more accessible churches were stripped and their metal melted down for

Where warring Hubba settled: Hubberholm

ammunition. Modern woodwork includes excellent benches and choir stalls from Thompson's Kilburn workshops; tiny church mice peep round corners and climb over bench ends.

If the church is locked find the innkeeper who holds the key.

In the seventeenth century the Tennants who lived in the skyline farm above the church were early Friends, suffering in York Jail and dying there for their faith. James Tennant was brought home for burial; his grave is in the stone-walled sepulchre to the west of Scar House. Climb the very stony track—the route George Fox took when guest here, and trod by many local Quakers who flocked to hear him. The views downwards are entrancing; paths which are very heaven—and pretty near to it—trail along the high limestone terraces above the Scar.

High level paths; keep right above Scar House and you come upon a faery glen, Cray Gill, noisy with falls, its deep pools reflecting ferns and rowans. Turn left for miles of hill top wandering, fair prospects of this delectable corner of a great, wide and wonderful world. Thyme-scented banks near crystal becks marginned with small flowers are made for idling. Feeling energetic? Then keep high above Deepdale where pre-Roman hillmen lived; of their village you may trace sunken floors and stone walls of huts, clustered below a sheltering limestone crag. At night when wild beasts came near they gathered the stock into enclosures walled in by slabs of riven rock and boulders. Deepdale Iron Age villagers had kin on Grassington High Close and Lea Green, on the platform where Arncliffe's Stone Men keep watch.

THE LENGTH OF LANGSTROTHDALE

Buckden to Beckermonds; the road rollicks updale, climbing high, dropping low to slow down by the river. With every mile the months roll back. Below Hubberholm, fields bright gold with buttercups are ready for the mower, some meadows lie in swathes; sheep shearing is still the full time occupation at Raisgill; at Yockenthwaite may-blossom still scents the breeze, pink and white petals falling on banks of primroses and violets—in July! A wash of blue on the fellside—bluebells; but on the high pastures drifts of lilac, purple, cerise run across them—what heavenly colour, and all due to the wild geranium, cranesbills of many varieties blooming there. Damp spots, and they are many, are gay too; by small runnels sending trickles down the slopes look for laggard flowers, pure blue butterwort's single head above green rosettes, among brooklime and forgetmenots, and the dainty lilac clusters of the mealy primrose rising from wet mosses. Summer is still far ahead.

The Norse settlements which became forest lodges, booths, and now are knots of farms; the road passes all of them. Raisgill stands low where Horse Head Pass drops from the toppling fell; climb up and over to Halton Gill and you tread the ancient packhorse route, ridden so often by the parson on his white pony on his way to Hubberholm where folk looked out for him and when sighted began to ring the church bell knowing there would be a service that day. Now tree felling and road widening has let in the sun at Raisgill.

The next community across the river was where a Norse Eogan cleared his land and named Yockenthwaite a thousand years ago.

Where Wharfe leaves Langstrothdale

The Percy's foresters lived here. Bridge—a lovely bow—goose green and south facing houses smile into the sun; ancient peace.

Deepdale follows on. The footpath passes a circle of stones, a Bronze Age burial place. In monastic times here was the largest of the Langstrothdale hunting lodges, with seven tenements. Waterfalls thunder in the gloomy places behind it. In the massive walling of the near crofts are medieval footing boulders.

Beckermonds is beyond a beguiling stretch of road. Reaching river level turfclad banks invite us to stay, watersmoothed pavements are kind to bare feet. What fantastic channels, undercut grooves, rounded cups and basins the river has worn in its bed. Bright water sparkles in the sunshine, turns to spray over ledges and falls into swirling pools to be churned white in millions of underwater air bubbles.

Beckermonds, where two becks meet, lies beyond a grey bridge, aged buildings caught in a welter of walls, a bleak windbreak of trees swaying as high winds sweep from the fells. It makes a memorable picture. Like the other hamlets it grows garrulous of more prosperous days. A lonely track runs off to Greenfield, another remote abbey grange, melting away into the mists; that way heads for Horton-in-Ribblesdale.

The road to Hawes passes north to the dale's farthest outback, Oughtershaw. It is less primitive than we expect with unexpected bits of Victoriana. Woodds, the land-owning family, lived in the substantial mansion with its ornamental shrubberies, stable block and commodious outbuildings. They raised the wayside memorial fountain, the memorial church—Norman architecture—and the roadside memorial cross. We look for stark unrelieved wilderness, and find a suntrap and an oasis blossoming like the rose.

One year a cry went out from Oughtershaw designed to melt the heart of officialdom. Give us a phone kiosk was the plea, for we are cut off from the world. "Thirty miles from a doctor, 13 miles from the district nurse. . . ."

The Roof of England is not far above. Take the farm road to Fothergill and Swarthgill and along the dwindling Wharfe to its first trickle high on the swampy ground 2 miles from the hamlet; an undramatic birthplace sighed over by winds; cried over by curlews. The watershed also watches the beginnings of Cam Beck, one of Ribble's twin sources.

Keep on the highroad and it is a straining climb to the Riding boundary and the highest point on Fleet Moss, 1,934 feet above sea level. As we climb, the whole circle of Pennine giants gather round, the swart fells fall into subservient places for there are the cloud-reaching, rain-bringing mountains waiting, brooding, Penighent, with Ingleborough and Whernside, links up with Dodd Fell and The Cam, with Drumdrace and Wether Fell and blue-headed mothering mountains, all of them 'strongholds for the proud gods'.

The bleak foreground, miles of bent grass, rushbeds, with stone cairns, broken walls and a summer as short as Scandinavia's. Will commercial tree planting invade here as above Beckermonds?

Nidd bank, Knaresborough

Three

NIDDERDALE

1. *Pattern of History by Nidd*

SINCE MICHAEL DRAYTON, the Tudor poet, wrote of 'the unquiet Nidd' the river has tamed down, its upper waters impounded by the Scar House and Angram reservoirs—to provide Bradford city with most of its water—a middle reach turned into a long and very beautiful lake below Gowthwaite, as compensation.

Why do we neglect Nidderdale so much? The fact that no highway finds a way out at the dale head should make it a walker's retreat; wild roads, though extremely rough beyond Middlesmoor, are just what the seeker for solitude needs, climbing over to Coverdale or making for Great Whernside, or striking east from Ramsgill to Dallowgill and moorlands which seem almost without end. Some of the best and least-known fell tracks in the Pennine country lie above the Nidd.

The lower Nidd is familiar countryside. A59 from Harrogate to Knaresborough and York cuts across the Nidd and its tributary, the Crimple; Marston Moor and Nun Monkton, Ribstone Park, Goldsborough Hall and Rudding Park, Red House of the Slingsbys, Spofforth Castle of the Percys, are but a few of the historic spots by lowland Nidd.

This book being of the dales, the river from Knaresborough to the dale head concerns us mostly. And who does not recognize Knaresborough when first seen? The posters of green Nidd and gay boats, pantiled houses in gardens on a tree-clad bank, and the railway bridge arching above all have been familiar all our lives.

The pattern of history in Nidderdale repeats the same theme—castle and abbey, Anglo-Saxon villages in the kind regions, Danish in the wild lands, hunting forest and chase on the enclosing fells, market town in mid-dale, and villages and hamlets in between. The variation in the theme has in this dale many lovely things to show us.

Before the Conquest scores of Anglian villages were thick by the river where it wound hither and thither, not over eager to join the Ouse, Ure and Swale combined. Monkstown (Nun Monkton), the Hammertons, Skelton and Ribstone were among them. Stockaded 'burgs' named Goldsborough and Knaresborough, and clustered by the river upstream Englishmen farmed the lands of Scotton, Ripley, Darley and Pateley. Danish invaders arrived later; Cowthorpe and Spofforth, Hampsthwaite, Thornthwaite and Gowthwaite, Ravensgill and Ramsgill and all the isolation of the dale head at Lofthouse and Middlesmoor were theirs.

2. *Knaresborough Castle and Fountains Abbey*

1066? After William's stormy reception at York all the lower Nidd region was devastated. English and Danish thanes alike were wiped out, their manors given to the Normans. That was when the Percys, themselves descended from sea rovers settled in Normandy, came over with William and 'by their good swords' won the Conqueror's thanks in the shape of Spofforth and other manors in the north east.

Serlo was given the Barony of Knaresborough and took his name 'De Burgh' from the English town. He built the castle on the high rock, work carried on a generation later by Eustace Fitz John, his nephew. He it was who took pity on poor monks living in extreme poverty by a little stream called Skell, reduced to eating bark of trees and wild herbs. He saw their wants were supplied while he lived at Knaresborough. But he took the losing side in the Maud-Stephen struggle and was faced with exile in Scotland, and took arms against England in battles to follow; he was not the only Norman-Englishman with the Scottish king; also, many who fought behind the English standards had sworn loyalty to the King of Scotland. Confused loyalties!

The castle all through its 'useful' existence was linked with kings and princes, with queens and favourites too. Henry II, remorseful after Becket's murder, sought to punish those friends who had done the foul deed; the four men hid here for a year, then away to seek other secret places. Richard I, his son, raising money to finance a Crusade, sold the royal manor and forest to William de Stuteville, for £2,000. This De Stuteville is remembered as persecutor of a holy man who prayed in a cell near the Nidd banks, living a hermit's life; he drove him out into the wilds where he raised a roof of branches for shelter and like a Saint Francis called wild creatures to his aid, yoking the willing deer to his plough. A penitent Sir Walter later called him back, granting him land between Low Bridge and Grimbald's Bridge. Saint Robert's cell and chapel are still to be seen—and much visited.

King John was frequently at the castle, enjoying hunting—his great passion—in his vast forest, with his retinue and '5 Spanish horses, 182 beagles, 38 other dogs, and 40 "vultra"' brought for the purpose. On the river banks the old manor house was used as the king's lodge.

The castle and barony passed next to a younger son of King John, Richard of Cornwall, and he founded on the levels below the Low Bridge a Priory of Holy Trinity; little is left but the name on Abbey Plain.

Though this priory had closest link with the castle another far greater monastic house arose not many miles away, Fountains, which grew from the poor cell on the banks of Skell, 'fitter for den of wild beast than habitation for men'. Who could recognize this in the Fountains Abbey we know, magnificent even in ruin?

As two lords of Knaresborough gave aid to early Fountains monks —Serlo's nephew who fed them, and Edmund Plantagenet, King John's grandson who gave them land at Brimham—a few notes on the abbey should not come amiss here. In wandering from Knaresborough we must certainly see Fountains; in roaming through the dales and especially in Craven we cannot avoid coming across the firm mark of the abbey, in history and place names.

The early twelfth century found many Benedictine monks growing dissatisfied with the lax discipline in their abbeys. The reforming adour of Bernard of Clairvaux spread to England and to St. Mary's in York where Prior Richard and twelve monks made up their minds to adopt the austere rule of the Cistercians. The archbishop was ready to help, their own abbot to object. The archbishop offered them land by Skell—which name means 'fountain'—and nothing else. The small band travelled in hope, settled in under an elm tree, with yews to screen them from winter cold, and nothing more than wild herbs 'boiled in a little salt' and leaves to sustain them; the little they had they willingly shared with the poor.

Prayer and work kept them warm. The wealthy began to show interest, land grants poured in, others with zeal for the reformed 'rule' joined the first few. Building was carried out with amazing speed, and rebuilding when the first was destroyed by fire. Within a century and in spite of many a setback Fountains Abbey was one of the most splendid, and the richest in possessions. Its reputation for sanctity brought scores of applications from the noble and rich for the right of burial within the church; they paid well.

The abbot was a colonizer. From the mother abbey small bands— abbot and twelve brethren—travelled to new sites, the gifts of noble lords, as did Alexander and his monks first to Barnoldswick in 1147, and five years later to a better site granted by Henry de Lacy, on Aire banks at Kirkstall.

Back to Knaresborough. After Edmund Plantagenet, the barony and castle reverting to the Crown was passed on to members of the royal house or favourites of kings. Edward II gave them to Piers Gaveston by charter confirming to the earl and his heirs for ever 'the honor and manor—the parks of Haye, Bilton and Hewyra [Haverah] —free chase in all the Honor—the judging of malefactors, one gibbet and gallows for execution of such offenders and all their cattle, goods and animals. . . .' This proof of the king's affection for his favourite was not to be enjoyed 'for ever', but for a very short time.

Soon after, in 1313, the town was taken and destroyed in part by Robert Bruce. Hardly had the townsfolk returned to rebuild their burnt down homes than armed forces again attacked their town and took the castle by storm. This time they were Thomas, Earl of Lancaster's men in revolt against the king; their leader destroyed all the borough charters, with the latest which had conferred upon them the right of 'free burgesses' in a free borough, with one market and fair, and freedom from paying unpopular rents, and tolls concerning bridge building, wall repairs and feed for swine in neighbouring woods.

Thomas of Lancaster was beheaded. Edward III, popular son of hated father, came to survey the castle, and make its walls and towers good. His high walls linked eleven or twelve towers and splendidly they stood above Nidd banks; the keep rose above all, the strong tower to harbour still more kings and queens, in times of joy and sorrow. Edward's beloved Philippa, the new royal owner, was here during the campaign she helped to fight against the Scots during the king's absence in France. Her son, John, born in Ghent, was next lord of castle and Honor; being keen on hunting he found the forest to his liking and there is a mound on the western limits near the Washburn valley called after him; he also took the death dues and rents from forest tenants to which he was entitled, and insisted the foresters maintained and repaired the castle when called upon.

Troubled times? During the Peasants Revolt John o' Gaunt's young wife, Queen Catherine of Castile, sought Knaresborough castle by night with torches blazing as her followers hammered on the great door. His nephew Richard II was to be a pathetic prisoner—the ante-chamber and state room on the keep's second floor were his— before Henry of Lancaster's men led him to Pontefract where he 'died'.

Many a street evokes memories of dark days, of skirmishes in narrow ways, bloodshed—English and Scots, Roundhead and Cavalier —of processions and cavalcades winding up the hillside lanes to castle and church. Sad eyes watched from the castle window slits. Do the imaginative hear dolourous moans and cries of anguish?

This is no grim, grey town. Roofings are orange, reddish-brown pantiles or old lichened flags, walls white and yellow, pink and buff, when you can see them behind a smother of orchard blossom, lilacs, laburnums or July roses. The sun always shines for me; the crocketed church tower, castle ruins and trees always cut into blue skies.

CURIOSITIES FOR THE CURIOUS TRAVELLER

Knaresborough's tourist attractions are most conveniently packed in between High and Low Bridge. Take the water-edge avenue called Long Walk—temptingly cool on hot days—and look across the river with the gay pleasure boats and tea gardens above The Moorings. That unusual old house, walls painted in black and white chequers, has a history all its own. This 'scheduled' Manor House has a thirteenth century King John room where that sporting monarch and his queen lodged. Here King Charles rested, and Cromwell stayed during his siege of the town. So old is the house that one can see, encased in a long cupboard, the 'roof tree', still rooted in the ground, around which it was built. Old tales tell of hauntings, a bundle of tattered clothes and a woman's bones! The narrow lane behind it climbs to church and castle as in medieval times.

The Long Walk makes for Tourist Attraction I—Mother Shipton's Cave and Dropping Well. The native-born witch uttered predictions believed in not only by her contemporaries. Some are today's common-places :

> Carriages without horses shall go.
> Thoughts around the world shall fly
> In the twinkling of an eye.
> Through hills men shall ride
> And no horse or ass be at his side.
> Under water men shall walk,
> Shall ride, shall sleep, shall talk.
> In the air men shall be seen. . . .

But the world did *not* come to an end in 'eighteen hundred and eighty-one' as she foretold.

The stream feeding the dropping well is impregnated with lime before reaching the rock which makes the drop. The fantastic assortment of objects suspended in the dripping water have been or are in the process of being 'petrified'.

Our woodland walk ends at Mother Shipton Inn—long, low and very old—on the busy highway by Low Bridge. Downriver are more 'attractions' so obvious that there is no need to draw attention to them. St. Robert's Cave which sheltered Knaresborough's own holy man was hewn out of the amenable cliffs; a century ago a bearded guide in 'antique costume' did the honours. High above St. Robert's rock-hewn chapel is Fort Montague, twelve years labour, though hardly of love, by a poor weaver wielding axe and hammer. Rock

King John's Lodging, Nidd side, Knaresborough

House was occupied by a family called Simpson in Victorian days. Other caves 'were doubtless retreats of lawless banditti who infested the Forest'. Plenty here to spark the imagination !

The town remembers a local murderer; you cannot avoid hearing about him. Eugene Aram and his accomplice hid their victim under the floor of St. Robert's Cave. Timber from the gallows is exhibited in a garden near the church. A novel by Bulwer Leighton gave the murderer 'an immortality he did not deserve', and Henry Irving acted in a play equally successful in keeping Eugene Aram's memory alive. But who reads about him now?

Far worthier of being remembered is a native genius, Blind Jack Metcalfe, who in spite of disabilities did far more to benefit England than many with all their faculties. He lost his sight as a child of four but he was full of spirit. He could guide folk unerringly across Nidderdale in darkness and snowstorm. People welcomed him as a cheerful carrier lad, and when English troops marching north through Scotland to Culloden were weary, who put spring into laggard feet but the merry fiddling Jack Metcalfe from Yorkshire? Later he was to cover the north country roads surveying for hundreds of miles of new turnpikes. He was the recognized engineering genius of his time.

> High deeds his manhood did
> And commerce, travel, both his ardour shared;
> Twas his a guide's unerring aid to lend,
> O'er trackless wastes to bid new roads extend.

From Low Bridge the highway climbs to the town; or Waterside and Castle Ings lead wanderers to gates entering the Castle Gardens. Children play and old folk meditate where kings and barons once paced. The keeper of the present, much diminished, castle shows us around the great keep and talks of kings and queens as though they were about to walk across the great chamber floor, and of tragic prisoners as though they still awaited the clanking of jailor's keys at the dungeon door. Where the garrison watched out for enemies from the north, we sit and scan the long fells of Nidderdale, looking out for nothing more fearsome than forbidding clouds hanging over Great Whernside, far away.

Street names are evocative. Briggate—armies marching up from the old bridge; Kirkgate—Bruce's men slaughtering as they forced a passage towards the church; Silver Street and Finkle Street taking countryfolk and townsfolk along to Cheapside and the Market Place which with rounded cobblestones underfoot and Tudor, Jacobean and eighteenth century buildings in pleasant proximity all around brings back the old days of trading and 'cheapening'; the early Georgian chemist shop claims to be among the oldest in the land, and it looks it. High Street is lined with tall-fronted Georgian houses, and many an inn with arch and stable yard reminiscent of coaching days which were the town's heyday. Off High Street—Gracious Street, on the line of the old town's ditch and defences. These are but a taste.

You cannot miss the church under its crocketed steeple; do not miss the Slingsby chapel in the north aisle for the memorials to this ancient family are a fascinating collection.

In the centre of the floor are the Elizabethan Slingsbys, Francis and Mary who had no fewer than seven sons, two of whom occupy their hollow niches in north and south walls. The parents lie in effigy on a splendid altar tomb, he in full armour, she in a long pleated robe. The sons look down on them; Henry, knighted, and twice High Sheriff of Yorkshire who died in 1634 has an angelic trumpet sounding above his head. Sir William who stands so non-chalantly on the opposite wall, a couldn't-care-less look about him, hand toying carelessly with his sword, belies his earthly character. He was a barrister, a gallant soldier against the foes of Elizabeth, M.P. for Knaresborough, and called by James I to be constantly at court. He—or brother Henry—were early discoverers of the virtues of 'Harrowgate's' mineral springs and might be considered founders of the Spa.

Always loyal to the Crown, Sir Henry in the next generation died on Tower Hill, a Royalist to his last breath; his is the dark marble tomb.

3. Routes into Nidderdale

FROM LANCASHIRE AND WEST OF THE PENNINES

The direct routes are A59 from Clitheroe through the Ribble Valley to Gisburn and on to Skipton, or through the Aire Gap from Settle and Hellifield, A65 to Skipton. The historic highway, as busy now as in the past, continues as the great cross-Pennine route to

Winter: farm on Greenhow Hill

York; by Bolton Bridge, Beamsley and Blubberhouses it is 24 miles to Knaresborough. As main roads go it is full of varied interest. Kex Gill, a fine bit of rock scenery with Raven's Peak at 909 feet above sea level, takes the road to the watershed and on to Blubberhouses through wild moorland and ranks of snow screens; beyond, the Roman Road coincides with ours. We pass from Clifford's and Bolton Priory land over the boundary of Washburn into Haverah Park and the once royal forest of Knaresborough. Exciting names on either hand: Timble and Dog Park, Penny Pot Lane and John o' Gaunt's or Bras Castle on the south; Kettlesing and Thruscross, Padside, West End and Hardisty Hill on the north.

FROM THE YORKSHIRE TOWNS AND AIRE AND CALDER VALLEYS

There is the A61 from Leeds through Harewood to Harrogate and Knaresborough. But far more exciting is the Bradford-Otley road which carries due north through the Washburn valley as B6451, crossing A59 at Blubberhouses and up into uplands airy from Hardisty Hill to wild, wide moorlands and Pateley Bridge. This ancient hill route carrying the traveller upwards carries him back in time. No part of the dales arouses more nostalgia, memories of 'dear, dead days beyond recall'.

This Otley-Pateley Bridge road; the Washburn which it follows is a string of long blue lakes and more are to flood the deep valley as Leeds needs more water. A hundred years ago natives were secure in their old homesteads, cultivating paternal acres on the sunny slopes below Padside and Thruscross, at West End and West House, at Fewston and Timble and Farnley. Yeoman families whose forbears had been tenants of prince, baron, lord or prior lived in comely halls, such as the upstanding Parkinsons at Cragg Hall. Thackray was home of the Thackerays. There were in Fewston, Swinsty Hall and Newhall where lived in forest days the keeper of the king's colts, and in King James I's reign a literary son of the Fairfax family who attacked several inhabitants of 'Fuystone . . . a wild place with rude people on whose ignorance God have mercy.' The folk, even the better sort, resorted to wise men and witches for help when cows gave no milk, and obeyed their instructions, even to burning young calves alive! His neighbours at Swinsty Hall were Robinsons out of Pendle Forest who must also have had a thing or two to say about witches. His kinsmen resided at Scough Hall farther downdale; here was born Sir Ferdinand Fairfax's eldest son, Thomas, later to become the great Parliamentary leader.

Travellers from Otley northwards have a route which should be an antiquarian's delight. First Farnley Park—with memories of the young artist Turner who visited the hall many times, making drawings for Whitaker's *History of Craven*, painting landscapes for his hosts, the Fawkes family, glorying in the light and shadow effects on the moors around, exulting in thunderstorms. To Blubberhouses and over to Pateley, thirty miles scenic, historic, and, of course, nostalgic. Nowhere are landscapes more uplifting than westwards over sad West End, over blue moors without end, from the road on Hardisty Hill, unless they be from Heyshaw heights beyond Padside, or from the breezy crag top where Yorke's Folly crowns Guyscliffe and all the Nidderdale landscape, in summer's glorious technicolour, is spread out to view. The air is like iced champagne on these tops. Then drop down to Bewerley and Pateley, through ravines which are like ready-made wild western film locations, to narrow precipitous lanes by Skrikers farm and every road bend 'It's an overcoat warmer'.

FROM WHARFEDALE AND GRASSINGTON

The Greenhow road crosses the watershed for 10 miles to Pateley Bridge. This also is a scenic route; you feel on top of the world, and what a great wide wonderful world it is. From Hebden Town Hill it is up and up, over Dibbles Bridge and Dib Gill, across heather moors—oh! the purple seas of August—to the grim places of Dry Gill and the summit on Craven Moor, 1,326 feet.

Winter can be fierce up here: note the snow screens. No gathering of cars and coaches then at the layby, the first hint a stranger has 'in the season' that there is something unusual laid on just here. Whatever drama lies subterranean in the Yorkshire fells, above ground is often without interest; Stump Cross caverns gave not a whisper of their whereabouts until discovered by miners in 1860. Then a new wonderland was opened up, tourists marvelled at the Pillars, the tall Sentinel, the Fairy Fountain, the Snowdrift and Crystal Column, the Church, and musical notes struck from stalactite's 'organ pipes'. By candlelight the underworld glittered with 'tints of irridescent spar'. By modern electric lighting and with coloured bulbs the sparkle is even more spectacular; also the light rays are causing moss to grow 'in the bowels of the earth'—as in the Cheddar caves.

Greenhow village, church, inn and clustered houses, is the only community on the moors; cottages huddle at Keld Houses and scores of abandoned cottages and holdings scattered over the landscape are reminders of lead-mining days. Digging into the grey hills for lead began with the Romans, the abbey of Fountains smelted it for abbey roofing, abbot and baron derived rich revenues from the workings which run like rabbit warrens through the moors. The many old lanes radiating from Greenhow were once busy with panniered packhorses bearing away the lead. The 1970s see improvements, 'conversions' of derelict miners' cottages; a new atmosphere of wellbeing.

Mournful such deserted places now. But soon the road starts to fall, to tumble down into Nidderdale, and the contrast makes of the patchwork landscape, pastures, meadows, cornfields in stripes, bands, and arabesques, a veritable Canaan. Sensational the descent, and kinder airs as we take the zigzag course, very slowly the better to enjoy the prospects, into old Bewerley and over the Nidd bridge to the grey sprawl of Pateley.

4. Up the Nidd from Knaresborough

The main road leaves Knaresborough for Ripley, keeps high to Summerbridge, then through Smelt Houses into Pateley. Alternatives are byways on the south bank of the Nidd through charming, rural, out-of-the-way spots, and through pleasant friendly villages like Hampsthwaite and Birstwith, Darley and Dacre, whose folk you hobnob with if you travel by the bus to Pateley.

Not a name on the map but has its history and some story to evoke the past.

VILLAGES OF THE DALE—SCOTTON AND RIPLEY

Take the village of Scotton, land granted to a Norman from Brus who brought the ancestors of Robert Bruce to Yorkshire; Bruces like the Baliols—both landowners in the dales—were to lose their English estates when they broke faith with English kings. Scotton knew a young man called Guido Fawkes, stepson of a local Roman Catholic. Guido was an old boy of the 'church' school, St. Peter's at York, but came to live here after his mother's re-marriage and was influenced to change his faith. When questioned after the failure of the plot to destroy king and Parliament he said boldly one of his hopes had been 'To blow the Scots back to Scotland', an early expression of the same wish which makes hands scrawl GO HOME YANKS.

At Scriven Hall nearer Knaresborough is the home of that family of Slingsby whose monuments—remember Francis and Mary and the two most outstanding of their seven sons—are such a fascinating feature in the north chapel of the parish church. The early owners of this estate, the Scrivens, were proud to claim descent from Gamel, a fowler to the king, in Norman times; his son Baldwin was forester and parker and so were many generations after him. In the Civil War, with troop movements converging from all sides on Knaresborough, the Slingsbys, staunch Royalists, with their household were in the thick of things. Sir Henry, a colonel in the king's army lost his liberty, and his life, during the Commonwealth. On the scaffold on Tower Hill he cried, "I die for being an honest man." The date: June 6th, 1658.

Ingleby's, like Slingsby's, were 'for the King'. The best-known story about Ripley Castle tells how Lady Ingleby forced to take Cromwell under her roof, her husband being absent, kept relentless watch all night with two loaded pistols at the ready.

A charming village, bypassed by the highway, only touched by the bus route; discreet cottages, trim gardens, immaculate roadway and never a sign of catchpenny tripperish souvenir shops or garish tea rooms: that is Ripley. Such complete harmony only comes of single ownership. Ripley has grown old gracefully under the eyes of the Inglebys of the castle.

Like Harewood at the great house gates, like East Witton rebuilt by the Earl of Ailesbury, Ripley is the creation of the family within its castle halls. Inglebys have had a long innings here, from the day when a young member of the family fearlessly dashed to the rescue of his king about to be torn by the tusks of a savage boar and was offered as sign of royal gratitude 'the lands of Haverah Park for ever'.

Tombs and memorials to the Inglebys are in the church, some older than the building which covers them. We are told that a much older 'sunken church' once stood in Chapel Flats near the Nidd, and was covered by a landslip; so at about 1400 a new church was erected at higher level. With a little knowledge of architectural styles it is interesting to detect which stones and objects come from the old site and which 'belong' to this.

Holes pitted in the outer walls, below the east window and on the west wall of the tower, tell another story, like the honourable scars on the Quai walls of Paris, on the Hotel de Ville walls in scores of towns in France and Belgium. Prisoners were brought here and firing squads shot them down; these bullet holes were from Cromwell's marksmen, the targets had been Royalists captured at Marston Moor.

An almost unique stone cross stands north of the church; the cross shaft has gone, the socket stone remains, and a larger base stone with hollow niches carved around it. Hearing it was so made—as a Weeping Cross for kneeling penitents, obliged to make a public show of penitance—we knelt too, and most uncomfortable it was, as intended. This certainly came from the 'sunken church' and was designed by Norman, or earlier, stone carvers.

Below the church an old lane passes the imposing outer gate of the castle and drops to a bridge over an ornamental lake with swans a-swimming. The castle looks down on pleasaunces, ornamental gardens and towards a fine timbered parkland across which goes a footpath, a walker's way upriver. Back to the cobbled streets, the 'foreign' Town Hall—a Victorian oddity built by a Miss Ingleby— past the fine tall cross, so to the outside world of roads and traffic.

WANDERING ON THE HEIGHTS, ABOVE GUYSCLIFFE AND BRIMHAM

The valley is completely charming, the villages smiling, the river running clear below wooded banks. It is pleasant, unspectacular, so we think but—be tempted upwards from any of the villages, up any of the lanes and we are hurled into those same airy heights crossed by the Otley-Pateley road and this is never unspectacular. Neither is the broken edge of the valley wall as we approach Pateley; now we pass below high ramparts of rock, riven into strange shapes, cut by dark gills. Guyscliffe is on the west and the dark places of Ravensgill, and special crannies, pillars and ledges with names Victorian travellers relished—Three Gaps and the Needle's Eye, Giant's Chair and Kate's Parlor. These have the added 'ornamentation' of the cliff-top Folly which Mr. Yorke caused unemployed labourers to erect for him; the mock ruined pillars look quite impressive climbing to Heyshaw in the dusk or silhouetted against the sunset.

On the east side of the dale those almost sheer fields which pattern

Dacre Banks with such decorative effect merge with the hillslopes of Bishopside—once the Archbishops of York's land—and they are broken by the fantasy of Brimham Rocks which cover acres of the high plateau.

This is Fountains Abbey country; roads across the moor make for the Skell valley. Edmund Plantagenet gave Brimham woods to the monks and they defined their possessions by the Monks' Wall which a seeing eye can trace quite easily across country. What the huntsmen of the Mowbrays, who were the 'top dogs' in Nidderdale in middle ages, thought of this menagerie of rocks crouching on the plain, or whether the monks of Fountains crossed themselves for fear of evil spirits hiding among the stones, we do not know. We know that the weather worn shapes are merely fragments of the Millstone Grits left intact when underlying and softer strata was worn away. Wind, water, frost and 'the wasting power of the atmosphere' graved the Idol Rock, the Druids Circle, the Yoke of Oxen, the Baboon's Head, and local imagination gave names to Kissing Chair, and Lovers' Leap and many another detached stone, some which rocked 'at the touch of the hand' and others which remained firmly anchored.

Guyscliffe belongs to a similar age and was formed by the same agencies. 'Storms and floods of unnumbered ages have washed away the soil accumulated round the rocks, exposing their bare sides in piles the Titans might have heaped up . . . corroding blasts sweeping from both Atlantic and North Sea unhindered have aided the distorted formation and created grotesque and singular shapes'. These 'corroding blasts' still blow on Brimham Moor and Greenhow Hill, as we know well, having battled into them during cross-country walking in March.

UP THE NIDD FROM PATELEY:
TO RAMSGILL, LOFTHOUSE AND DALE HEAD

Pateley Bridge—with Bewerley—is one of the bridge-end and road-side communities caught up in the traffic and commerce of a great abbey and lead mining which has in later years become just a small market town where narrow, cramped and climbing streets with hidden away lanes and alleys are being given a face-lift or falling beneath a spate of demolition and rebuilding fervour. Pateley's high street gaps are—inevitably—car parks, small gardens of rest with flower beds and seats, the ground paved with old roofing flags, and the usual public utilities.

Pateley has a long history. The Archbishops of York being lords of its manor, granted early fair and market charters and the folk celebrated by a September feast known as Pateley Rant. They still hold the feast but it is shorn of the old rumbustious rowdyism and is more of an annual family reunion.

They 'talk o' Feasts, Wakes, Tides and Fairs,' as a centuries old song says, but here all agreed that 'Pateley Feast will quite outdo All

Inn yard in Old Pateley: "Cross Keys"

others hollo'. They are proud of Pateley. I have heard it called a
'Shangrilah', holding them and never letting go!

Updale, the Nidd waters a fair, quiet countryside where long ago
Fountains Abbey shepherds, and Byland's, cared for their flocks.
From Sigworth and Wath, byways wander through woods and dells
where, 'they say', Robin Hood drank from the well given his name;
and why not? Skell country is not far over the hills, and Friar Tuck's
abbey.

We have our own views about big cities which seek deep valleys
and lonely fells for water supply. You may understand how apprehensive Nidd-side folk felt when Bradford surveyors arrived around
Gowthwaite eighty years ago. Edmund Bogg tells how his collabo-
rators about to sketch near a farm were refused lodgings, being
mistaken for some of 'them prospectors'. Even 'cocks and hens flew
away cackling alarm and distrust' when Bradford's agents appeared!

The waterworks won and Nidd's dale head was dammed; Bradford's
reservoirs at Scar House and Angram provided the city with most of
its requirements. Down at Gowthwaite, not far north of Pateley, a
lake was created, compensation for water robbed from the head
streams. After the lapse of years it is beautiful as a natural lake, a
fine place for observing wintering wildfowl, and flocks of geese from
the far north feed on the banks, from a distance looking like snowdrifts. On October days when mists are persuaded away by morning
sunlight and the lake is pearly bright, and in May when gay green
is repeated in the still waters—enchanting! Then we almost agree

with Bogg who hoped when he saw the lake in making 'it would add rather than detract from the picturesqueness of the valley'.

They drowned the old Hall of the Yorkes; stones were built up into a new Tudor-style house at higher level.

Ramsgill beyond the lake is a pleasant surprise, very bright, trim, prosperous-looking and especially so seen after the crossing of wild, barren fells from Fountain Earth Fell or Dallow Gill, the contrast is so complete. Wherever there was space for flowers, flowers have been grown: before the handsome and imposing inn, in front of· the cheerful cottages, round the immaculate green where each dwelling has feet in flowers.

Byland was a landowner round Ramsgill, the abbot had a chapel here. Old buildings have gone, but we appreciate on these rainy days when we wait for a bus to Pateley the use to which old stones have been put in a well-built shelter.

Who is interested now in Eugene Aram, that 'native genius', a schoolmaster turned murderer, who was born here? Victorian tourists knew Hood's poem—and relished the discovery of the victim's remains.

> Blood for blood atones!
> Ay, though he's buried in a cave
> And trodden down with stones—
> And years have rotted off his flesh,
> The world shall see his bones!

They had seen Henry Irving play his part carrying—a gruesome prop—Eugene Aram's own lantern! They gloated over places associated with his story, at Knaresborough, and here. But today no place is less concerned with what is unpleasant.

Trippers early in the century came updale on a light railway, its terminus—Lofthouse.

Lofthouse and Loftus are old Yorkshire place names, with a namesake on the Hardanger Fiord. One looks from the Cleveland coast, another is near Wakefield. The Lascelles swept away a Lofthouse when planning the ornamental lake in Harewood park and the new Harewood village was its replacement. Part of Sedbergh east of the church was Loftus. And the comeliest of all, Lofthouse, a hamlet high above Nidd where the site was that of a Norse 'saeter' a thousand years ago. Even now Lofthouse seems more ready to wander away on fell tracks into the cloudy sky rather than down into the dale. Ancient farms, picturesque cottages, are grouped haphazardly beside the winding street which beyond the top farm gate continues as a moorland track. Above Backstone Gill it is joined by hillways from Ramsgill and Bouthwaite and there is exhilarating walking eastwards on what was the ancient corpse way to mother church at Kirkby Malzeard.

What lonely miles they are. Little wonder that centuries ago folk from Nidd faced by the dangerous journey waited till babes were old enough to walk to their christening. The ride to the wedding was a hazard. Ponies carrying the dead for burial had snowdrifts to struggle through, and always boggy ground to face. Small wonder that dale head parishioners pleaded for their little chapel at Middlesmoor to be granted the right to christen, marry and bury their own: in 1484 they had their way.

Middlesmoor, hamlet and church, crowns a green mound 'which catches all the sun that's going, and all the four winds of heaven too'. How quiet it is, and so remote from towns we forget lives are organized by timetables, whistles and bells, by car, bus and coach. Is there a more tranquilizing scene anywhere than that about the green hill on April days with young lambs playing and all the larks in the sky giddy with song?

If you see young men with ropes and torches striding purposefully along the road, with no eyes for tranquil countryside or the mountains

Woodale farms, upper Nidd

ahead, they are pot-holers, cave explorers and hot foot for the gates of Nidderdale's underworld. There is How Stean, the gorge 'an example in miniature of a canyon in Colorado', and from it entrance into Tom Taylor's Cave, where a hoard of Roman coins was hidden in a cranny and never called for. Beyond the mouth of Elgin Hole opens an underworld, made for troglodytes.

In this surprising hollow underworld the Nidd does her disappearing act. Two miles north of Lofthouse are Goyden Pot and Manchester Hole involved in Nidd's secret life. Two miles out of sight and the river rushes into daylight like a prisoner released, and many never even notice. The road actually passes over the limestone near its exit—on one hand dry ground and on the other the flowing waters!

Though packhorse routes, thronged with traffic two centuries ago, make from Middlesmoor over to dale head at Angram and then over Dead Man's Hill to Coverdale they are not easy going today. We

were diverted by the advice of a Middlesmoor man to the low way—
the route of the reservoir builders—a former 'tramroad' and, with
the young Nidd for company and a succession of comely old farms
in the loveliest of settings to give constant and varied pleasure, we
came to dale head.

Because there is no 'made' motorable road here it is quiet beyond
belief. A kestrel's cry, curlew's wailing, the bark of a grouse, the
belling voice of a kenneled hound, all sound clear though far away.
The old farms of Woodale have dark windbreaks, deep gills cut into
the fells above and thorns are white with may, and rowans bright
with berries within them. Thin silvery waterbreaks seam the slopes
after rain—so often rain, for which Bradford gives praise!—and
clouds which seem high indeed stroke the mountain ridges, and
herald more rain.

Two high dams hold back the headstreams of Nidd; Scar House
and Angram waters are held within the arms of bare brown fells
which come down from sky-reaching Great and Little Whernside.
We look up into dark cloudwrack which shadowing the hollow cwms
makes of them sinister cauldrons boiling over and mist wreaths hiding
the way we wish to go.

WAYS OUT FOR WALKERS

Ways out of the dale? Walkers only—the packway from Lodge,
through the gap between Little Whernside and Dead Man's Hill to
Arkleside, down Coverdale to Middleham: 9 miles.

Or from Lodge, a long mountain slog south of Little Whernside,
to follow the saddle to Great Whernside, along the spine where at
2,187 feet the Nidd has its springs. The summit is higher—at 2,310
feet—a rocky gritstone crown, and Kettlewell and the Wharfe away
below.

Lodge is kingpin in so many fell walks. After rough going to Little
Whernside, or from the saddle between the two Whernsides we have
made a quick descent from Pally Hut down to the Cover Head road,
not far from Hunter Hall and Woodale.

Each Nidd side farm has an escape route—track and sheep pads—
from its back gate to the fell tops. All eventually join forces with
better defined routes forging east towards Kirkby Malzeard, or dropping alongside Leighton reservoir into the altogether lovely valley of
the little Burn. A good road goes downstream and lanes make from
hamlets like Healey and Fearby to either Masham or Swinton. A
great possibility for happy wandering before reaching the main highway, A6108 from Ripon to Middleham. This is a far cry from the
green and gentle Nidd.

The old high ways signposted from Ramsgill, or from Lofthouse,
are good walking too. You cross wide moorlands, where I for one
should not care to stray in mist or with night approaching. But given
a long day of swift changing sun and shade and the ways converging
on Dallowgill are the best of upland walking.

Windsor of the North: Middleham

Four

WENSLEYDALE

1. *Pattern of History*

WENSLEYDALE IS A wide and welcoming valley more like my native Ribblesdale than any other. Some dales are green grooves, narrow corridors, but above the Ure you may throw your arms wide and drink in the space. On the airy galleries, those high limestone terraces which run the length of the dale, there is uplift and exhilaration. The men who live by Ure are built to match, they are tall, upstanding types, ruddy faced, broad backed. They stride forth like independent spirits, their voices ring loud and clear; they have never needed to struggle for elbow room. They are great trencher men.

Nothing is secretive here. Outsiders have had easy access to the dale ever since the Ice Age ended. The glaciers which ground out their wide troughs at the dale head and smoothed the walls of the hills prepared the foundations of great highways from Ure Head and Garsdale Head to the great Plain of York.

The pattern of history is easily seen. The limestone terraces were chosen by prehistoric hunters and herders for their homes, the proud gritstone caps of hills like Addleborough for forts of Brigantian tribesmen who were a threat to Roman invaders. The Romans knew the valley, a moraine pile above Bain and Ure providing a readymade site for Braccium; their military highways came striding in from the wild passes, The Stake and The Cam.

Homely sounding Anglo-Saxon names are thick in lower dale and on the rich lands near the river—the Tons, the Hams and the Leys; they bestride the highway from Ripon to Masham and Middleham. Ripon with its cathedral of St. Wilfred and its ancient see has usurped by Ure the role which castle towns like Skipton, Knaresborough, Richmond and Barnard Castle play in other dales. Ripon is Wensleydale's market centre—not its castle town of Middleham.

Danish sea rovers were early comers. They probed from Ouse to Ure and settled in many a minor dale, not too far from existing villages. Theirs are the Bys and Thorps; look for them in small hamlets and farm names. Behind them, or rather coming in ahead of them and a century later, by Pennine passes and dale head—the Norse land seekers. They took the Anglian and Danish leavings. They gave names to their saeters or setts, to the gills, becks and fells, the hill farms and remote hamlets, where becks frisk and waterfalls splash.

The castle and abbey theme plays around Middleham. Here the Conqueror's kinsman chose to overlook his lordship and wide forest lands of Wensleydale, and two abbeys, Jervaulx founded by families from Ravensworth and Richmond, Fitz Hughs and earls of Richmond, and Coverham in which Fitz Ranulphs, lords of Middleham, had prior interest.

Earls, lords, Nevilles and Scropes, the two abbots—they were owners of lands; they shared rights in the hunting forests, chases, parks and warrens of Wensleydale. The rise and fall of each, their fortunes and misfortunes following foreign wars, civil wars, rebellions and risings make Wensleydale's history a very full book.

MIDDLEHAM AND ITS LORDS

Ruined walls, broken towers, still proud in decay, Middleham Castle chronicles the centuries. Standing on its high windy slopes above the river it seems as unaware of the cottages and the village beneath its walls as Gulliver striding through a crowd of Lilliputions.

The castle may frown, but the village smiles; its houses gay, open squares are welcoming. Women talk at doors and invite us in to show where castle masonry is built into their homes, where castle woodwork was used for interiors; cheerful fires are inviting on the cold March days when the castle courtyards and roofless halls have sent us seeking shelter.

Winds rush down the Hall of the Presence where high and mighty Nevilles held court; winds keen in the corner tower, the prince's chamber where a future queen of England gave birth to a child, a future Prince of Wales. We climb to the highest battlements of the great Norman keep take a comprehensive sweep of landscape, dale and fell, and are chased to ground level by fierce gale force gusts. Cold comfort castle-dwellers must have had. The huge hearths; they must have devoured complete woodlands for fuel; winter shivers in hall and solar in spite of fur lined cloaks.

Lords of Middleham were first of Breton stock, the sons of Ribald, younger brother of the earls of Richmond and son of the duke of Brittany, who threw out the original occupants of the manor on William's Hill. Ribald's grandson began work on a Norman castle, the hard core of the one in ruins today. Generations later his line ended in an heiress, Mary of Middleham, who in marrying a Neville brought that family to Ure dale. They remained the great power in the valley for generations to come.

The names of the Nevilles are like battle cries sounding across the dales. Robert, Peacock of the North, died in combat with Earl Douglas. John, lord of Raby, lieutenant of Aquitaine, Victor over the Turks, was taker of eighty-three walled towns. Ralph, he was acclaimed Hero of Neville's Cross; and Ralph, Earl of Westmorland, he brought blood royal into the strain when marrying John o' Gaunt's daughter, Joan Beaufort.

This Neville, so close to royalty, decided the time ripe to make of Middleham a castle to vie with palace and king's court. Around the Norman keep he built enclosing curtain walls linking corner towers, above vast courtyards rose walls of proud halls. No wonder Middleham became known as Windsor of the North, where Nevilles held semi-royal state, where the course of history was to be shaped. Here

Warwick, King Maker, Last of the Barons, was to prove most powerful, his end most disastrous in the Neville story.

Power games were played at Middleham. The pawns—daughters. Cicily, Rose of Raby, her parents' twenty-first child, mother of two kings, was one. She was married to the Duke of York when Nevilles were for the House of York. She was 'Aunt Ciss' to the little Anne Neville who in her short life was bride of Edward, Prince of Wales—when her father changed sides to give support to the Lancastrians, and after her tragic widowhood was married to Richard of Gloucester, became his queen and was mother of a little boy who might have been king. Middleham saw the shaping of both dynasties and destinies.

It was written of Warwick that in his castles he 'feasted thirty thousand persons daily in their halls; he could rally thirty thousand men under his banner and carry them like a troop of household servants from camp to camp, as passion, interest or caprice dictated'. And so came the weary and hungry, the noble and great, limping, riding, or marching with banners towards Middleham's gate. In the reign of Henry VI, Warwick and his brother, George Neville, Archbishop of York, gathered around them the greatest in the land. One can imagine among the wise churchmen and the proud lords, the children of the household running around the courtyards—little Isabella and Anne, and their playmates, the sons of noble houses, and among them young Richard of Gloucester, 'Aunt Ciss's son', and his friend young Lord Lovell. So many were to become pawns in Warwick's 'power game'.

It was 'the trumpet call from Middleham' in 1457 which mustered five thousand Yorkshire men to follow the Neville banner south; imagine them issuing from the great gate, over the drawbridge and away, the earl's men wearing his badge upon their arms. The Neville who led them to battle at Blore Heath was Earl of Salisbury. His son Richard who succeeded him, was proud Warwick, and he was to lead armies—and cause navies to go out to war.

When the War of the Roses was 'sparked off' Nevilles gave their support to the Duke of York, Cicily Neville's husband. A time came when, with Henry VI taken prisoner by his enemies and safe within the Tower, Warwick began to exert his influence upon Edward, his kinsman. The Duke of York slain in battle, Edward was now king, but not the willing tool Warwick hoped. A marriage with a French princess was Warwick's plan for him; but Edward had married Elizabeth Woodville and pleased himself. Middleham Castle had the new king in its walls, held captive under the not too close surveillance of Warwick's brother, the archbishop, whilst counter plans were sending Warwick to Queen Margaret to work upon her—by promises of men and ships—for agreement to a marriage between the young Prince of Wales and daughter Anne. A complete change-over followed, the Nevilles now on the Lancastrian side—a short-lived allegiance for after the Battle of Tewkesbury Anne Neville was a widow, and prisoner of Richard of Gloucester and the Yorkist victors. Edward IV contrived through smuggled letters and friends lying in wait outside Middleham to escape his 'jailor' and was away south to rejoin his armies. In 1471 at Barnet great Warwick was tumbled down—and with his death toppled Neville fortunes.

Edward soon repaid Warwick's disloyalty by confiscating the Neville estates and handing them to his brother Richard who much liked the Middleham Castle of his youth. Often he stayed here with his court, as duke and later as king. And he married the widowed Anne and here their son Edward was born one joyful day in 1473. Those were happy times though destined to be short lived. Richard and Anne kept court at other Neville castles, at Barnard Castle and Penrith. And Middleham's halls—now roofless and silent—echoed with merriment. Martin the Fool would amuse the assembled, especially 'my lord Prince' the light of his parents' eyes. Fine horses were kept in the stables, and one for the little boy, and grooms with the good local names of Metcalfe and Peacock ran alongside the young prince when he went riding in Middleham Park. A pack of hounds streamed out over the fells of Cover and Bishopdale and Semerdale when the duke and his friends went hunting.

Richard III was not the black villain of Shakespeare or Tudor historians to the dalesfolk of the north. We have heard how writers pinned upon him the brutal slaying of the Prince of Wales at Tewkesbury (yet Anne the widow married and loved him); that he went hot foot to London from Middleham when news came of his brother's death and soon brought about the murder of the two Princes in the Tower, his nephews, so that he should win the throne; that a whole series of necessary imprisonments and deaths followed, eliminating all aspirants to the crown.

They did not believe this of him in Middleham. They rejoiced to see Anne Neville as queen. They sorrowed with the distraught parents when their son Edward died untimely; they did not whisper, 'the sins of the fathers. . . .' When the sad queen 'bid the world good night' they mourned her. When news came of the fate of Richard on Bosworth Field and the tragedy was played to its bitter end, the people of Middleham knew an epoch had come to an end. No more the pomp and circumstance.

Nevilles' hopes were quenched when the King Maker died, and when the Tudors won the throne. Henry VII had no time for the Nevilles. In Henry VIII's reign they were at Raby Castle, and there —with the Percys—brought about the Rising of the North in Elizabeth's time; that was the end of the family. By then Middleham was neglected, half ruinous. It was suggested to the queen that parts could be rebuilt as a lodge to enjoy hunting in the royal forests of Wensleydale; nothing was done. By the time Cromwellian orders were slighting the whole castles in the north, Middleham's was already 'decayed'. But the walls remained in spite of attempts to blow them up by powder. Fitz Ranulphs and Nevilles had built them well.

It is easy to imagine Middleham as a market town, secure in the protection of the castle. It had two markets, one for cattle, one for swine. In the past its November fairs were the most important in the dales—held on the breezy moor outside the 'town'.

To have the best view of the castle, walk over the pasture on its south side, climbing the slopes of William's Hill, a most interesting site. Middlehammers of a thousand years ago toiled up the hill to answer the call of their manorial lords, the forerunners of Ghilpatrick who dwelt here at the Conquest. It is said to be 'the most perfectly preserved example of Anglo-Saxon burh in Yorkshire; a burh or 'bury' being a defensive place, a military post, quickly constructed fort with earthen ramparts, deep ditches and timber palings to form a stockade. Here there are double earthen banks—well used for children's rolling and tumbling, and hide and seek and chasing games. A large platform in the depression on top was a court wherein stood the thane's homestead.

Anglo-Saxons, Danes, and the Normans who were followers of Ribald all took stock of lower Wensleydale, and Coverdale, from this hilltop. One might expect it to have some legend long remembered. William's Hill hides great treasure, folk believed, and 'whoever shall run nine times round without stopping will find a door opening to him' admitting into the cave where fabulous hoards lie, untouched!

COVERHAM ABBEY

The castle and abbey theme? The first Norman Lord of Middleham towards the end of his active and fighting life retired as a monk into St. Mary's Abbey, York, his eldest son Ralph succeeding him. If he and his family occupied the William's Hill site it was his son Robert who moved downhill to see to the building of the new castle. His wife, Helewise, daughter of Henry II's Lord Chief Justice, at the same time devoted herself to good works, founding about 1190 an abbey at Swainsby not many miles east, near Bedale. This was a house of White Canons, Premonstratensians, the puritans among Canons Regular, followers of the Rule of St. Norbert and not unlike the Cistercians though all their members were priests. Her son about 1214 offered the Canons a better site not far from the new castle, by the Cover banks. Helewise was buried at Swainsby but re-interred at Coverham. Ranulph Fitz Robert dying in 1251 was buried here with due ceremony.

By this time a great Cistercian Abbey was already standing on Ure banks just east of Middleham, well endowed by Fitz Hughs of Ravensworth who had founded the abbey at Fors, and the earls of Richmond who had translated it to 'Yore Vale', at Jervaulx.

So, in Wensleydale, we have a castle with two abbeys close at hand, the greater provided for by great earls and rich landowners outside the dale, the lesser enjoying grants from the lords of Middleham.

Coverham Abbey is far less known than Jervaulx. There is far less of it. It is remote from highroads, in a quieter valley, sheltered in a veritable suntrap. A large hall was built on the site, its farm buildings incorporating abbey masonry in their walls. The garden and orchards are protected by the cloister walls; carved door heads, pillars and fragments of window tracery appear in unexpected places. Of the tombs of generations of lords of Middleham who were brought here for their last resting place nothing remains but mutilated effigies, 'dug up while constructing some outhouses'! Two are of knights in battledress of the thirteenth century, one of the founder, the other possibly of his son who willed his body to Coverham but his heart to the church of Greyfriars he founded in Richmond. Other tomb fragments are possibly of early Nevilles who gained Middleham through marriage and continued the family interest in the abbey.

Coverham came off very badly during ferocious Scots raids; then some of the early tombs were sadly mutilated. It suffered acutely at the Dissolution—its valuation in 1535 was £160 compared with Jervaulx £455—for it became a handy quarry for local builders once the king's agents had done all the stripping and demolition they thought necessary.

The fine and complete round archway of Norman period, the abbey gate, can be seen from the road above Cover Bridge. The precincts are covered by private property, and have been so occupied since the Bainbridge family were the first to buy the site soon after the Dissolution.

Coverham canons like Jervaulx monks were great producers and consumers of cheese. It was made from ewe's milk according to their own recipes. It is said that after the abbeys were closed the monks, harboured and well-treated by local farmers, handed them details of methods they used, so starting a 'home industry'. They produced the famous, creamy white Wensleydale cheeses.

Also both abbeys were interested in horse breeding, a fact the king's agents reported to Henry in 1535. Their 'stallions and mares were well sorted'. They were practising selective breeding. The region still breeds the best bloodstock.

JERVAULX—ABBEY OF YORE-VALE

One wild day in 1156 a band of weary, white-habited monks with their abbot, John of Kingston, were travelling through the thick woods of the Ure valley when they realized they had lost their way. They were bound updale for the wild outpost in the waterfall country at Fors where for some years the brethren had been labouring painfully to establish a daughter house of Byland Abbey. As they stood wondering which way to turn they beheld a vision of the Blessed Virgin who stood in their way and led them to safety. A voice was heard to say, "Ye are late of Byland but now of Yore Vale."

Yorevale was the name given to the new abbey they later began to build on land near Ure and Cover given to them by Earl Conan of Richmond, a kinsman of the lords of nearby Middleham; out hunting near Fors he had offered the much distressed pioneering monks land in a far more comfortable district. Yorevale was later, in its frenchified form, Jervaulx.

The first time I visited the abbey I walked from Middleham to the Cover and the fine bridge at Ullshaw—Ralph Neville of Middleham gave money for a bridge here in 1424—and so by a pleasant riverside way to the precinct wall. The gardener in a picture book cottage had the key to the ruins; I paid my admission sixpence and had the abbey all to myself.

Jervaulx with gifts of land from many great lords soon owned half the dale. Abbotside, the north side, was the lord Abbot's. Sheep walks, rights to hunt game in the hills, iron mines in Colsterdale and coal pits too, the livings of several rich parishes, all these they possessed. Apart from the interest of earls of Richmond the abbey also was sure of the help of the Fitz Hughs of Ravensworth and Cotherstone; their ancestor, Akarius, founded Fors and their descendants for generations came here for burial as effigies and graves slabs show though many lie in unidentified graves.

At the start of the last century when the earl of Ailesbury took up residence at Jervaulx the site was overgrown and hidden beneath a wilderness of weeds and heaps of rubble. Clearing began with enthusiasm and care, stage by stage the extensive ruins being laid bare. And what a good job was done. The clear Cistercian plan was revealed. Now our feet tread lawns and pavings where monks' sandals trod and flower borders bloom against walls which gave the brethren shelter and trapped the sun.

How noble the proportions of the abbey church, built on a large scale to accommodate not only the brethren but large numbers of working lay brothers, illiterates whose motto was 'Labour is Prayer'; they laboured, the monks prayed and meditated. Look for the two altars, the monks' choir, presbytery and the lay brothers' nave with a processional way around them. And in the centre of the church, the effigy of its most noble benefactor, Henry Fitz Hugh.

How many times a scrap of carving, a slender spandrel, a touch of rare beauty brings us to a halt. In the roofless Chapter House— fragments show how lovely were the six delicate marble pillars which supported its roof. Even the 'offices' were extensive; separate refectories, dormitories for the literate monks and illiterate lay brothers, and as for the abbot, his own lodgings were fine enough to be approved of—as accommodation—for the most noble guests. Enough remains in spite of demolitions and the sales of 1539 to show that Jervaulx ranked high among the greatest religious houses in the north.

When the first Tudor came to the throne Jervaulx, as foremost religious body in the dale, as greatest landowner, was carrying out its wonted role. Church services, estate care, entertainment of the wealthy and poorer travellers, doling out large annual sums to the poor, it obeyed the Cistercian rule to the letter. In its employ were servants who lived in the booths in the fell country, shepherding many sheep and accounting for the large sheep clips to the abbot. They also milked the ewes and made cheeses which were part of the monastic diet, bred and trained fine horses, mined the coal pits and worked the iron forges of Colsterdale. The abbey employed many officers who saw to the management of outlying estates, who collected tithes of churches, tolls from fairs. And constantly masons, wood carvers, and craftsmen in wood, stone and metal were at work. Building was always going on.

The abbots were not unaware of coming change. Outside criticism of their wealth and power, business and financial activities came to their ears. When Henry VIII's agents arrived to pry into their monastic affairs they allowed them to 'see the books', and were apprehensive. Already they had submitted to royal decree that no more payments of good English money had to go to the pope. Adam Sedbergh, Abbot of Jervaulx, waited for the blow to fall.

In September 1536 Henry ordered closure of all religious houses the earlier survey had found to be possessed of small incomes and valuation. Especially in the north were men angered by this, above all those families whose ancestors had founded the many small abbeys, priories, friaries, nunneries, chapels, hospitals and almshouses which came under the royal edict. They banded themselves together, chose a banner carrying the Five Wounds of Christ, compelled many who were unwilling to join their numbers, chosing for their leader Robin Aske, of the Swaledale family of Aske Hall near Richmond, though his brothers stood for the king in the rebellion of 'the Commons'. They were anxious to draw into this 'Pilgrimage of Grace' the heads of the powerful abbeys. Many an abbot as a man of God was a man of peace. Like Abbot Paslew of Whalley, Adam Sedbergh was far-sighted enough to see the rebellion would end in disaster and he, unwilling to be implicated and bring a terrible punishment to Jervaulx, thought it best to get out of the rebels' way.

It is a sad story. On September 29th from two to three thousand rebels from 'Mashamshire and Kirkby [Malzeard]shire' converged upon the abbey and battered at the great gate. The abbot escaped before they entered, with a small number of companions, one a boy. He made to the lonely places behind Witton Fell. Orders were sent to the abbey servants to save all the goods and cattle they could before the rebels got at them, and to return to their homes. The Commons withdrew for a while, forcing a way into Coverham Abbey, then north to Swaledale. Word reached them of Abbot Sedbergh's forbidding any tenant or servant to join them. So—back to Jervaulx; no abbot there! He had returned by secret each night, put heart into the brethren, and away by morning.

"Your abbot has deserted his abbey. Elect a new one," the rebels commanded. The brethren refused, until a dire threat sent them to seek Sedbergh 'in a great crag' on the fells. If he did not return the abbey would be fired by the men who massed within its walls. The abbot had to face them.

In his own courtyard he was torn among the rebels, threatened, compelled to take the pilgrims' oath, borne away on his weary mount —then eventually allowed to return. He was, in the final reckoning up, considered to have supported the rebels and so acted treasonably against the king. The next year, after imprisonment in the Tower, he was taken out to his execution at Tyburn.

In 1548, the brethren were dispersed, the abbey silent, except for the gangs of breakers employed to strip the building of all that was of value. They stripped the lead from the roofs—365 tons of metal; they brought down the bells, but found they could sell 'for no more than 15 shillings the hundred'; they piled everything ready for removal.

That winter proved so bad and the local ways 'so foul and deep no cariage can pass' that further destruction had to wait until the spring of the next year. Then the waggons rumbled away, week after week and the abbey once so proud and great, lay open to the wind and the rain.

The king granted the abbey site and the Manor of East Witton to the Earl of Lennox. You can find out more about him at Temple Newsham on the fringe of Leeds, another property formerly owned by a religious order of Knights Templars; he was father of the young Darnley who was to marry Mary, Queen of Scots.

Later owners, the Earl of Ailesbury in particular, were responsible for the changed face of abbey, hall, and the surrounding landscape, at the beginning of the nineteenth century. There is certainly a landscaped charm about it, and at the village of East Witton a complete rebuilding of cottages, and church too, similar to plans carried out by other wealthy landlords at Milton Abbas, Harewood, Holker, and Ripley.

Stalling Busk : a saeter above Semerwater

2. Daughter dales of Ure

If you enter Wensleydale from the Great North Road, striking along Ure from Ripon or Northallerton—by A6108—you learn to appreciate the gentler beauties of the valley floor. Coming from the Eden valley and the north, downdale, you follow the river from near its source and see the Ure landscape growing, expanding with every mile.

Those of us whose usual approach is from Ribble or Wharfe have an introduction from the minor dales. We tell others that ours is far better, that the best of Wensleydale is 'just off it'. Is any dale entry more exciting than from Ribblehead by Widdale to Hawes, the lonely defile and its solitary farms beneath valiant windbreaks leaving a lasting memory? Or to drop from the tops of Fleet Moss when we come from Langstrothdale into the almost-as-Nature-made-it ravine called Sleddale? Or, delight reserved for walkers, looking on Semerdale from the Roman Road over The Stake? Even coach and bus travellers can share what Bishopdale offers, amazed at the green-floored dale below them as they remain poised for a moment on the top of Kidstones Pass. Coverdale awaits the pioneering motorist, an enclosed world for long kept secret to all but the walker coming over the Park Rash wilds from Kettlewell. And there is little Waldendale and West Burton waiting at the end of it.

> Still Aire, swift Wharfe, with Ouse the most of might;
> High Swale, unquiet Nidd and troublous Skell.

They are the much looked on rivers, now as in Drayton's days. The seeker after complete quiet linked with melting loveliness is more likely to find them by the daughter dales of the greater valleys, especially these feeders of Ure.

IN WIDDALE AND SLEDDALE

At the west end of Hawes, '16½ miles to Ingleton' reads the sign-post. Seven uphill miles of grey fell road and you are flung up to the treeless wastes of Redshaw Moss and Newby Moor; and that was Widdale!

At dale head are the 'horrid wastes and frightful deserts' which quelled the spirits of eighteenth century travellers, the only bright spots being the 'one lonely house' formerly the Newby Inn, and Gearstones. These inns were resorts of cattle-dealers who drove beef 'on the hoof' from over the Border; the Wednesday markets and autumn sales when thousands of beeves were bought up for Martin-mas killing were well attended. On these gale-ridden heights, where winds come 'piping loud' and June can have the bite of December, John Ruskin came to a halt one April day. He 'leaned on the wind as on a quickset hedge' and surveyed Ingleborough amazed 'that it should stand so still without rocking'. Ingleborough, 'that creature of God' which after seeing Croagh Patrick in Mayo and peaty waste this so much resembles—only turf stacks and turf cutter's donkeys missing—I feel should be respected as a 'holy mountain'.

Mountains ring Widdale head, all drawing down the sky for caps. The swift weather changes! Rain and rainbows chased by sun-gleams and 'searchlights' resting on rose-gold bracken patches, a colour which persists till the new green takes hold in June; a solitary white-walled farm under a valiant wind break, a line of washing pulled about like a distress signal; farmer and dog silhouetted on a skyline and a file of sheep moving on dark trods below them; these are Widdale for me.

Widdale is known to most folk in summer dress, gay and busy, when every farm stands in a patchwork of green and gold and all the dalesfolk are out of doors working from morn till night to cut, dry, lead and house the precious hay. They still 'make hay' in this dale though the horse-drawn sled, once so familiar pulling loads up meadows steep as a barn roof, is replaced by the obliging tractor with performances as staggering.

Widdale Fell, Wold Fell and Snaizeholme Fell shut in the dale, not to shelter it but to make a flue for the north-east winds. How they blow! Early farmers set their homesteads deep in the gills and for extra protection planted trees; wherever you see green domes of sycamores, or any trees, look for human habitation.

This is true of Snaizeholme, an offshoot of Widdale, a lonely, un-visited defile with only a farm track deep within it, and no way out. Bare fells, The Cam, Dodd and Ten End grip it tightly. Wander on foot from the old Widdale school, or from the bridge half a mile below it, to find this last outpost of change.

East of Snaizeholme is another back o' beyond, Sleddale, as wild and bare as any in the Pennines, a deep groove ground out of the sombre fells. Farms lie far from each other, one rough track linking them. More often than not this is a landscape without any moving figure upon it. The Hawes to Kettlewell old fell road toils up the steeps; from Gayle, the only village, the climb is over a thousand feet in less than three miles, and the last struggle, though straight, is formidable to the heights of Fleet Moss. Here we feel on the top of the world, and in summer we return into spring. Far below in Sleddale bottoms haygrass is waving before the wind, 'rippling with mirth', bright with buttercups. Here, at 1,934 feet, violets and prim-roses and pale mayflowers bloom in the verge.

Gayle, only a mile from Hawes, has character. The huddled dark stone houses, once homes of famous knitters, turn their backs to the road and mutter secrets in dark alleys. "We're far older than Hawes," they whisper, "and what tales we could tell if we'd a mind to." In Hawes they tell you that "Gayle's a rum shop, and rum folk to go with it!" Everything about it is standstill; the men loitering on the bridge look but say never a word. The beck however is never still; it falls over broad and wide monumental rocky steps, into stone-paved pools, making a merry din.

Converging upon Hawes from its satellite hamlets are many stone-paved church paths. One from Gayle's West Lane runs direct to the parish church; this is also signposted THE PENNINE WAY.

SEMERDALE—AND SEMERWATER SIDE

Semerdale? This is gathering ground for three mountain streams which run into the tarn, Semerwater, then at its outflow become the river Bain. A short life but a merry one, sing the Bain's bright waters as they drop under the grey arch at Bainbridge and flow to meet the Ure.

Semerdale's three forks are Bardale, down which walkers find a path from the Roman Road, Raydale, which has no access except to Raydale House, and Cragdale, wrapped in deep gloom when we look into it from the stony tracks under Addleborough. No part of Yorkshire is so impregnated by old memories, such a hoard of history.

I have talked with dalesfolk whose parents attended a dame school overlooking Semerwater where the blacksmith husband taught boys and girls the knitting skill he had had from his father. I heard at first hand how one returning late to Countersett called 'Goodnight' to a passing woman. She turned to face him and her features showed strange in a sudden burst of moonlight; she went on uphill from the Carlow Stone. A farmer coming down the same brow swore later he had seen no one at all! Stories too of horse's hoofs heard on the drive of Raydale House, and no one there, and no hoofprints to be seen.

Countersett Hall

Semerdale a century ago? William Howitt visiting Countersett, 'a cluster of cottages in lovely Simmerdale', felt the times of George Fox had indeed returned. He joined the Friends at worship in the Meeting House near the hall and noted that all, men as well as women, 'carried in their hands nosegays of sweet smelling herbs, useful stimulants to those unused to being within close and crowded rooms'.

Walter White stayed in the dale in 1858 and helped with the hay. He wrote, 'Forks are not used except to pitch hay from sled to barn; all the rest, turning swathes, making cocks, is done with rake and hand. So I took a rake. . . .' Later he confessed haymaking in the Tyrol was a 'much more sprightly pastime than with Quakers in Wensleydale.'

A century before this, in George III's reign, it was said that Semerdale folk lived in such a state of primitive simplicity that when the king died they thought the crown elective and that 'the Lord of Raydale from his wealth and consequence was likely to put in a nomination.'

According to White, when the first tea merchant arrived in the dale a local farmer ordered a stone, 'to try this new leaf from China'. His wife decided to tie it in a cloth and see what it tasted like boiled with the bacon. The resultant brew? "We couldn't abear it, nor sup a drop o'broth."

The hollow of the hills was scooped out by retreating glaciers and boulders dammed the outlet, leaving a sill to imprison the lake. But dalesfolk believed it had a magical origin.

Everyone knows how the selfish folk of an inhospitable city in the dale floor were punished. A poor old wayfarer, refused alms and shelter, turned to a lone cot on the brant hillside where a humble couple welcomed him in. At daybreak the guest rose up, raised his arms over the dale and the proud city, calling down a curse upon it.

> Semerwater rise and Semerwater sink,
> And drown all the town but the one little house
> Where they gave me food and drink.

And from that day waters have hidden all that was there, king's tower and queen's bower. Hard fact points to prehistoric lake dwellings—and inherited memory.

The Carlow Stones at the lake foot remain, monster stones of the moraine sill, but legends insist that the largest was an altar 'where druids practised unmentionable rites', and that the devil himself in a trial of skill with another hurled the two rocks here and one 'has t'ould lads fingerprints on it'.

Climb to Addleborough with its steps and terraces, a typical table-topped hill of which Wensleydale has several on its south side. Our Celtic forefathers, the Brigantes who proved the hardest nuts for the Roman heel to crack, had a fortified stand up here. The one-inch map marks many sites of antiquity. At Carpley Green, on its southern slopes, is Stone Raise; on the northern is the Devil's Stone.

> Druid, Roman, Scandinavia,
> Stone Raise on Addleborough.

This is a cryptic 'quote' associated with the tale of a local giant borne down by the weight of a chest of gold he was carrying on an unlikely journey from Skipton Castle to Pendragon. He found himself on Addleborough, sank wearily to the ground, dropped his burden and declared—note well, in rhymed couplets like all self-respecting giants—

> Spite of either God or man
> To Pendragon thou shalt gang.

At once the earth opened and swallowed the chest, and stones by magic covered it up. And there it remains! There was a list of complicated rules to be followed by any who cared to recover it.

Climb and see the site for yourself.

The Brigantes of Addleborough's fort made the Roman occupation 'not a happy one'! Like Celtic people since, they seized upon the invaders' preoccupation with other enemies to get their own back, if only temporarily. Maybe local tribesmen joined with raiding Picts to destroy Pennine forts when left unprotected; several times the fort at Bainbridge, Braccium, was attacked and had to be rebuilt again when the Romans returned.

From the bridge in Bainbridge climb a steep grassy bank, up Brough Hill a moraine knoll conveniently left by the Ice Age. There is a wide and comprehensive view along the main valley and into the hills, just made for a defensive post. Wander over the turf, among the grazing young cattle and trace the line of stone walls, foundations of dressed stone and cornerstones left uncovered by excavation. The plan of Braccium is particularly clear seen from the Roman Road where it strides down from Wether Fell; the earthworks show as enclosing a rectangular area, across which goes a modern field wall.

Early settlers, Angles and Danes alike, avoided the devil-haunted site and ruins of Roman camps. The saeters or setts of Norse herds-

Bainbridge from Braccium

men were thick on the slopes above Semerdale but the village of Bainbridge was a much later starter, springing into existence when the Norman lords of Wensleydale decided that this wolf-infested hinterland, overrun with deer and wild boar, was ideal hunting ground. The Conqueror's kinsman, Ribald, lord of Middleham, appointed forest keepers, and their lodges clustered at Bainbridge well below the green hill of Braccium.

'Ancient customs are wellnigh immortal in our country', commented White when he heard a 'stiffjointed greybeard' blow Bainbridge's forest horn. A century later the horn is still blown. Its origin goes back to early times, for Saxon dalesmen blew horns to warn of danger, to start the hue and cry against game poachers, and Norman lords ordered that strangers entering forest or chase should blow loud blasts as a signal they came without ill intent. In Semerdale horns sounded when wolves were seen near the folds of lonely 'setts'; then all animals were hurriedly driven to shelter. And the horn was still heard after the last wolf was slain as a signal to herdsmen in outlying places to move flocks and herds to fresh pastures. The horn's note reaches far.

Old custom dying hard, the forest horn continued to be used long after forest days. Wayfarers benighted on the tracks above Semerdale listened for its welcome sound and so found their direction to safety. If you do not know the vast loneliness of the Cam road, or the Stake, at the edge of darkness, in rainstorm or cloudwrack, you cannot imagine the hazards of travel 'up ont'tops'. We have crossed from Ribblehead on March and November days, hurrying to beat the darkness, glad to find ourselves between the walls of the Roman Road on Wether Fell knowing Bainbridge was not far ahead. We always reached the village before hornblowing time.

One night we stayed at the horn blower's cottage looking on to the green. When the time drew near we set out with him to perform his nightly ritual. It was wet and windy, and very dark until doors opened and chinks of light splayed across the ground. "Folk set their clocks by me", he said, "not by t'wireless time." And he and his predecessors have never failed them—except during the war years when horns and bells were silenced. The local opinion was that 'jerry planes' hearing their horn 'would know where they'd getten to, and that would never do.'

Every night from who knows when, between September 27th and Shrovetide—the black season of the year—at nine o'clock the cowlike crooning has sounded over the silence of the hills.

When not in use the horn hangs on the wall of the inn's entrance hall, and handsome it looks, bright and shining. This horn is a century old; an older one, of buffalo horn, is in Castle Bolton museum.

To explore Semerdale. A good road, though steep and narrow, climbs up, then down, to Countersett, a haunt of peace, Greystone farms cluster in sheltering hollows above the lake. In one dip is the hall of seventeenth century Robinsons, who were George Fox's hosts in 1677 and later suffered so much as Friends. Fox slept in the room over the porch; his bed was preserved.

There is a brooding peace lingering in the austere room where generations of Friends gathered for Meeting.

Among Countersett's distingushed visitors was Lady Anne Clifford, *en route* from Wharfedale to her Westmorland castles, her transport the first two-wheeled carriage ever to be seen in the dales. More humble travellers stayed at the 'Boar's Head', the inn lying low and sheltered in the hollow next the hall. Now it is a farmhouse, recently modernized, but I remember its old-fashioned kitchen and the roaring fire which once welcomed us in. A March day it was, and thawing out on the hearth were new born lambs in blanket-lined baskets, early arrivals with life only feebly flickering in them.

Marsett, an early Norse saeter like Countersett and Burtersett, stands sturdily above the lake head. Dark gritstone farms with heavy stone roofs, and mistals with large through-stones designed to shed dripping water away from their walls, occupy the sites of herdsmen and forest tenants. Climb above the hamlet and in the tree-filled gill behind Bella Close is the roar of waterfalls; wander upwards towards the head of Bardale—looking out for lone bulls—and you reach the rushy wastes by the Roman Road, and the heights of Fleet Moss.

Raydale folded within the arms of bare fells is so tranquil a backwater it is wellnigh impossible to picture it full of fighting men, as it was in June of 1617 when the belligerent Sir Thomas Metcalfe led forty, 'armed with guns, bills, pikes, swords and other war-like instruments', against the hall. The master being away, they were bold in attack. Mistress Robinson and her small children escaped in their nightclothes across the lake delta marshes to Stalling Busk. That siege of Raydale House made quite a stir in local news circles.

Semerwater; in winter a steel shield in a sere setting, in autumn a blue jewel in a bronze frame, in summer pure enchantment, twinkling in the sun. A sight to rejoice the heart. But *not* on summer weekends. Lake water laps upon the shores by the Carlow Stones and licks around the litter. Gone is the quiet when motor speed boats take to the water, leaving a trail of oil—and petrol cans on the verge. Notices, not the surrounding beauty, draw the eyes. KEEP OUT. PRIVATE LAND and—because farmers at last decide to make the best of a bad job—MINERALS. SWEETS. Also—£10 LITTER.

Escape over the fields to Stalling Busk where is still 'peace and quiet kind'. Cuckoos shout, curlews call over the deserted churchyard beneath the waving sycamores; folk from three dales built at their own expense the little church above the lake, in Elizabeth's day. They came to worship even though a clergyman was not always available. When the roof began to leak and rain poured on them, they met, for worship in the churchyard, their praises mingling with the birds'.

The hamlet was Stallion's Bush long ago, a high-placed saeter on a ledge between lake and fell. The buildings all face to Semerwater. A long windbreak of tall trees is full of perpetual roaring like the waves of the sea, for the wind never sleeps up here.

Stalling Busk wears a welcoming smile when we descend from the gale-swept Stake, the first sign of human habitation since we left Cray. So it must have appeared to travellers who used the same Roman way to Bainbridge, to George Fox battling through the snow, Lady Anne jolted in her carriage, and a thousand others before and after them.

Behind the hamlet, above the Roman Road, are fairy hills, and Addleborough. Eastwards, beyond the fells lies the long groove of Bishopdale.

BISHOPDALE

In Anglo-Saxon days sporting prelates came hunting in Bishopdale—it was then Archbishop of York's preserve—and Norman barons took it over for their own pleasure. Richard II granted the Nevilles of Middleham and their heirs 'for ever' right to hunt herein and over to Pen Hill, and power to punish any who trespassed on their domains.

The deer lingered long in Bishopdale but now they too have gone and the hunting horn of bishops and barons is silenced.

There is nothing secretive in this long green dale. The road B6160 coming over Kidstones Pass from Buckden plunges down from the riding boundary, 1,392 feet high, losing height rapidly in the first three miles, levelling out below Ribba Hall into 'the lovely sylvan dale where tree-lined lanes are beautiful as Berkshire's and the floor rich in meadowland', a scene which so delighted travellers long ago.

It pleases all who come over from Wharfedale, the riders in cars, buses—on market days in summer—and luxury coaches, but they are only aware of the merry becks and hidden falls after heavy rains. Then torrents leap over the rock ramparts, the becks go frothing through the fields and behind every farm the babbling becks which usually croon evening lullabies under bedroom windows keep families awake with their loud raging.

Water music and water falls are 'the thing' in this dale. Find your way to Foss Gill, 'one of Yorkshire's finest sights, where a continuous chain of falls and cascades, fourteen in all, leap, plunge and disappear into deep abysses—the final drop one hundred and fifty feet !' That is something worth finding. So is the Silver Chain, in The Gill near Thoralby, where falls and cascades chase through woods 'silvering through scenes of remarkable beauty'.

Thoralby, settled by a Viking a thousand years ago, is at the dale end, a nook-shotten place which the road enters diffidently as though having no right to intrude. The first time I came in by bus I thought the driver had gone off the rails !

The village history is very 'local', except for a few incidents with repercussions farther afield. The lads distinguished themselves by their alacrity in springing to arms when Napoleonic invasion was expected. The signal to muster for the loyal volunteers of the dale was beacon fire on Pen Hill. Naturally when Pen Hill watchers saw a glow on far away Roseberry Topping they were not to know it was only heather ablaze. Neither were the local lads to know their own beacon gave a false alarm. Soon they were marching with drums beating down the road to Middleham and Thirsk. Later, Parliament notified its appreciation of their loyalty.

Soon afterwards, when the national hero was Wellington, a bridge was erected near Littleburn House. A tablet read 'In memory of peace and security under God. Dedicated to Wellington'.

Thoralby's maypole was a giant, dating from the young Victoria's coronation. Forty lusty lads bore in two gigantic larches and set them up with due ceremony.

The villagers once considered the year's highlight was their Martin-mas Feast. Everyone who could return home did so, and enjoyed a

week's merrymaking, mumming, feasting and dancing, especially a
local 'jumping dance' loud with stamping boots.

WALDENDALE

What Thoralby is to Bishopdale, West Burton—a jewel among dales'
villages, with friendly villagers to match—is to little seven-mile
Waldendale; two miles of road link them.

The village-round-a-green plan is completely satisfying, ringed
around by smiling cottages, there is an old-fashioned inn, a squatting
smithy and, for centrepiece, an obelisk on ancient market cross steps,
this being suitably decorated with garlands when the May Feasts of
long ago were days of old English—therefore old Yorkshire—merrymaking. Here 'Times ambles withal'. In June the air is drenched
with scent from lime trees. After rains, thunder of waterfalls.

To the back garden walls sweeps down Pen Hill's western escarpment. Eating back towards the mountain slopes of Buckden Pike,
Walden Beck makes three miles or so of delicious solitude for the
loiterer who is content with his own company, sharing the vast tops
with the buzzard, and the walled-in peace of Waldendale bottoms
with wheatears, dippers, water wagtails and birds which have for
their haunts peat-brown pools and splashy falls. There are lingering
banks of cushioned moss with wild thyme and starry saxifrage, and
on the heights acres of ling and heather.

A 'walkers' only' dale; tracks to the Pike and over to Wharfedale;
to Park Rash, or Starbotton, or Buckden. Exhilarating fell ways due
east from Cote Farm climb 700 feet in the first mile before levelling
out on Pen Hill's shoulder, where red and fallow deer were chased
by Neville huntsmen; we pass Howden Lodge and a shooters' hut
before dropping to the long green dale of the Cover.

Four miles between Waldendale and Coverdale at Carlton, on foot,
but 10 miles by car on the highroad from West Burton along the
floor of Wensleydale. A devious route it is, to Cover Bridge which is
the end of Coverdale. From West Witton a byroad climbs up and
over Melmerby Moor, reaching Coverdale in 6 miles; wonderful
prospects!

THE DALE OF THE COVER

Coverdale; an enclosed world of its own which after more than
two centuries of isolation is again invaded by wheeled traffic.

The fifteen miles from Cover Head to Cover Bridge until the
eighteenth century was the most hazardous stretch of the London-
Richmond coaching route. What a straining, and pulling, and hard
'slippering' it must have been.

Long before coaching days the dale road was thronged with traffic,
this being the main castle to castle and abbey to abbey way north-
ward through the Pennines. Often it was loud with troop movements,
armies riding and marching through to Scotland. When Middleham
Castle at dale end was recognized as a minor Windsor, cavalcades of

nobles, courtiers and royalties wound their way over Park Rash and
slowly towards the 'palace' of Neville's, earls of Warwick.

For two hundred years or so the pass became deserted by all but
farmers, dalesfolk and drovers. I remember it as a rough, partly
grassed fell road, crossing a veritable no-man's-land where to meet
anyone else was surprising. Then, the war over, the improving hand
of road makers put a surface on the track and now cars which can
first surmount the 1 in 4 gradient on the Wharfedale side may venture
safely into Coverdale—with great care at every one of its many dips
and bends.

There is a smack of the Norseman in this landscape. Swinside and
Arkleside began as saeters, Woo Gill and Woo Dale were outlying
farms, so were Gammersgill and Melmerby, naming their settlers.
Clearings were made at Hindlethwaite Braithwaite and Brackenrigg.
The noble hills called Caldbergh and Harkers were of their naming.
These dalesmen were so fiercely hostile to the invading Normans that
their new lords found it necessary to liquidate them, raze their homes,
wipe out whole communities.

Anglian villagers were thicker at dale end, round Middleham
where the great thane had his manor house, at Coverham low by
the river, at Carlton and Scrafton. They suffered as sorely as their
Norse neighbours in the Harrying of the North.

There are alternative roads up the Cover as far as Carlton. The
highway from Middleham sweeps over its open moor, passes Coverham church—the abbey is lost below—so on to Melmerby and the
first houses of Carlton. Here a much more desultory byway, quieter,
narrower, has wandered in from East Witton—you come into it from
the highway A6108—by way of that most interesting specimen of
a dales hall now a farmhouse (open to the public) at Braithwaite,
by Cover Bridge and West Scrafton.

You will dilly dally, playing ducks and drakes at Cover Bridge, a
pretty spot. Coverham Abbey is a private house, but you may look in
at the grey archway to the garden borders within. The roadside
church reminds you of a famous son of the dale, that Miles Coverdale
who when Henry VIII ordered that each parish church in the land
was to have its copy of the bible printed in the mother tongue was
able to make this work, so important in the reformed church, possible.
Our Psalter—his 'matchless phrases'.

Melmerby village is flung high; below, the Cover hides in deep
woods. A path creeps down to Simon's Wath, an ancient ford, where
long ago the dalesfolk came to pray at St. Simon's Chapel. This saint
was highly thought of formerly, his day was Coverdale's Feast when
everyone let himself go, too much according to James I's liking. A
chaplain updale at Horse House let the congregation dance in chapel
—to the playing of a piper! Only the Cover's voice and bird song
now where the holy hermit prayed in his cell.

Carlton is Coverdale's natural centre, and has been since village
elders gathered round the Carl Motte for law making in pre-Norman
times and foresters courts assembled in the days of the hunting earls.

The forest limits were Coverdale's horizons; within was a deer park and a warren for small game. One inn is the 'Foresters', most suitably.

Behind the inn take the path down the Gill Hole to a Cover foot bridge and scramble through half-choked old packways, or climb the wide strip lynchets' steps of ancient cultivation terraces, so into West Scrafton. The servants of Coverham Abbey lived here caring for the abbot's flocks which roamed the vast Caldbergh sheep walks; an abbey grange was here.

We think Scrafton was once deeply religious; so many chapels to so few houses! A little-visited hamlet, with country quiet wrapping it round. Streams fall into basins of rich red rock from Caldbergh's sides and disappear into mysterious depths. Up Caldbergh, a most exciting upstanding hill—like Pen Hill, and Addleborough, and Yorburgh which look on Ure from the south—run tracks to old coal pits and over to a monastic Coalpit Road, and Colsterdale. This is exciting walking country, the winds cool and sweet, blowing over miles of heather. In summer ripe bilberries are for the picking and a local rarity and delicacy, cowberries which grow low to the ground, small juicy threesomes.

Names on the map; why Honey Pots, Flagstone Pin, and why did Jenny Binks have a moss called after her? None of the local Binks can tell.

The Binks tell me of local characters. Old Scouring Jack fifty odd years ago obtained loads of 'donkey stones' required by farmwives for their doorsteps and flagged floors, Scrafton quarries his source of supply. He and his sister earned extra by hiring themselves for muck-spreading at 'ha'penny a heap and luncheon'. Poor souls! When Jack died his hoardings were found in his Melmerby cottage, jam jars full of money.

Coverdale cows gave full cream milk. To test a good milker the old grandmother ran an egg over a bowl of cream left standing. 'If it was from a good milker the surface was like leather, so the egg rolled.'

They liked rum in the dale but referred to it by other names; the rum bottle was the 'old grey hen', and that drop which made cheese tarts all the better was 'a dash of the black cow's milk'.

It was always a valley for nonconformity. In penal days fell-top cairns, like one far above Gammersgill, marked a route to places of secret worship; a Lofthouse raised one. Scrafton had at one time two chapels to cater for very small minorities who thought differently about Methodism. The Primitives won at Horse House—the second hamlet passed going updale from Carlton, Gammersgill in between.

Horse House—where the piper played in the church on St. Simon's Day—terraces the Cover hillside, a tight knot of grey stone houses with an inn, and teas at the Old School House, quiet enough now but once busy with pedlars and badgers—they bought up farm surplus of butter, eggs and cheeses—who gathered here after hard journeys over from Wharfedale or Nidderdale.

The wayside chapel was built by the Primitives in 1828 and, as two members told us one September day when we peeped in to watch how Harvest Festival preparations were progressing, 'in its time it has sent forth clouds of witnesses'. No less than six local preachers have they sent out into the larger outside world of Methodism. 'Some Sundays there are more preachers than congregation', but however few gather their voices wellnigh lift the roof. 'The church is much quieter. Chapel has the boys for the singing'.

Out of the golden afternoon women bore in armfuls of flowers, ripe corn, berries from the hedgerows. Willing hands worked, following patterns set by other 'Harvests'. A towering centrepiece of sunflowers, golden rod, phlox and dahlias hid unbeautiful stove and stove pipe. The preacher on the morrow would have to restrain his movements as he peeped out of a cornucopian overspill of massed flowers and piled fruit. Heads would look down from the balcony through bowers of flowers. Even the black iron coat pegs in rows against the entrance wall were transfigured, each with its dangling posy of red rowan berries and golden wheat heads.

Carlton with its mile of happy cottages and gardens in the best tradition—the rockeries in April, the borders in July!—Gammersgill settled and placid as a contented matron, Horse Head watching old roads come in, and the farms of Bradley and Woodale watching the lonely road sweep up to the dale head, all are pleasant communities taking interest in any incomers from over the watersheds.

Now Dead Man's Hill, on the old fell road crossing from Horse (originally 'Hause') House to Scar House at Nidd head, hints at macabre. Taking an unnatural interest in travelling men who stopped overnight at their inn were the sinister landlady and her son who 'made away with' three Scots pedlars, and might have murdered a fourth in his bed had he not become suspicious. He, Angus his name, met the son lurking at his bedroom door, knocked him down, and like the wind flew over to Middlesmoor for help. The searchers returning discovered the bodies of three victims in a croft by the inn. The murderers were caught and hanged.

There is nothing secretive about Cover Head. The road toiling from the last outpost of Woodale is open to all the winds that blow. And how they batter us when we walk towards the watershed, not a stick or stone for shelter, except that battered boundary mark, Great Hunter Stone, where in the middle ages the rangers of Wensleydale Forest and Langstrothdale and Littondale Chases recognized the limits of preserves under their jurisdiction.

The occasional car crawling very slowly to the skyline does little to break into the age-long solitude. We enter into silences such as the Coverham shepherds knew as they toiled over to the abbot's Scale Park sheep walks, and Percy and Neville huntsmen riding their boundaries along long lonely skylines—just where the single farmer with his dog stands silhouetted against wild skies, his shrill whistles blending with the mewing of hawks.

Peace waits among these fells where Cover is cradled.

3. North side of the dale: Leyburn to Askrigg

LEYBURN AND VIEWPOINTS

What is this place called Leyburn to which all roads appear to be signposted? There it is, flung out on a breezy hillside—very much as Reeth and Grassington with which it has much in common. Each is a market town, each was founded on lead, each continued in reduced circumstances when lead no longer boomed.

Its market place is vast, enough to take a cattle mart, corn market and all the stalls and stands from which folk from the lower dale expected to do their market day buying. Two royal charters, one from Charles II and a second to confirm it from James II, gave Leyburn its markets. The local lead mines boosted it, the coming of the railway in 1870 gave it an additional fillip; now mines are no more, the railway is closed and the place is not quite what it was. Look around the outer perimeter of the square where tall Georgian houses and many inns wear the airs and graces of past centuries; the upper floors are unchanged though the twentieth-century shop windows are sometimes a concession to the present.

Leyburn Shawl and Scarth Nick are two outstanding features of the five mile long limestone scars extending westwards. From the town wander two miles through the woods, a 'promenade' of which the natives are inordinately proud. "The views! The good pure air!", they boast. They tell that Mary Queen of Scots, managing to escape from her Castle Bolton guards, reached this terrace before capture, casting down her shawl. That the word 'schalle' or 'skali' meant huts or shelters to early Norse settlers they repudiate if romantically inclined. They also forget to refer to the horse-shoe shaped depressions below the Shawl, foundations of prehistoric hunters' dwellings.

Look at the view, they insist. And fine it is, along the wide green dale we are setting out to enjoy.

Three miles along the same scars and overlooking Preston-under-Scar is Scarth Nick, and prospects are so magnificent that travel writers gave it five star rating. Wrote one: "Glorious! a wealth of quiet beauty . . . to come upon it suddenly from dreary moorlands, enchantment is in the far spreading views". Speight and Bogg agreed it was one of the most beautiful viewpoints in Richmondshire, to the stranger's eye a veritable 'Eldorado or the Land of Promise'.

The impact of the 'surprise view' comes only for those who cross the bleak moors from Grinton or Halfpenny House which are pitted and spiked with derelict mine workings, coal and lead. We feel as travellers in a barren land confronted with a paradise flowing with milk and honey.

The zig-zagging roads and paths dropping to the valley were made by the eighteenth century miners whose homes were at Preston under the Scar.

WENSLEY AND REDMIRE

From Leyburn we head for the milk and honey vale, one and a half miles into Wensley, the most neat and smiling village grouped to make a perfect picture at the park gates. Before its big elm fell crashing before a fierce gale of summer 1946 it looked even more idyllic; even worse gales of February 1962 sent hundreds of the park trees crashing, bringing down scores more like ninepins, raging along the dale leaving a wide path of devastation in its wake. I was sad when I watched woodmen at work on the old elm in '46; I was far more saddened at the skittle alley havoc in the woods in '62.

What was so important about Wendeslaga of the Anglo-Saxons that its name was given to the valley? The church gives part of the answer. It was an early religious centre with a school of artists who possibly learnt their skills from Italian artists encouraged to come to England by St. Wilfrid of Ripon; they carved tall crosses with intricate designs in plaitwork and scrolls, interlacing patterns with trailing vines, chevrons, and with panels of birds and beasts, and sometimes with the figure of Christ. Look inside the church for tablets naming priests who laboured at Wendeslaga when warring Danes fought their way along the dale: Donfrid, Eadbricht, and Aruni.

The church is mostly thirteenth century work, the arcading and the wall paintings showing the Fall of Man, Adam and Eve with the Archangel Michael sword in hand, casting out Satan from Eden. The woodwork is from many periods. Ripon craftsmen worked on the chancel stalls and old pews. The iron barred reliquary of St. Agatha and the exquisite parclose screen incorporated in the hall pew were brought from Easby Abbey after the Dissolution by the Scropes whose ancestors had been lavish in gifts when the abbey was new. The pew is more like a self-contained parlour, screened and curtained in the old days when the family wanted privacy in their worship; with the Bolton alliances blazoned in panels of red, blue silver and gold it is a typical Jacobean period piece.

The present Lord Bolton is a successor of the dukes of Bolton who built the hall in 1678, thereupon vacating the vast, draughty towers of Castle Bolton, home of their forbears the Scropes. A drive leads to the hall and paths go through the park, the most enchanting through woodland glades and by the riverside where long beech boughs trail their leaves in the water, above brown pools ringing with trout, where dark fish cruise around with barely a flick of fin. Lord Bolton is a great lover of trees. Where tall conifers strain towards the sky and avenues are needle-soft, look for small nesting boxes fastened high up the trunks. A sanctuary for birds! June evenings are a joy. Always there is drowsy crooning of wood doves. Always pheasant, the cocks handsome as any peacock, are feeding in the open pastures at the wood edge.

Redmire is rather more than three miles west of Wensley, walking through the park or by road north of the park. There is more to the village than first meets the eye; unexpected nooks hide round corners. A small green with original cross steps, 'commemorative' parish lamps, a town hall on a very small scale, a doddering oak crutched in extreme old age, and an assortment of pretty cottages—that is Redmire. It had aspirations to be something more; a discovery of a sulphur well led to big talk of a second Harrogate.

Where the footpath from Wensley leaves the park for the open fields, there is Redmire's ancient church, with fine Norman door, and massive walls pierced by pointed lancet windows, looking on a quiet landscape such as John Wesley surveyed when he came to preach in 1744. The people resented his coming, eyeing him suspiciously 'as if we had been a company of monsters', he complained.

An octagenarian born within the walls of Bolton Castle tells me of childhood and boyhood days hereabouts. Poor folk used to go to Bolton Hall for broken meats and soup doled out at the kitchen door when times were bad—lead mines on short, or no work. The field by the keeper's cottage, that was where the village children came for pace egging, boys throwing their hard-boiled eggs, girls more decorously rolling theirs. Then rough play followed. Every self-respecting ten-year-old boasted a brand new, red silk handkerchief in his jacket pocket. Lively teasing lasses liked to snatch and run away, the boys chasing. "I remember the lass who took mine", he says. "I rolled her down the bank but she tucked it away where I dared not try to get it. For all I know she has it still." After eighty years—I wonder?

Redmire Feast was on the same day as Castle Bolton's; the one in the afternoon, the other in the forenoon, and there were silver teapots to be won for quoits, and prizes for races, wrestling, walloping and knocking down pegs, and grinning through collars. Happy days!

For six centuries the local cottagers have been tenants of either Scropes or Lords Bolton, at Redmire and at Castle Bolton little more than a mile away and at higher level. Men laboured for and fought with the Scropes, and continued to work in Lord Bolton's mines. The annual Rent Day dinner is still a great occasion.

THE SCROPES AND CASTLE BOLTON

The first Scropes arrived on the scene in 1284 when William le Scrope was granted East Bolton, a small estate. The Scropes were already a name in the dales, for in Edward II's reign a Scrope who had received lands from a Constable of Richmond rebuilt part of Easby Abbey by Swale and there the family chose to be buried. Then they were known as Scropes of Masham, and to Mashamshire they returned in the Tudor times to their seat at Danby Hall. The years between saw the rise of their castle at Bolton.

The Nevilles were then the recognized 'top dogs' by Ure, inclined to resent interlopers. But Richard Scrope was high in royal favour, a chancellor when young Richard II was king, a trusted adviser, Treasurer of the Exchequer and Keeper of the Royal Seal. Scropes were so well thought of that the king readily granted Richard the right to raise the walls of and add fortifications to his humble house at Bolton. That was in 1379. A battlemented hall by Ure would help stem the Scots. Also it would effectively curb the too-uppish Nevilles.

Neville's underlings reported on the activity on the far hillslopes. Scropes were employing gangs of masons and labourers; quarrying on a large scale was going on. Long trains of waggons were bringing in timber. Nevilles did not like it. Scrope certainly went beyond his permit, but King Richard kept quiet. Let the Nevilles realize there were other big fish in the Yorkshire pool.

Eighteen years a-building, £12,000 the cost; many changes came during that period whilst Scrope coffers were emptied. The king, for whom the Scropes founded a chantry chapel in the castle, fell before

Scropes' stronghold: Castle Bolton

the forces of his cousin Henry Bolingbroke, Earl of Lancaster. The Nevilles were for Henry, their star was to blaze brightly. The Scropes, loyal to Richard, were to suffer greatly. Lord Richard's son Henry and his brother, the great Archbishop of York, were in the forefront of rebellion against Henry IV; both lost their heads and their possessions. And Castle Bolton walls mortar hardly dry!

You cannot keep good men down for long. In the downs of the House of Lancaster and the ups of the House of York many Yorkshire families went up or down, and Scropes made rapid returns to favour. The family produced two who became earls, twenty barons, two bishops, four high treasurers, two chief justices, as well as the first at Castle Bolton, the lord chancellor and the lord archbishop—and numerous Knights of the Garter.

The Neville's downfall after the defeat and death of Richard III—Anne Neville's husband—meant the Scrope's ascendancy. They were leaders of the dalesmen who marched north to fight the Scots at Flodden. They took no part in the Pilgrimage of Grace which was death knell to many dales' families, and helped to crush the Rising of the North planned by Nevilles of Raby and Percys of Northumberland. They were recent 'hosts' of Mary Queen of Scots on whose behalf the Roman Catholic families rose against Elizabeth.

Elizabeth was not too sure of the wisdom of entrusting her 'cousin' to Scropes. Lady Scrope was sister to the Duke of Norfolk; he was known, through letters intercepted, to have a burning desire to marry Mary and with her to depose Elizabeth, to restore the Old Faith and the fallen abbeys. After six months sojourn at Castle Bolton the Scropes said farewell to the royal 'guest', her six ladies, her retinue of servants, and watched the procession of twenty carriages and twenty-three saddle horses wend its way southwards. It was a cold January day; she had arrived on July 15th of the previous year. The Scropes sighed with relief; the villagers also, for Mary's retinue had been billeted in their small cottages, uncomfortably.

Just as the great castle towers, even in decay, overshadow and dwarf the village stretching away from their walls, so did the Scropes lord it over the dalesfolk, their tenants.

The castle, a farseen landmark in Wensleydale, the walls gleaming silver when the woods and fells behind are deep blue in cloud shade, or dark and grim, frowning in deep gloom when the background hills are glinting gold, never fails to recall memories of 'ancient far-off days' and stirring scenes enacted within its walls. It is 'open to the public'. Very rewarding it is to walk through the spacious apartments where Scropes feasted and entertained noble guests, or to linger in the rooms given up to the captive queen, to look from the windows which framed the same prospects for her—the long dale and the blue fells westward over which came the road which brought her from Scotland—and to stand in the bedchamber from which was no chance of escape. How often must Mary have chafed, though her 'guards' treated her as an honoured guest and allowed her to ride out hunting, towards Nappa, or Cover, or Leyburn; the chains were there though invisible and the Scropes dangled no keys.

The stone stairs spiral up to the leads of high towers; we grip the parapet as the wind tugs and whips us. Far below—the roofless chapel; away from the walls the long village green and small moving figures, children, and a woman leading the tiny grey donkey with milk kits shining at its flanks. Down we go, through the dining-rooms—where they produce at short notice the best meals you are ever likely to have put before you—and to the cold, damp and dank dungeons; no one lingers long here but a minute is long enough to appreciate that to be a Scrope prisoner was an unpleasant experience.

Outside the walls look at the church, of normal proportions but small measured against the towering walls. From the field gate at the west end is a pleasant short cut through the pastures to Beldon Beck, West Bolton and Carperby village.

TO CARPERBY

The road drops below the castle and turns updale to Carperby, a grey village 'of linked sweetness long drawn out', all its parts so neat and comely it has twice won the prized trophy for the Best Kept Village in the Dales National Park. If it has a centre it must be the green around the high-stepped market cross, where the 'prize' seats are. At the hall lived the Willis family whose breed of Wensleydale rams is known far beyond the Yorkshire dales; I knew one proud long-nosed patriarch called Carperby Wonder who put the curl in the fleeces of many cross-bred sheep in Ribblesdale.

You must be familiar by now with the Wensleydales, those large, white-faced and hornless sheep with permanently waved fleeces, silken and pale fawn when 'fettled up' for the show ring. Most likely, in all pedigree stock the Carperby strain will be present.

Around Carperby the rolling hills between village and river are stepped and contoured by wide, strip lynchets of medieval cultivation. How well they show up as the sun dips and shadows are thrown over the banks. For a thousand years this part of the dale has been continuously ploughed and tilled; a timeless landscape, green and smiling, as Dorothy Wordsworth saw it in the September of 1802 : 'beautiful each way, the bright silver stream inlaid the flat and very green meadows, winding like a serpent . . . the sun was not yet set and the woods and fields were spread over with the yellow light of evening which made their greenness a thousand times more green'.

To carry forward above the Ure brings us to Wood Hall, glorious in autumn flame and gold; a Warrener cared for the small game here in forest days when deer were confined within the park by an unleapable wall. Not far ahead where the road runs on the levels above a limestone scar, grey towers rise from the trees below; this is Nappa Hall and here we are in Metcalfe country.

THE METCALFES AND NAPPA HALL

In the fourteenth century members of the clan Metcalfe arrived in this dale, of the family of a certain Adam Medecalf of Middle Tongue high up Dentdale who was slain there during the reign of the first Edward. They were to prosper and multiply greatly during the next two centuries; as high ranking officials large tracts of forest land came into their hands, enough to supply the needs of sons and nephews. At Military Musters the head of the 'Meccas' rode forth proudly leading men of his own name. In 1534, of ninety-six mounted 'Meccas' sixty-two were from Nappa. On one historic occasion one, as High Sheriff, collected more than three hundred Metcalfes to ride with him to do him honour in York, all mounted, the story goes, on white horses—which were most probably York-shire greys.

Now you see the name on shop fronts, inn doors, cattle waggons—and no less than two and a half columns of the telephone directory covering Wensleydale lists twentieth century Metcalfes.

The Nevilles rode with kings to war; the Metcalfes followed the Scropes. So it was James Metcalfe who fought well at Agincourt who was rewarded on return from the French Wars with land at Nappa whereon stood a small tenement called jokingly 'No Castle'. James had ambition and family pride. Soon he was to obtain a licence to erect a battlemented hall which was to prove anything but a joke. His high roofed 'halle' stood between two tall, strong, battlemented and castellated towers, his capacious stables and outbuildings enclosed a large paved courtyard to which access was by a deep gated archway. And so it is today, though none of Metcalfe name live here now.

The Nevilles showed suspicion of Scrope's ambitions when Castle Bolton looked like a threat to Middleham's position. So did the Scropes feel qualms and had second thoughts about giving land to the Metcalfes. But too late. Metcalfes were not content to stay down on the fourth rung of the feudal ladder. They would hold up their heads among the Nevilles and Scropes; let them wait and see !

James, the second of Nappa, was chancellor of the Duchy of Lancaster and high in offices in Richmond and Middleham lordships

Nappa Hall of the Metcalfes

during the reign of Henry VI. The third James was able to keep his feet on the slippery ladder from which Scropes had fallen when Henry IV ousted their patron Richard II, and from which the Nevilles were to topple in the fall of the House of York to which they were so closely bound. The third James had followed Richard of Gloucester in his travels and from the duke had received ranks and honours in the lordship of Middleham. He was made master forester of Wensleydale, Raydale and Bishopdale, high honour indeed with many 'perques', and became high sheriff of the county.

When Richard became king and then fell before Henry Tudor the Metcalfes clung to the ladder and kept their hold, persuading the new king that they were too valuable to go down. Metcalfes were in full force at Flodden, and in the forefront whenever Henry VIII needed support of north countrymen. They continued to prosper.

Thomas Metcalfe added to other family estates disafforested lands in the upper dale, when hunting preserves were becoming vaccaries or cattle ranches. In his time the family fortunes were firmly consolidated. In young Sir Christopher's days the Metcalfes were their most resplendant, for he was a typical Tudor type, fond of good living and lavish entertaining, the hall ringing with feasting and merriment, the court yard filled with horsemen returning from the hunt or riding away to visit other wealthy and noble families in other dales. One day a hunting party came through the gateway, with Mary Queen of Scots among them; Sir Christopher entertained her right royally. His wife was a Clifford, daughter of the first Earl of Cumberland who gave a graded scale of dowries according to the rank of the bridegroom. Sir Christopher was good, but not good enough. Elizabeth's dowry was a modest 900 marks, he being but a mere knight.

Sir Christopher entered his inheritance with a liability. When old Sir James died the Scrope of the time with great malice set lawyers to find what claim the family had to the estates his forbear had bestowed on the first James Metcalfe. No legal right at all! So to buy the lands they had enjoyed for so many generations the new owner had to sell and mortgage Nappa estates. After his high living the possessions were even more depleted, his grandsons dividing the residue. A century later the South Sea Bubble took what was left. Soon there were no Metcalfes at the hall.

Nappa Hall is a farmhouse now; a bull croons in a nearby coppy, children and sheep dog puppies play around the doors, men are busy at the sheepfolds in the croft where 'No Castle' once stood. Indoors the kitchen is full of life and movement, but the high hall which was once so noisy with Metcalfes roaring in their cups, singing and roistering, is silent—unless it is a wet day when the children of the house are careering around.

The towers are tall; from the trefoil-headed windows in the thick walls are fine views over countryside Metcalfes once were able to say "All that is ours."

The first Metcalfe at Nappa founded a chantry chapel in Askrigg church; three generations of the family lie there—but little is to be seen of chantry or tombs.

IN OLD ASKRIGG

There is no mistaking Askrigg for an old market town though the long street is never thronged now as in the old days with drovers and packmen, merchants and pedlars, colliers and miners from the fells, knitting men and knitting women from outlying farms, and no merchandise is put down on the cobblestones or round the cross near the church gate. However quiet it is—and footfalls echo on the pavements when we walk through Askrigg—it is not difficult to imagine 'better days'.

Look for the Georgian façades of decorous houses, and for archways opening into old inn yards. Their 'day' was when this street was on

Main Street, Askrigg

the busy Hawes-Leyburn turnpike, and the London to Kirkby
Stephen and Kendal stages coaches pulled up with a flourish at the
Red Lion door with "All change!" shouted and great commotion on
all sides—just like an animated picture from a Christmas card 'Olde
Tyme'.

Before going into the churchyard, turn round. The cobbled area was scene of lively bull baitings. The ring for tethering is still imbedded in the stones. But the fine hall with a gallery admirably suited to the participation of Georgian 'sportsmen'—that has disappeared. There is a local story of a baby abandoned on the cobbles long ago, cared for and named Luke Stones because of the place where he was found.

The church as we see it is mostly fifteenth century, the period of the first Metcalfes at Nappa and their newly founded Chantry of St. Anne. The arcade pillars are far older, probably Norman work salvaged from the abbey the Cistercian monks of Byland were endeavouring to establish at Fors, or Dale Grange, near the village. They were having a hard time of it, pioneering in a wild outback fraught with many dangers not least of which were wild beasts and wolves. According to legends they were able to translate themselves to kinder country down dale at Jervaulx through the offer of Conan, Earl of Richmond who stayed with them when hunting in the forest near Askrigg and had pity on them.

Among natives of the village who carried the name far outside the dale were the Caygills, skilled clockmakers. I know one fine specimen owned by the old man born at Castle Bolton. This grandfather clock was bought from the Caygills by a farmer who lived on the tops above Leyburn. Later, having being 'passed down', it was left to a relative in London. Transport proving too difficult it was collected and had a shorter journey to Castle Bolton. Nevertheless it travelled well to its present home in a cottage on the Lancashire moors, its proud possessor a Moore.

Yoredale now has a new grammar school in spacious grounds below the village. At the annual summer sports boys take part in a special local race, a strenuous run as originally intended by the maiden lady who 'thought it up'. The Garland Race, she decreed, was to be run from the station door to the top of Garland Hill—this being the climbing road out towards Muker—in three minutes. My informants tell me, "She had been disappointed in love and likely wanted to get her own back on marriageable men i'Askrigg. Likely she meant race to kill 'em off!" The prize money came from a field rent; the victor was suitably garlanded.

Askrigg's falls or fosses named the twelfth century abbey of Fors. Unlike Aysgarth's—which do their raging and roaring in full view of passers by on the bridge—Askrigg's need tracking down in deep ravines which can be pure enchantment in the penetrating sun of early morning or evening light, or sheer drama after heavy rains. Beyond the church go along to Mill Farm—you will see the outsize cheese press stone 'in situ' here—and follow the beck to Mill Gill bridge—now a concrete slab where, before winter ice split it, was a huge monolithic stone 'clapper'. Upstream in a tree-filled glen full of undersea mystery, a veil of white water comes dropping out of the sky. This is Mill Gill Force 'which Nature keeps as a shrine approachable only by the active foot and willing heart'. Another path and a scramble to an ancient ford called Slape Wath, where an old packway crossed the shallows, and you come to Cogill Beck. This has slowed down after a tremendous drop over a dark wall of rock, sixty feet of a leap, all in a secret gill; this is the Whitfell Force which once brought all Victorian tourists to stand, to goggle and gape.

It is a delight to give up a summer afternoon to these lovely places, then to return to the village along trodden ways across flower-filled pastures, and to have as landmark the church tower and grey roofs of the clustered cottages.

Church paths, close set paving stones trailing stile to stile across the fields, are short cuts to Bow Bridge—near the site of Fors—and over the valley to Bainbridge. The road updale crosses the Ure too. Below, a flat valley little cultivated, looks like the glaciated floor it was, the river looping often-flooded acres.

4. South side of Ure

Coming updale from Leyburn to Askrigg we have travelled high above the dale, looking south to the limestone terraced fells above which rise the distinctive table-topped Pen Hill, Addleborough and Yorburgh and watching the play of sungleams and cloud shadows on the dales gripped between them. Byroads follow those limestone terraces; small villages are strung along them, airy hamlets too, from which folk look down on almost birds'-eye views of the dale floor.

Now for another journey up the Yore valley, from the 'mouth' near East Witton, to West Witton, Swinithwaite and down to Aysgarth, for the sake of the falls, rising again to breeze-ridden heights of Thornton Rust before dropping to Worton, there to meet our north-side route from Leyburn to Askrigg.

Our last route from Leyburn to Hawes by unclassified roads north of Ure: 18 miles. This, starting from Masham, through Middleham, 8 miles on A6108; and westwards to Wensley, West Witton, Aysgarth and Hawes, south of Ure, 18 miles on A684.

HISTORIC SPOTS BY LOWER URE

The highway A6108, along which we come from Ripon by the wide and dignified waters of the mature Ure, passes through a rich, comfortable countryside of cornfields and contentment which has so many sites of history, and prehistory, that if tempted to digress we should never reach the beginning of the lower dale of the Ure, let alone dale head.

Rising above the wooded banks upriver from the stately Tanfield Bridge is the grey tower of the castle raised by John, Lord Marmion, as defence against the Scots, with Edward I's permission; here had been a 'humble Hermitage in Tanfield Wood'. Beyond the tower the fine old church wherein are buried under splendid effigies those Marmions, of proud and honoured name, descendants of the Fitz

Hugh heiress who married Robert, Lord Marmion. He like many of his forbears was Royal Champion of England.

Minor roads go off across the valley to Well—where Roman retired officers had dwellings as pleasant as those down river at Aldburgh, with tesselated floors in their villas. There an early Latimer of date unknown slew a dread dragon, and centuries later another Lord Latimer was to marry young Catherine Parr, destined to be queen. The last Lord Latimer was Sir John Neville. Earlier Nevilles, when lords of Middleham, founded the picturesque hospital, or almshouse, of St. Michael for a 'master, two priests and twenty-four poor brothers and sisters'. If you wander away to discover the whereabouts of Well you will find an ancient church and the hospital nearby.

The byways link Well with Snape too, a quiet sleepy village with a grey and formidable castle at one end, half occupied, half ruinous. Look carefully; this was built by the same lords of Middleham, the Fitz Randolphs who were at work on raising Middleham Castle. Like other Middleham estates this also came into Neville hands and carries the Neville 'saltire' on a wall, the date 1587.

North of Snape, the long avenue leads to the lovely hall called Thorpe Perrow, with gardens and ornamental lakes of exquisite beauty. North again and lanes come to Bedale, a pleasant old market town with the grey tower of the church of the Fitz Alans looking on. But we are wandering; back to Masham—or on to Leyburn which is only 11 miles due west.

'MASHAMSHIRE'

Masham is disposed round a market place with a cross, centre of activity every Friday from the year 1250, and even more thronged for its September cattle and sheep fairs, when of sheep alone thirty-five to forty thousand were brought here annually for sale. No longer, alas, do the villagers keep open house 'offering roast beef, pickled cabbage, drink and other necessaries for travellers, welcome rich or poor'. The church is old, the tower first stage is Norman, the lantern thirteenth century and the prominant landmark spire fifteenth century. Visit the tombs in the north aisle Wyvill Chapel for the sake of Sir Marmaduke and his lady who lie there in effigy, she meek with closed lids, and he tinted 'realistically' with red lips, pink cheeks and alabaster eye balls painted blue; mourning over them—cherubs blowing alabaster soap bubbles, and Death, skull in hand.

Mashamshire is Scrope country. Whereas the main line of Scropes were at Castle Bolton and through the marriage of a daughter continued at Bolton Hall, Sir Geoffrey, a younger son of Lord Scrope, bought the Masham lands from the Waltons; his descendants founded the Masham line. The main line lived for generations at Danby Hall, the park on the north side of Ure, across from the lands of Jervaulx.

Above Masham town narrow bylanes ride high, looking in at the tiny hamlets of Fearby and Healey if you hanker after closer acquaintance with the remote dale of the Burn. This is the Colsterdale wherein

Jervaulx abbots had coal and iron works, and a coal pit road which
sets walkers off to the dale head and over Caldbergh side into Coverdale, a glorious moorland day. It is wild, lonely landscape, and easy
to lose the way if clouds descend. The body of one who perished on
the moors of Grewelthorpe, and whose remains were given a resting
place at Kirkby Malzeard, was discovered a century ago in a peat
bog. Peat preserves as well as any embalming. This 'young man lost'
was a Roman-Briton; his cloak was green, his tunic scarlet, his
stockings yellow and his feet wore leather sandals.

The same byway turns north out of Masham for Ellingstring, a
delightful village flung far above the Ellingtons from which it takes
its name. Elingstrengge was a string or vein of lead owned by the
people of Ellington, and the Ellingtons were the farms of Ella's folk
more than a thousand years ago. The village does not advertise its
whereabouts; it has never hit the headlines, and if it had not had a
very small youth hostel in Lilac Cottage I doubt if I would ever have
come to know it. Half a mile long, one street with pretty cottages in
gardens to match, a village store, a homely inn, the 'Boot and Shoe',
aged farms and Victorian chapel, a green with a tiny school upon it
—that is Ellingstring. But what a setting, and what tremendous
prospects !

Villagers take evening walks to the crossroads just to see the world
stretched out, to feel the perfumed breezes in their faces, to look over
the vale of Ure, a tapestry of golden cornfields, meadows, pastures
and a twisting belt of dark trees to tell where the river coils. At
sunset with the landscape drenched in gold, the warm light bathing
the ridges above Yore dale and Vale of Mowbray—milk and honey
country there—and the rolling, rose-flushed ramparts of the far away
Hambleton Hills, the Cleveland Hills, and Roseberry Topping which
so often blazed with beacon fires—it 'beggars description'. When the
colour pales and blue dusk wraps the Plain of York, then is the 'heart
called home to quietness'. From Ellingstring the bylane sweeps roundabout for 2½ miles then joins the highroad near Jervaulx, the abbey
domains wide and fair below.

For walkers only : a monastic forerunner of the same route starts
out near the inn, following Wood Gate, a flower-choked monks' road
to Mellwood cottage and dropping to the valley road near the abbey
gate; also a field path way to East Witton starts from the same point,
going west to High Newstead, over the bylane to Hammer Farm,
so to Low Newstead, and finally to Thirsting Castle and Low Thorpe,
on the outskirts of East Witton where its ancient church once
stood.

EAST WITTON—AND WEST

The Masham-Middleham highroad also pays a call on East Witton
after passing Jervaulx parklands.

Early in the last century when many of our byways were busy
highways the London to Hawes and Kirkby Stephen coaches ran
through East Witton, and doubtless their passengers looked out,

quite charmed with what they saw: the Earl of Ailesbury's new village.

Actually East Witton is very old, an Anglian village where the monks of Jervaulx as the largest local landowners were anxious to obtain a royal charter to hold markets and an annual fair; this they obtained in 1306. The fairs lapsed in 1563 when a terrible plague swept through the dale 'so hot and awful many fled'. Both East Witton's and Wensley's Trinity Fair so ended. Later they were remembered only for feasting and merrymaking, old East Witton folk telling of maypole dancing, sports and foot races on the green— 'twice round the green to the mile!'

We can only guess what old East Witton looked like. St. Martin's church was at Low Thorpe—in a secluded site shadowed by tall trees; the earl had it demolished in 1809, the stones used for the new parish church by the highroad to commemorate George III's fifty years as king. The ancient gravestones remain, and their epitaphs 'teaching the rustic moralist how to die'. Three eighteenth century specimens:

> Death does not always warning give.
> Therefore be careful how you live.

> The grave that opens next may well be thine.

> Reader remember what we are
> And in thy youth for death prepare.

The earl must have kept his tenants well employed, pulling down the old cottages, building the neat new decorous houses spaced evenly on both sides of the green, clearing the abbey site, and creating garden walks among the ruins, as well as pulling down the old and putting up the new church.

Not knowing the old we find the 'new' very pleasant. Take a good look at the fountain on the green, base for games and children's play. In 1859 a team of sixteen straining horses dragged the boulder base to this spot from the hillside where it had lain since the Ice Age glacier dropped it there.

West Witton, often confused with East, lies six miles' crowflight west, but much more by highroad and bus route which must proceed roundabout by Middleham, Leyburn and Wensley before returning south of the river. By linking a series of byways, a pleasure to walk, and possible for car-users exerting care, we may leave East Witton at its west end and keeping parallel with the Cover river, passing Braithwaite Hall—owned by the National Trust and open to the public, cross the river just below Coverham Abbey. Beyond the church turn left, updale, and in less than a mile take the first right turn, a short lane up to Agglethorpe.

Now we are up, on the moors which were Coverham Abbey land, where the monks' pastures became horse raising uplands and where now hopefuls from many a racing stable are led out on the shaven gallops for exercising. When Henry VIII's commissioners were spying out the abbey lands in 1535 they saw what excellent high ground the monks had for their horses: 'the finest galopping horses, I mean swift horses, horses as we call it bred for the light saddle, that is to say for the race, the chase and for running and hunting'.

This breezy plateau is a high terrace on the limestone wall running the length of the dale, broken only by the dales coming in from the south. Sudden drops and high level byroads come down to the low level, main roads—one into West Witton.

Here is a typical road-edge community, facing the valley, sheltered by the high fell escarpment behind. A farm called Chantry reminds us that the monks of Jervaulx had a small chapel here, and to help guide wayfarers on Pen Hill to safety they fired a warning—as the foresters of Bainbridge blew their horn. This was an act of Christian charity. The annual ceremony of the Burning of Bartle smacks more of pagan sacrifice. Travel through West Witton about St. Bartholomew's day and you will hear all about it, and have chanted for your benefit this old doggerel, a rhymed tour of Witton's environs.

In Penhill Crags he tore his rags.
At Hunters Thorn he blew his horn.
At Capplebank Stee he brak his knee.
At Briskill Beck he brak his neck.
At Wadham's End he couldn't fend.
At Briskell End he made his end.

So if you are tempted to follow the steps of Old Bartle it should be simple!

Swinithwaite, West Witton's neighbour, now a pretty tree-embowered village, road side and high above the Ure pastures, was named from the swineherds' clearings; pigs rooted in the acorns and mast of Wanless Park. Nevilles were owners of the hunting preserves and Metcalfes were parkers.

AYSGARTH AND THE FALLS

Riverside paths make for Wensley. The road carries on updale and into Aysgarth, where if no one told you, the odds are you would be through the village and out again, the falls unseen.

Aysgarth has a life of its own apart from its scenic attractions. Once the villagers were joined by merrymakers from the length and breadth of the dale to share in the annual fair and feast, for maypole dancing, wrestling, and 'men racing stark naked', a common north country attraction, included in all sports programmes of a century ago.

The falls were never 'discovered'; they were raging and roaring when the Britons of pre-Roman times lived in their stockaded village above the 'ais'—which means a waterfall. Ancient mills used the water to drive their wheels. The parish church, to which the Scropes gave carved woodwork from Jervaulx, for centuries looked down on the dramatic reaches of the Ure where in no less than three mighty staircases the river plunged down and down in its rocky channel.

Curious travellers of the eighteenth century admired the romantic river scenery, and many wrote about it. Artists and writers left records which brought more to enjoy, until the railway era carried a flood of tourists to the conveniently nearby station (now closed, of course).

Because everything is laid on so conveniently for the sightseer, naturally these falls are much frequented. If crowds spoil scenery for you, then wander away from the bridge along quiet paths. Where Nature works on such a grand scale, people have little effect.

We in the 1970s know what happens when men strive 'for sordid ends to deface the natural beauties of our countryside'. Those words were uttered by one of the many Victorian V.I.P.s who formed the Aygsgarth Defence Association a century ago when it was planned 'to build a huge brick or stone viaduct on skew arches, so ruining for ever one of the most exquisite landscapes in England'. The objectors who succeeded in making their voices heard numbered Ruskin, Lord Leighton, Alma Tadema and Ouida, a mixed bag!

Folk lean and meditate on the mossy parapets of the sixteenth century bridge—and how many thousands before them? Wanderers find rock seats to rest on, the better to ponder on swirling water, glass bubbles, air currents and, after spate, the ferocity of roll-back waves beating against rock walls and boulders.

I follow the downriver path from the Lower Falls, through hazel woods in April floored with anemones and primroses, and along banks in June gay with wild roses, of which wrote a Victorian botanist, 'there are no less than thirty different varieties near the Falls'.

Let Beauty at Aysgarth speak for herself.

TERRACE ROAD AND PRIMROSE PATHS

Back to the village, out on the road forking left from the main highway which climbs the southern scarp of Addleborough, to the 850 feet contour along which Thornton Rust lies. These are indeed uplands airy, the air like wine—and there are many children tumbling about, bright-eyed and rosy-cheeked. Room for everyone up here, space for houses, tall trees between, gardens about them. St. Restitutious added the Rust to its name. It adopted an unusual way of bidding to village funerals; a bell ringer walked the long street, 'bidding' as he rang. Can you easily credit anyone dying here where life-giving airs should bestow a kind of immortality?

Addleborough rises southwards. Celts watched from its summit hill fort, monastic herdsmen trod out the paths over its shoulder and flocks and herds defined the straggling track making away from the village.

A path down the scars to Worton, that must have been made by fairy folk—like Beetham's Fairy Steps. To find it look out for a wall gap just west of Thornton, then squeeze through a crack in the rock face, below which narrow steps carpetted in ferns and mosses make an enchanted staircase to the woodland verge, from shadowy places starred by primroses into pastures awash with bluebells, and sunny fields gay in May with cowslips, purple orchis and anemones. What a path for dallying!

Thornton has a birds-eye view of Worton. Worton, clustering houses—with interesting doors and doorheads—where roads meet, in turn looks across the dale to Askrigg and Nappa. Highroad and bus route turn updale, sweeping into Bainbridge, round the green and out to Hawes. For the last few miles, below the road the river coils over the flat dale floor, above the road hamlets and farms stand high above flood level. On our south side is the dark gritstone hamlet of Burtersett austere, windbattered, and across the river linked by a minor lane are tiny communities, Shaw Cote, Litherskew and Sedbusk, all 'satellites' of Hawes.

AT 'THE HAWES'

In the middle ages when all about it was hunting preserve of lord or abbot, at Hawes there was nothing more than a hause or hawes foot hospice for travellers trudging in from the wilds. At Gayle was a village, but here very little until Richard of Gloucester as lord of Middleham and Wensleydale gave the herdsmen and forest dwellers a 'Chapel at the Hawes'; that was in 1480. When forests ceased to be and game preserves became farmlands Hawes came more into its own. Population increased, Hawes grew, trade began to centre here and passing drovers, packmen and merchants stayed a while. Cattle market, inns for reception of market traders and travellers from other dales, the turnpike act and improved roads down the dale, the coming of stage coaches on the Lancaster-Richmond route, the Kendal and Kirkby Stephen and London routes, Hawes receiving house for the royal mail—these led to its growth and prosperity. It has never been ousted from its position as first in importance in the upper dale.

Old Hawes: Steppe Haugh

Tuesday is market day; come then if you wish to see Hawes spring to life. On other days it may be 'dead quiet'. Tuesday sees the long main street and highway, A684, 'throng' from end to end. Hill farmers and dalesmen, and their wives, come to town, but they bring nothing of the rush and bustle of city shoppers with them. There is a lot of standing and staring, as though time had no real meaning. Men with stick over arm and dog at heels brood at corners or talk in small knots—of yowes and tups, hoggs and gimmers, lamb crops, and wool clips. When they have departed and quiet falls upon the street Hawes lads meet on the bridge; their talk is cricket, football or fishing.

Interesting features? Look for the Quaker house with the date 1668 and pious text carved over its door; George Fox had many friends around Hawes. Not far away is Steppe Haugh, as old, and between the two 't'auld smiddy' recognized by outside steps with wrought-iron railings and an old half-door so covered, wooden jambs, lintel and all, with heiroglyphics little of smooth woodwork is visible. These are the individual marks used by local sheep farmers to make their flocks easily and unmistakably identified, ear or lug marks, horn burns and smits. The smith made the tools for them; these are the trial marks, and a sort of reference book.

Old Hawes: Quaker House

If you know little about sheep Hawes is the place to find out. Can you recognize the 'Sward'l'? It is the lithe and hardy horned sheep, the native hill sheep crossed with Scots Blackface, and well able to fend for itself on peaty heights, rather like the Lakeland Herdwick in its goatlike athletics. The larger Wensleydale sheep found in lower country looks down its long patrician nose at the unkempt, wall-leaping Swaledale; its fleece may be longer, silkier, more tightly waved but its expression is like the 'dumb blonde's'. When a Wensleydale ram is crossed with a Swaledale ewe the ill-assorted match produces the Masham which has some virtues of both breeds.

Cheese-making is another local talking point. I remember pre-war days when there were tables piled with farm house cheeses at every gate on the roadside up Widdale and into Garsdale head. Now a local factory copes with the trade.

When we first walked over the fells to Wensleydale, very tired and hungry, the local constable directed us to Hardraw and the Green Dragon Inn. An excellent choice we discovered it to be, for we had the dramatic gorge and the magnificent waterfall—going great guns after a rainstorm—just outside the back door. The inn bars access to Hardraw Scar; you walk through the passage into the 'scenery'.

'Worth seeing and worth going to see', that is Hardraw's fall, which makes one tremendous 99-foot drop, without a break. Whether Fossdale Beck is a mere trickle to fall in fine spray or a foaming curtain obscuring rocky ledge and rock walls it is a rare spectacle, not to be missed. Once lusty voices of choir parties and strains of brass band used to compete with the natural water music; unfair competition.

5. *From Hawes to Ure Head*

Now we are heading for the dale head, into countryside which might at first delude you into thinking gentle pastoral landscapes are to be with us to the end. Appersett is such a comfortable huddle, its farms all white-walled and under substantial flagged roofs. The road and river go side by side. When we see them in summer with blue shade from avenues of trees thrown on road, and children paddling in rock-paved pools holding amber-brown water, with fields adrift with golden buttercups and marginned with blue cranesbill and creamy froth of meadowsweet across the valley floor, and the high fells, Widdale and Great Knoutberry, Sails and High Shunnor, dreaming under innocent skies, this we think is bliss and go home to dream of it in 'hours of urban depression'.

Winter paints a different picture. That bare gale-ridden Nordic landscape beyond Thwaite Bridge—3 miles west of Hawes—where the barren lands begin, treeless as Iceland, is like something left over from the Great Ice Age. It was certainly so in '47, '62 and '63. The weather forecasts, summarized, read 'Rainfall heavy. Floods expected. Snow accumulating to enormous depths' all too often.

The names fit the scene, hardbitten, muttered between clenched teeth. Norsemen named them; their summer shielings and shelters were at Appersett, Bearsett, Hunesett and Pickersett, they named Broad Mea and Jinglemea, Melbecks, Lunds and Hell Gill where the infant streams run down from cloudwracked mountains. Early topographers liked to think of Hell Gills as haunts of the devil; they gave the bridge here the devil's name though in fact Norsemen spoke of all spouting water as 'hell', and as dalesmen agree 'there's a gey lot o' that in t'daal, to be sure'.

Not once have I walked towards the Moorcock but I have had the wind in my face or behind my back. The inn stands at 1,000 feet, its white walls a welcome sight. Travellers bear down upon it from Garsdale Head, and from the highway which follows the infant Ure and was the 'new' turnpike of the 1820s linking Wensleydale with Mallerstang and the Eden. Wild watersheds are to be crossed, and great loneliness, in spite of their being main highroads.

Many a traveller's tale has been told behind the shelter of the Moorcock walls. 1963 must have added its quota.

Will they equal Harry Speight's stories of the 1890s—of farmers with jaws frozen together, and caps which had to be thawed before they could be removed from the head? As for the vicar of Hardraw taking midwinter services at Lunds church, he often had to crawl on hands and knees along wall tops in snowdrifts, or as precariously when floods covered church paths.

At Lunds you must needs read Meg Merrilees' only book, 'the churchyard tomb'. It is a silent, lonely spot now, and never was otherwise. Lack of incident prompted one clergyman who ministered to its scattered flock to say to the meagre congregation, "At Lunds you do not love each other and God does not love you. Since I came among you there has not been one wedding, or a single funeral."

If you are a walker, and one who enjoys 'walking with history' look for the Cotterdale gate, about 3 miles out of Hawes. A lonely grey road strikes north for 'Cotterdale Only', a place of solitude and poignant melancholy, as are all places where 'men have been and are not', with disused lead mines and derelict miners' cottages; beyond The Town two of the most romantic waterfall-noisy gills in the dale.

Not far from the Cotterdale gate began the pre-turnpike road to Hell Gill and Mallerstang, climbing the shoulder of Cotter End fell and running along the 1,500 feet contour line, far above the Ure to the watershed of Ure and Eden and the county boundary. It was a short cut to Lunds church too. Now—grass-grown and rough walking.

This was the road Hugh de Morville travelled—the Becket murderer—and the Veteriponts and Cliffords bound for their castles, Lady Anne the last of the line swinging along in her two-wheeled carriage, the timber waggons carrying Inglewood forest trees to the building of Castle Bolton, the procession of personal attendants and guards bringing Mary Queen of Scots to her first Yorkshire prison—and Scots for centuries on their unlawful and, later, their lawful occasions.

Imagine the Highland drovers playing their bagpipes on the last long rise to Hell Gill bridge, to encourage their weary cattle upwards. Picture if you can the many dalesmen who came this way to Brough Hill Fair and how they smacked their lips seeing how the farmwives of Mallerstang had set out stalls of good food for them. You will have to depend on your own resources if you walk the old road now. But for miles you will have walked in good company, if only with the ghosts from the past.

The road says good-bye to the Ure half-way between Shaw Paddock, a former inn much frequented by farmers and travellers from many dales, and the railway-men's cottages at Aisgill; as every railway enthusiast knows the line just here is over 1,000 feet above sea level.

Walkers cross the stripling river half a mile south of Hell Gill bridge and are over the watershed and looking on the Eden. It is a grand if extremely spongy climb to track down the Ure springs; the Pennine mountainscape is magnificent, if the day be fine. But who in his right senses would penetrate a cloud pall just to say he had been in at the beginning. The best of the Ure is far and away below.

6.   Crossings to Eden and Swaledale

Ways out of Wensleydale: Continuing from Hell Gill—on foot— and Aisgill—by road—all wayfarers follow the Eden north to Maller-stang, the ruined towers of Pendragon and Lammerside Castles and the Tudor hall of the Whartons across the river. At Nateby this is joined by the road from Swaledale and Keld; both converge on Kirkby Stephen. Ahead is splendid countryside, rich in ancient buildings, full of the same border history we have tapped in the eastern dales, lush farm lands in the valley, the wildest mountain scenery close at hand.

For routes from Ure to Swaledale turn to the Fell Ways section in the next part of the book.

Upper Swaledale from Satron Side

Five

SWALEDALE

1. The Swale and the Pattern of History

IF I HAVE a preference it is for smaller dales, therefore Swale which is more like a big sister of Coverdale or Littondale than Ure or Wharfe pleases me well. Steep fells almost crush and crumple the dale floor fields, so close they draw together. The farms facing each other across the valley seem near enough to pass the time of day.

The Ice Age never completed the smoothing out of this dale's uneven outlines as in others. It created no right of way to encourage large scale entry at the beginning, and though escaping ice flows are responsible for the pretty bits of gorge scenery below Richmond they never opened out a welcoming way from the plains. All roads, in or out, are minor.

Come over from other dales and gradients of 1 in 4, or 1 in 5, are to be anticipated in the last quarter mile. High perched farms, gripping clawlike into the fell edges as their predecessors did when each was a Norse 'saeter', look down on rooftops and a pattern of fields hundreds of feet below. All face to the sun. About the walls of Summerlodge and Oxnop, Marrick and Kearton, Keld and Stonesdale farms fields are fresh and green when middle England is dried up and dusty. Theirs are Alpine pastures and meadowlands gay as spring when summer is well advanced, which means July and August are not second best months. Come before haytiming—date dependant on the weather clerk—to enjoy the full flush of Swale's flowering season, every pasture 'embroider'd o'er', every meadow a waving sea of flowers, hedges tangled with roses and honeysuckle, walls hidden behind tall ranks of foxgloves, campanulas and St. John's wort.

This feast of colour, travellers on the fell crossings to Swale have for a welcome. Those who come updale by the low roads have a feast of beauty too for the Swale's windings and the twistings below wooded headlands make of them infinite variety in every mile. It has been said with truth that 'the ten miles from Richmond to Reeth are the loveliest in England'. The next fifteen miles to the last community at Keld are even more so.

Therefore—go high, stay low, as mood dictates and it is always the 'best of England'.

Swaledale history follows the same pattern as other dales but—excepting Richmond's major role—on a small scale.

Lack of main line communications kept the main flow of history outside its limits. The dalesfolk heard what went on over in Yore dale, over Stainmore and along the great highway from York to the border; not often were they called on to share in it. Not unless they were close to the earls of Richmond, or involved in troubles which affected Askes or Darcys, Swales or Whartons in later years.

Prehistory? Where there are limestone scars there are marks of hill men. Harkerside near Grinton has long dikes, earthworks and Maiden Castle. Iron Age men held out against the Roman invaders from these fell-edge fortifications. And at dale foot where Brigantian peoples had their strongpoint, the Romans took over and made of it the great fort, Cataractonium, from which a network of military roads radiated.

The Angles who made of Eboracum their Northumbrian capital knew of Catterick and Gilling as halls where their kings went for relaxation. Many Angles became farmers near Swale though few ever penetrated much farther than Grinton.

Swaledale is associated with the Christianizing of the pagan Northumbrians. Bishop Paulinus, who had baptized their king Edwin at York, had a missionary journey into the dale's outback, if Gunnerside was place of the mass baptisms on Christmas Day, A.D. 625.

'He did regenerate by lively baptism above ten thousand men besides an innumerable multitude of women and children. Having hallowed and blessed the River, called in English "Swale", he commanded by the voice of criers and masters that the people should enter the river confidently two by two, and in the name of the Trinity baptize one another by turns', recorded Pope Gregory. Wonderful example of organization! And 'notwithstanding so deep a current and channel, so great and diverse differences of sex and age, not one person took harm'.

Danes infilitrated from the plain of York to lower Swale; Norse settlers found the dale head waiting for them. Scandinavians find themselves very much 'at home' where saeters are perched high above gill and waterfalls, and the very names smack of Norwegian.

The Normans? The Conqueror's kinsmen who were given Richmondshire—and Swaledale—were sons of the Duke of Brittany.

As we shall see later, the Breton earls left their mark in castles rather than in signs of devotion to mother church in Yorkshire. Christian charity, founding of great abbeys and provision of fitting burial places for their dead, they carried out in their native Brittany. Exceptions—Ribald who died a monk at York, Ralph Fitz Ranulph who founded Greyfriars at Richmond, and Conan IV. Conan we met in Wensleydale taking an interest in founding of Jervaulx; he also befriended a small local priory and a larger abbey by Tees.

The abbey nearest Richmond is at Easby. The Breton earls had no part in its foundation but one of their castle constables, Roald, was responsible in the year 1152. The White Canons, followers of the Norbertine rule—as were the brethren at Coverham and Egglestone Abbeys—were here for four centuries. Only thirty years before their arrival, Norbert, a courtier at Emperor Henry V's palace, had retired from the world and worked out a rule for life and worship which made of his followers 'Puritans among the Canons Regular'. Premontré in France was to be their centre; priors were to attend annual chapters there and deliver taxes collected from all their houses, these to be used for the good of the order.

The White Canons of St. Agatha's were a great influence locally. Like the Augustinians they were assiduous in preaching, teaching and work in their parishes, they were concerned with education, with hospitality to wayfarers great and humble, and of course shared in the wealth brought in by sheep and wool crops.

From Roald's descendants lands passed to the Scropes and with them responsibility for Easby. The Scropes always pride themselves on being 'the abbey's second founders.' They gave lavishly to new building. Generations lie at Easby. When the abbey was dissolved John de Scrope in 1547 obtained a lease on St. Agatha's, St. Trinian's and other church property by Swale.

Religious orders were 'like blackberries' around Richmond. White Canons at Easby, Greyfriars and Benedictines in Richmond town and White Canons from Eggleston abbey as priests within the castle. The white-habited Cistercian nuns were at Ellerton and the black-robed Benedictine sisters, at Marrick updale on Swale side.

Tenants of abbot or prior, and abbess or prioress, pursued their various occupations in field and fold with little deviation from the daily round: until rumours of change trickled updale. That all was not as it once was they had known from the days when John Wycliffe cried in no uncertain words his criticism of the 'religious', especially the 'poor' friars of Richmond. Their lives were to be turned upside down at the Dissolution; new owners for abbey lands—only the land remained unchanged.

As for the upper dale, the great ones, earls and royal princes who were lords of Swaledale and who possessed rights of the chase, had only remembered it existed when anxious for good sport. This wild hinterland, where wolves and wild boars as well as the usual beasts of the chase could be hunted, stretched from Swaledale's fells over Arkendale Chase and New Forest to the wilderness of Stainmore.

Dalesfolk who were the earls' tenants were involved in herding and farming, or in preservation of the game. They rarely went beyond the confines of their own dale.

Swaledale's history is very local, the locality being not much more than 25 miles from the outskirts of Richmond to the last habitation at Birkdale. Church history is richest around Grinton which for centuries drew all parishioners to mother church, and funeral corteges along the Corpse Road from dale head; Muker later collected its own complete parish history. Then non-conformity took root; tales of chapels, travelling ministers, of Wesley's coming, of love feasts, summer festivals and preachings add colour to the rest.

After the Dissolution when all Swaledale's religious houses were closed down and lands passed into lay hands, lead mining, and its ups and downs, plays the biggest part in the dale's story. As we shall see.

The Breton earls and English royal princes, the Askes and the Darcys, important families who suffered in trying to stem the king's plans to close the abbeys, the Huttons of Marske, the Whartons, the Swales (three families who were of outstanding importance in the past)—these names are forgotten or rarely mentioned, whilst the family names of Norse farmers, they were with us a thousand years ago, persisted after the Dissolution, the end of lead mining and are still here today.

2.   Richmond—Castle and Town

First impressions matter. The first time I looked on Richmond was at the quiet end of a summer evening, after a long walk over the heights from Reeth, and how our perceptions were quickened and heightened. Every narrow wynd or alley held mystery, round every corner waited drama; all the shoppers and visitors were gone, the square was half deserted, the castle walks and the angle seats sheltered by the ramparts enjoyed by only 'linked loiterers'. The second time, walking over the moors from the south, winds blowing and storm clouds gathering, we saw the castle towers and battlements glowering above Swale, and could imagine the mutterings of native dalesmen who eight centuries ago saw that massive citadel as threat to their liberties. When the sun burst through the clouds and lit up the towers with dramatic effect all that was missing was an array of fluttering banners to bring back the days of high romance and chivalry.

Richmond's site is superb. And this was the 'Rich Mount', the fair hilltop which so pleased the early Breton lords, the earls of Richmond and a succession of royal princes who owned it, one calling his new town on Thames side after it, the Surrey Richmond. On this hill dwelt the fair lass—Miss Frances l'Anson—whose sweet smiles broke the heart of the lyric writer; it was at Hill House in Frenchgate she lived. She died at the early age of twenty-nine.

What a slice of north country history Richmond contains; what a lavish wedge of history the castle wall enshrines.

Because of the vagaries of the Ice Age and the great glaciers which swept through the dales, Richmond occupies a high-flung site where the Swale, leaving its original river bed, pursues a new sweeping course south of the rock. Long before the Normans—or rather the sons of the Duke of Britanny—arrived there was an old settlement here, an occupied site on the heights and dwellings near the river where the ford was, and where later the Devil obligingly allowed himself to be taken in by a shepherd but kept his promise to build a good bridge. Of these communities the invaders took no notice when only a few years after the Conquest they arrived in full force to 'consolidate their position' as new owners of the Gillingshire earldom of Anglo-Saxon Edwine.

Norman William's followers, rewarded by wide estates, rarely chose for their headquarters the manor halls of the Anglian lords they ousted. His kinsman, Roger of Poictou, chose to build a stronghold at Clitheroe near Ribble rather than use Blackburn to oversee the old Hundred; Robert de Romilly saw the possibilities of Skipton's rocky ridge as a strong point, ignoring Earl Edwin's manor house at Bolton. Parallel cases can be found throughout the land. Alan the Red, whose considerable aid with many men and many ships had played a major part in William's victories, decided Richmond was the best possible site to build a castle, considering the Hall of Gilling three miles north of the Swale site quite inadequate.

At Gilling the earls of Mercia had long held rule; here they had governed their northern domains; Anglian kings of Northumbria had occupied the hall as a 'country palace'; Gilling had been only behind York in importance. After 1071 it began to wane; few now even remember its greatness, so quiet a village it is.

After 1066 for four years the men of the north grew to dread the name not only of the Conqueror but his henchmen, the sons of Eudo of Brittany, who were with him in his harrying and slaughter-

Quiet street : Castle Terrace

ing of the Yorkshire countryside and its people. As reward for his
loyal support Alan the Red was given 199 manors. He came, and
saw, and surveyed the mount above Swale. The flat platform—here
his castle would rise. The rocky ledges dropping to Swale—here impregnable walls would be planted. The coiling Swale—that would
be added protection from the turbulent natives, none of whom had
cause, or would have cause, to love him. The sooner a defensive wall
was put up between his folk and the locals the better.

The Anglian dwellers by Swale remained on sufferance, outside
the new walls, which first were earthworks, but later built of solid
masonry. Within the castle walls the Breton brothers—Alan Rufus,
then Alan Niger and later Stephen—with their households and
armed men saw the fortress take shape, and so did Stephen's son,
Alan III who married his cousin, the daughter of the eldest brother
who had remained in France as Duke of Brittany. Remember, as the
years passed the owners of Richmond had two allegiances—as earls
of Richmond to the kings of England and as Breton dukes to the
French sovereigns, which all led to most interesting situations when
wars developed between the two countries.

The Breton brothers' story could fill a book. And of their descendants wanderers in Yorkshire find traces in the works of Fitz Henrys,
Fitz Ranulphs and Fitz Roberts, Ribald's line, in the Fitz Alans of
Bedale from Brian, brother of Conan fourth earl of Richmond, and
in Swaledale in the projeny of Earl Stephen's daughter, who in marrying William de Gant founded the family of the lords of Swaledale.

Stephen's son Alan succeeded him in 1141. In 1171 a king of
Scotland, William the Lion, after defeat and capture, was a prisoner
at Richmond, waiting for the collection of a £100,000 ransom. On
his release a truce was signed and for about twenty years the two
kingdoms were officially at peace; during which period Earl Alan's
son, Conan, married the Scottish princess Margaret.

Conan, who was the fourth earl, built the great keep—a mighty
hundred-feet-high tower—which completed the castle, apart from
rebuildings and the addition of top floors, and minor works belonging
to the thirteenth and fourteenth centuries. His brother, Brian, was
founder of the Fitz Alan family, lords of Bedale, who in the days of
Edward I built church and castle in that old market town. Conan's
outside interests were in the small Richmond priory of St. Martin—
a gift of Earl Alan's chief steward to the Benedictines of St. Mary's,
York, and built by a band of monks sent out to establish the small
monastery. Out hunting in Wensleydale Conan pitied the poor
labouring brethren at Fors and offered them the fairer site of Yorevale which they accepted and built upon as Jervaulx abbey. He was
close friend of Henry II, and of his father-in-law, king of
Scotland. Conan and Princess Margaret to cement this royal friendship betrothed their daughter, Constance, to Henry's son, Geoffrey
Plantagenet. Through this marriage Geoffrey became duke of Brittany as well as earl of Richmond. We all know of their little son,
Prince Arthur, the pathetic victim of his uncle John's ambitions.

In the centuries to follow, Richmond and its earldom were possessed by the Crown and in the gift of kings. His father, Edward III, passed it to John o' Gaunt who enjoyed the rare sport and had a small lodge for hunting updale at Healaugh. John's son, Henry IV, handed it to his friends and in-laws, the Nevilles. Later kings were pleased to pass Richmond and the title to sons of favourite mistresses. There was usually someone of royal blood in possession, until finally a son of Charles II, Charles Lennox, was given the dukedom of Richmond—and so it passed to his descendants into modern times when the duke of Richmond and Gordon handed the castle into the care of the Ministry of Works. Long before 1911, the date of handing over, the castle had been a ruin.

What makes the town such a fascinating place to wander round and muse upon? If it has an un-English look about it this is only to be expected. For the first century of its existence castle and environs were quite definitely out of bounds for the Englishry; the descendants of the native English were 'without the walls', huddled by Briggate or Bargate foot, clustered beyond the bars and under the ramparts. The vast Market Square where we catch the bus, meet our friends, do shopping, and watch the summer weekend crowds milling around—a goodly proportion in khaki, for Richmond is surrounded by 'the military'—is actually within the castle walls and covers the outer ward. Here the language spoken was Norman-French or Breton. The retainers of Alan and Conan and their families, with the wealthier folk, settled close against the town wall in what became Frenchgate. When they were in need of money in came the Italian money-lenders; it is likely Lombards' Wynd was so named. A mixed population has known Richmond.

Probably the first survey of the town we make as visitors is from the Market Square, standing somewhere near that very mixed building block islanded there, incorporating the ancient church of the Holy Trinity and other useful premises. Some authorities dated the church from Paulinus' days because, they averred, that good bishop when baptizing folk in the Swale blessed them with the name of the Holy Trinity, and churches were founded near the pools where so many converts became Christians—hence the Holy Trinity at Richmond. If this be true the church was here serving the folk of an earlier settlement—maybe Hindrelagh—and considerably older than the Parish church of St. Mary which was possibly a foundation of Alan the Red. It is a venerable edifice, and less given up to secular uses than seventy years ago when Speight wrote of 'dwelling house and shop between steeple and nave, and other shops including a tobacconist's built beneath the south wall gallery'. At the same period the curfew bell—which continued to be rung at eight each night ever since William of Normandy ordered the covering of fires, and at six each morning as signal for the uncovering of hearths—was suspended in a convenient place just above the town crier's bed so that he, or his good wife, could pull the rope at the right hour, in comfort; his house was at the base of Holy Trinity Tower.

The church stands in the middle of the outer ward. The wide circle of houses, shops and many inns—the 'Bishop Blaize', the 'Golden Lion', the 'King's Head' among them—either stand against the site of the medieval barbican or follow the line of the outer bailey and town wall. Breaches in the buildings are King Street and

Richmond Town Wall: Cornforth Postern

Friars' Wynd, a narrow way with Greyfriars' tall tower at the end of it and one of the archways in the town wall, a postern gate, halfway along it, Finkle Street which led into the market from Rosemary Lane and Newbiggin, and New Street. Curving round under the ramparts to Castle Walk and the platform above the Swale, another

opening leads into a quiet corner with houses sunning themselves
and sheltered by towering walls. Old houses flank the hilly street
dropping quickly to another relic of the town defences, Cornforth
Bar, an exciting archway with peeps up or down equally fascinating. East of Holy Trinity, is the street of the French incomers,
Frenchgate, from which narrow inlets probe into alleys, discover
Castle Wynd, the pleasant eighteenth century houses of Castle
Terrace, and again we are close to the outer defences and walking
above the Swale.

If you have the right sort of curiosity, allow yourself to be tempted
through archways, down alleys and into odd corners and you will
find Richmond your element. On dazzling sunny days it reminds
me of Blois or Chinon, of many a French town with a castle of the
same period, and open 'place' with the same air.

At Richmond, as in York and all northern towns with Danish or
Norse street names, 'gates' are not gateways but streets or roads.
Gateways into walled towns were always 'bars'. Entry into Richmond
town was by three bars. From the north, folk approached from
Gillingate to Frenchgate by Frenchgate Bar; nothing remains. From
Swaledale the road from Reeth and Grinton came over the heights
and entered the town by Finkle Street Bar. From the south, over the
bridge, travellers climbed from Briggate up the steep 1 in 7 gradient
of Bargate to a bar therein, entering the town in Cornforth.
These bars are no more, but there are the two posterns, one in
Friars' Wynd and the other, the one with the peeps through the
archway, at the top of Cornforth Hill, an ascent so steep that a
handrail is provided, and you may distinguish residents from strangers
by their fleetness in negotiating it.

Although Richmond seems to turn its back on Swaledale—an
aloof and proud place it always was—it drew in crowds of traders
for its fairs and markets. The Market Place contained formerly no
less than three market crosses—only one tall obelisk now around
which buses line up—each collecting about it sellers of barley, wheat
and oats—'beer, bread and porridge'—whilst fishmongers and flesh-
mongers had their own space, and dealers in wool and fleeces, traders
in yarn and—in later times—in locally knitted stockings and caps.
Later it was in Newbiggin, at the part of the town where the steep
Bargate Hill levels out—now a very pleasant cobbled street with
avenues of chestnuts and limes, and houses with fine Georgian doors
—where the Horse Fair and Beast Market were held amid loud
clamour and confusion of incoming and outgoing flocks and herds.

Among less familiar commodities carried into the markets a
fourteenth century list for tolls includes these: 'mulnells, conger and
stikar eels', many lampreys 'before the Passover', 'fine cloths, and
silken cloths with and without gold thread, and sendal, and for lining
robes for winter warmth the skins of kids, foxes, cats [polecats?]
and squirrels'. Men bought woad in Richmond market, and great
quantities of garlic, and much honey. Horseloads of ashes were
brought in, loads of faggots, waggon loads of coals and brushwood.

Richmond worthies have resurrected from oblivion a rare bygone, the old Theatre Royal in Victoria Road; in the war years it was a salvage dump!

In mid-Georgian days this theatre was 'a £15 house', admission one shilling. The auditorium was circular, the stage in a sunken pit. Elegant pillars supported the galleries where playgoers wishing to register disapproval were provided with a special 'barracking board'. Below the gallery, the space was divided into boxes, many with front panels bearing noble arms; here Yorkshire dandies quizzed the actresses, and endured the hammering on the barracking boards above their heads. Lighting, by candelabra, was regulated by the pulling up of the long chains into holes in the ceiling. Edmund Kean, the young man and the well established actor, was a familiar figure.

The castle? It is worth looking at, gazing from, and certainly worth a visit. Guide books and leaflets are good and with one in hand wanderers may track down the works of the early Breton over-lords and ponder on the roles of the inner 'apartments' and halls. We are told that Robin Hood's Tower was William the Lion's prison. The chapel of St. Nicholas below is a little gem with arcaded walls, place for meditation; remember this small oratory when you look at Egglestone Abbey in Teesdale for the earls of Richmond ordained that six brethren should serve here as priests 'in perpetuity', unless war swept across the land. Gold Hole Tower appeals to lovers of buried treasure stories; also there is a frightening drop into dark depths far below. Scolland's Hall, at the south-east angle of the castle court, was among many domestic buildings where the earl's chief butler organized the castle household. Scolland, Earl Alan's butler, was a great man in his own right, a lord of Bedale. The hall named after him has many fine early features, many round-headed Norman windows, and masonry showing herring-bone work.

The keep is waiting, every step of its hundred-plus-feet. From a gloomy vaulted ground floor, the ribs springing from an octagonal central pillar, we climb to the imposing chamber above, also vaulted, and after winding up spiral stairs reach the second floor. The castle dwellers could walk out from upper doorways onto the ramparts, or climb out to look over miles of dale and fell from airy battlements. We may look out of 'wind-holes' and cast our eyes about over town, courtyards, river and outspread countryside. After the climb we feel we deserve it.

My favourite spots at Richmond: a bench in a sheltered angle on the Castle Walk where river and bridge and rooftops make a happy picture. The wooded banks sweep down precipitously to the river, and somewhere hidden away therein is that cave mouth which opened to admit Potter Thompson and which swallowed up the valiant little drummer boy long ago. Both made for the underground halls wherein —so tradition has it—King Arthur and all his knights sit in an enchanted sleep around a table laden with untold treasure. The potter found his way in, his astonished eyes beheld the sleepers and their long beards entangled with hunting horns and drinking cups—and the fabulous treasure; his hand he stretched out to touch, a sleeper moved—and out ran Thompson a voice ringing in his ears:

> Potter Thompson, Potter Thompson,
> If thou hadst either drawn
> The Sword or blown the horn,
> Thou'dst have been the luckiest man
> That ever yet was born !

But there was no returning. The cave mouth had closed up behind him.

This old story was centuries old when soldiers stationed in the castle decided to find if it were true by sending into a cave the youngest among them, the drummer-boy. "Beat your drum", they told him, "and never stop. We'll hear it under the castle floors. . . ." They heard the rat-a-plan, growing fainter, fainter. The boy was never seen above ground again. But folk report ghostly drumbeats heard below Clink Bank.

A lovely spot for a warm summer day is the far bank of Swale away into the shadowy woods. Bridge, bridge end houses—the new council houses less picturesque than the old pantiled dwellings—and the castle ramparts and towers above—a scene 'half as old as Time'.

Richmond has a strong hold on the imagination. It could hold you for days—if the pull of its dale did not prove equally strong. In the Market Place are buses bound for Reeth and Gunnerside, Muker and Keld—and Swaledale's outback.

3. Roads to the Swale

Roads into Swaledale are many. From Lancashire and the south the routes leap over from Wharfe or Ribble to Wensleydale and over again by the most spectacular highlevel crossings which are the highlights in north country 'scenic touring'. After travelling over the Border into the Eden valley, or approaching from Lakeland, very exciting roads enter by way of Nateby and Tailbrigg, Birkdale and Keld, or, more exacting, by hillways to Tan Hill. From the Yorkshire plain off-shoots from the Great North Road come in from Scotch Corner or Catterick Bridge.

FELL WAYS FROM URE TO SWALEDALE

Six crossings from Wensleydale; most dramatic by Buttertubs, almost as thrilling Muker Pass falls into wild western ambush locations in Oxnop Gill. Another, from Askrigg is hurled into Summerlodge Gill—for walkers only—and a surfaced fellroad to Low Row. Less secretive routes make high level from Redmire to Grinton and Reeth, and one from Leyburn goes up and over moorland to Downholme and Richmond.

THE BUTTERTUBS

Buttertubs Pass, 6 miles of it and the summit 1,726 feet, enough to make us quail when black clouds hide the tops and the road, a

black snake disappearing. "It leads you straight to the pit of hell".
One July we stood in Hawes, lacking the courage to walk into the
heavy cloudwrack. A man of Hawes took pity seeing us dripping by
the bridge.

"I'll get out the van. Once on Buttertubs likely the wind will
blow a change." It did, sun splaying through a widening cloud rent
and picking out Swaledale farms where children were smiling for the
first time for two days. Sports and Show were on the afternoon's
programme. Later we found all had 'kept to schedule', whilst in
Wensleydale—the rain it poured all day!

The Buttertubs naming the Pass are an amazing natural feature,
a number of sinister potholes gaping at the road edge. 'One of 'em
has no bottom and t'others are deeper than that!' They say farmers

Farm on fell road to Low Row

used them to dump unsold butter when market price offered was an
unacceptable sixpence a pound. Approaching the verge—carefully
for the ground is wet and slippery—we look into yawning chasms
into which becks fall, waters blown back by high winds into fine
spray. Ferns grow in crannies and rowans find roothold on ledges.

The 'pots' are impressive; equally so the sheer drop below the road
to the deep, deep groove where Cliff Beck is a thin silver thread and
into which countless white waterbreaks tumble after rain, seaming
the raking slopes of Lovely Seat.

The first time I looked on the dale from this road was 'after rain'.
We huddled under a wall, in company with a tramp who talked of
the Buttercups; the sky opened and enchantment at once transfigured all we saw, trembling with rainbows. On all hands 'a hundred
nameless rills' leapt down to the Swale, and what a roaring from
waterfalls!

In dropping to Thwaite the road negotiates many acute bends, one 'suicide corner' because of wheeling spills. Such hazards mean little to travellers now; in summer a Saturday bus has ventured over from Hawes, coaches have attempted a slow crawl over the pass, hazards at every bend, on every gradient. NOT to be encouraged!

MUKER PASS

From Askrigg by Oxnop Gill to Muker: 7 miles and at the highest point 1,633 feet. For the first mile the backward views are splendid, into Semerdale where sungleams catch the surface of Semerwater and pick out the striding Roman Road down Wether Fell, or linger in Bishopdale, or chase shadows over the sides of Widdale Fell, Buckden Pike and Great Whernside, Addleborough and Pen Hill. Above, the lonely grey road is defined on the tops by concrete posts, which have replaced the tipsy poles, to show the way in fog or snow. The curlew's cry only accents the quiet. At Oxnop Beck head, not a sigh or sound; the limestone ravine seems to be waiting for hidden bandits to pounce. It would do admirably for a screen set, or as setting for deeds macabre.

Away from the gill a grouse barks, in June cuckoos call and sounds of field and farm burst on us from High Oxnop. The Swaledale scene has its impact too; how different the crazy patchwork of the high intakes, dark walled and with scattered 'laithes', from the grey and white limestone, steps and ledges, of Wensleydale. Here are limestone pastures too, for centuries providing grazing for cows which produced milk unexcelled for cheese making. Suddenly, below Crow Trees farm with its gyrating 'weatherbird', we are hurled to the dale floor and Muker is in sight.

BY SUMMERLODGE AND CRACKPOT

From Askrigg to Gunnerside, by Crackpot: 6 miles—and for walkers only. We take the surfaced Reeth road from Wensleydale and at the sign post 'Reeth 5 miles' leave the windswept tops—where the bare fell is torn by old lead 'hushings' and scarred by many lead mine workings—for the downward track to Summerlodge farm, a long stony slither and slide. Soon, nearing the wooded gill, we are conscious of bird song, warmer airs, and sweet perfumes. Small wonder Norse farmers came here for their summer pastures. Sun side is above Red Mea, and Bloody Vale sends a beck down to the first farm, the upper limit of farm land. Oak trees dip to the gill over banks of primroses and violets, beeches stand among drifts of bluebells, bird cherry sheds snowy petals from the same sheltering hedgerows where lilac is in bloom. A green oasis among birdsong and water music; that is Summerlodge. Here the Brodericks lived in their generations; in 1840 ten youngsters ran down the lane to school at Crackpot.

Crackpot—meaning a cleft or cranny where crows chose to nest—is a farm group where two ways meet, now a quiet homespun sort of place but once centre of social life and education. That empty plot at the lane end was site for a school which had its Victorian 'bulge' of home-produced children. Ruth Garth founded it, left money to encourage the young in learning; the moneys now are dispersed every year in book gifts to the youngsters of the community, and a dictionary for each setting out for higher education at the Richmond schools when they reach eleven plus.

Crackpot's lanes are quiet now where once they were thronged. Drovers herded Scots cattle and shepherds drove huge flocks past the farms, heading for their night stands above Summerlodge where the animals were let out on the high intakes; the following morning they were off to Askrigg or other cattle fairs farther south. Dalesfolk walked by, carrying butter or cheeses to sell at Askrigg, all knitting as they went. Old women reckoned to complete one stocking on each journey. Knitters went by to the old Yarn Mill by Swale banks for here many collected their wool for their next stint. Now Crackpot's windows see little passing.

Journey's end from this crossing is Gunnerside.

TWO MOORLAND CROSSINGS

Redmire to Grinton and Reeth; this is an 'open road' climbing to over 1,500 feet, with vast 'sky-ey' scenes usually displayed in glorious technicolour. The highway runs hither and thither to avoid peaty places and many still pools, and sheep wander as they will and stand and stare from roadway or heathery knolls. Autumn's palette is richest; the heather's dying crimson, the claret of whins, tawny brackens, yellows and umbers of the grasses, the silver-gilt of reed beds are the colours of an oriental carpet.

The skyline tops have exciting names; Whitaside and Harkerside—with prehistoric sites—are to the west. Rising above 1,500 feet on the tops at Golden Groves, names like Grovebeck Mine, How Level, Devis Hole, Wellington Vein are reminders of times when for miles the landscape, now so empty, was bristling with coal pit winding gear, lead mine chimneys, shafts and smelt mills.

Leyburn over Preston Moor to Grinton and Reeth: 8 miles, rising to 1,333 feet at Robin Cross Hill. This high route, like that from Redmire, passes over moors riddled with countless coalpits and lead mines, where there is nothing but an immense loneliness broken only by moorbirds' crying, and how that can add to the brooding melancholy. The views are, as on all the moor crossings, wide-flung and uplifting.

Middleham to Leyburn, Bellerby and by Halfpenny House to Downholme and Richmond: 13 miles on the highroad A6108. This is lower level, running across the shoulder of the moors, reaching rather more than 820 feet. The landscape unrolls eastwards over the dreamlike plains to the ethereal, filmy blues of the distant Cleveland and Hambledon hills. North-east from Halfpenny House forks a long lonely road where I can never throw off a feeling of apprehension. The first time we walked this way we ignored red flags and 'got mixed up with the military'. I remember a clear, bubbling wayside spring and as we stopped to drink a shattering roar of many guns which sent us racing madly onwards to safety. This was the Hart Leap Well of Wordsworth's poem.

The highway continues north passing against the grey walls and under the oriel window of Walburn Hall from which, tradition says, 'Mary Queen of Scots looked out'. The thick, outer walls breached by the gateway were formerly embattled defences of a pele; horsemen gathered in the inner courtyards when danger threatened from the north, for Walburn played its part in Yorkshire history long ago when Scots rampaged down the Great North Road.

Beyond stretches the dale, floored with rich farmlands, cradling peace. There is a timeless quality about this Swale landscape where history in passing has left few scars. The Anglian farmers who toiled here when their overlords were the great thanes went on in pretty well the same way when the Norman earls took possession. The sweet serenity of the nunnery estates was shattered when Scots descended upon Ellerton Priory, and when Henry VIII's commissioners put an end to Ellerton and the neighbouring priory of Marrick, but the same smiling tranquillity soon returned and is still an essential part of this part of the valley.

Surveying all is Richmond, its castle both proud and fair in splendid ruin.

FROM THE GREAT NORTH ROAD TO RICHMOND

Catterick is 'all change' and turn west for travellers on the Great North Road now heading into Swaledale. The highway is jading and we are in no mood to dally. This is a pity for modern Catterick of the military camps and race course in any other setting would be a tourist venue.

Caer Caratauc had its Ancient British camp and doubtless Brigantian charioteers careering over the same ground. The Roman military experts saw the importance of Caer Caratauc and created of it Cataractonium, a top ranking army camp and road centre with the native Britons later holding their own rights in the region and establishing their own mint. But in spite of its ancient importance you can see nothing more than a platform of land near a farm, site of British and Roman station, known locally as Thornborough City. You need imagination's enlivening eye to reconstruct the remote past. Once Catterick was site of a royal palace, a residence of the Northumbrian kings, where King Edwin and his queen bade Paulinus 'god speed' as he set out to convert the pagan dalesfolk; that was in A.D. 625 or 626. Years later invading Danes came fighting mad upon the palace, yelling for blood.

Of course Catterick has its centuries' old roadside inns; look well at that by the old bridge. Seek out the quiet of the parish church too; look at the shields of arms of powerful Swaledale and north country families on porch, font and on altar tombs, of De Burghs, Fitzhughs and Scropes, Lascelles and Nevilles, Urswicks and Lawsons.

A mile away across the Swale, in Bolton churchyard, lies that 'ancient of days', Henry Jenkins, who lived to 'the amazing age of

169'; who shortly before his death in 1670 was able to recall memories of a hundred and twenty years and so settle a legal squabble; who remembered as a lad taking a horse-load of arrows to a military muster before Flodden; who could tell of visits with his lord to the abbot of Fountains. A tale was told of a lawyer seeking him out at his cottage in Ellerton. A feeble old man at the door referred him to 'his feyther, a more shrivelled relic of humanity' who, in turn, directed the caller to his father, old Henry himself, who was found busily chopping up sticks in the garden, hale and hearty, and possessed of all his faculties—and still going strong at 166 years! So you see what good Yorkshire air plus 'temperance, a life of labour and a mind at ease' can do.

The Richmond road—B6271—follows the north bank of Swale through a valley rich in history and the 'might have been'. Possibly Paulinus performed his mass baptism of 'ten thousand men' with their women and their babes too numerous to count not at Gunnerside but in the river near Brompton. Less probably, Hipswell claims to be birthplace of John Wycliffe; another village of the same name on Tees bank is more likely to have cradled this great northern reformer.

The exciting variety in the river landscape was work of the Ice Age glacier which here cut out deep cleft and rocky channel between dale and plain. Broad meanderings, horseshoe farmlands, wooded bluffs thrust towards the Swale, sunny plots and gloomy depths follow one upon the other. Small villages appear, and old houses with history gaze upon road or river—like Colburn Hall, ancestral home of those Darcys who rode out with the Askes of Aske Hall, joining the Commons against the king in the Pilgrimage of Grace and losing their lives thereby.

Easby is the abbey nearest Richmond but not a foundation of its earls. Roald the Constable made it possible for the White Canons to settle here in 1142 and build the house dedicated to St. Agatha. Find it down a quiet lane, trees on either hand and the Swale not far from what remains of its walls. On a sunless day what a melancholy spot with rooks and jackdaws chattering among the ruins. A place like this has unnumbered charms for musing minds, but first of all visit the nearby church, old when the Canons arrived here.

Easby was a Danish village and a Danish yarl lived at the manor hall, the last to worship here being Tor. Later, in the reign of Henry III, the folk made great efforts to beautify their church. What the mural artists made of it the walls of the chancel show us. Nowhere will you see more lively wall paintings than here, or more complete. The north wall is given up to the story of the Fall of Man—Adam and the creation of Eve, the casting out of Eden—whilst the south is covered with beautiful paintings in yellow, grey and red-brown, line and wash, of the Redemption. The artists clad all their figures in the costume of the period; the seasonal activities—as shown in the four deep window embrasures—were those of dalesfolk in the thirteenth century.

For the murals alone the old church should not be missed. Then

Cistercian Priory, Marrick by Swale

to the abbey where a plan of layout speaks for itself. A quiet place where we find ourselves pacing deserted cloisters and transepts with measured sacerdotal tread.

From the riverside the scene updale is dominated by the castle of Richmond—as for centuries. A timeless quality is about the landscape

4. Richmond to Reeth

TAKE THE LOW WAY—RIVER LEVEL

The main road updale which leaves Richmond bridge to follow the curving Swale across comfortable, friendly countryside is a 'new' highway, that is brand new in the 1830s, replacing the old coach road running up and down, high level, along the fells north of the valley.

No two roads could be more unlike. The low way keeping close to the river passes within sight of the two priories, the house of the black-robed Benedictine nuns of Marrick and that of the white-robed sisters of the Cistercian nunnery at Ellerton. Though more than four centuries have passed since the two were closed down there is certainly a stillness and orderliness in the pleasant landscape carried over from monastic times. Not that all was sweetness and light in the two nunneries, or in their relations with each other. The prioresses and the sisters included the saintly and the worldly wise, the truly religious and the proud and ambitious, the inefficient and muddlers, the keen business organizers under whom the houses prospered—or not. What life was like under Christine Cowper, the last prioress, who succeeded in winning a reprieve of five years for Marrick when Joanna of Ellerton submitted at once to Dissolution, most meekly surrendering all 'without murmure or griefe', you may read in that splendid novel by H. F. M. Prescott, *The Man on a Donkey*.

Sheep and their lambs safely graze in the green pastures about the priory church tower and the modern farm buildings on Ellerton's site not far from the highroad. Across the Swale more was preserved of the wealthy priory at Marrick, tall tower and the church where the tenants had always worshipped, but farmstead and barns now cover the ground where once were the nuns' well-filled garners, well-plenished barns and storehouses, orchards, herb gardens and quiet cloisters.

Once three bells sent out sweet notes to be heard afar. I remember a flat-bottomed boat which carried one across the river. I have watched young folk working merrily to restore old buildings as a church youth centre. And leaving the priory behind I have climbed that staircase path called Nuns Steps, between raspberry canes, ferns and flowers, up limestone scars to breezy uplands and Marrick village. This half-forgotten spot is also reached from the Old Coach Road between Richmond and Reeth, or by footpath from Grinton bridge, where on a quiet day, especially in the evening, you feel 'peace come dropping slow' and the past drawing nearer. On the busiest week-ends when everyone with a car is suddenly possessed with the urge to tour up Swaledale, the pastures around Marrick are still and silent, save for rural sounds and birds crying.

TAKE THE HIGH WAY—OLD COACH ROAD

Choose to take high road by Marske or low road by Downholme from Richmond to Grinton and Reeth; the distance is the same, 11 miles. Before 1830 choice there was none, only the straining coach road over desolate heights. One byroad joined it from aptly named no-man's-land—a journey in which Marske in its sheltered hollow was a veritable oasis, welcome as the palm groves and water wells of the Sahara.

It is an exhilarating route, good walking—and hilarious wheeling. The backward views cover the blue infinity of the hills beyond the plains. The country ahead is wild, lonely, and on grey, misty days so eerie it does not need the keenest imagination to conjure up footpads lurking in Clapgate Gill or highwayman racing to crossroad hold-ups.

From Richmond the road climbs above Whitcliffe Scar, a limestone cliff with green turfy slopes above it and thyme cushioned slabs to sit on whilst surveying the dale so far and remote below. Farms on the river level are tiny as toys, their animals moving specks. A certain horseman who leapt over the scar and after three bounds arrived— both he and his mount—in one piece at the bottom gave his name to the place. The Willance who named this Leap was Robert; the year 1606.

Marske is a surprise, a delight. So much colour and sunny stillness, the wild places and windy tops shut out; so many flowers, trees so tall, and bare, and the uninhabited miles above. Small wonder early owners held on to it, from Norman lords who paid three roots of ginger each Christmas to the earl of Richmond, to the Huttons who remained in possession for centuries. One was the Tudor archbishop, Matthew, a later one a military Hutton who loved his home so well he willed that his body should rest in the old deer park near Marske. His monument marks the spot, at Gallop End.

Marske is unlike any other village in these dales. There is an air of some cosy caught-in-a-combe Cotswold community around the Big House. But no sooner do you climb out of the place than the open fells take over and going on to Fremington and Reeth it is windy skies, great clouds and moorbirds crying.

A signpost names Marrick and there the curious traveller must go. Only a short mile, and you are lost in another world which in no way belongs to the present. The lane runs between pastures where the nuns' shepherds cared for the priory flocks. The priory tenants lived in humble cots where the present village is sited. All the land we wander through was the priory's, well farmed and a far cry from the wolf infested wilderness northwards and from the lonely hunting preserves westwards. Whyomar, ancestor of the Askes, did well for the Benedictine nuns when he endowed them with Marrick.

MARRICK—A VILLAGE ASLEEP

I first knew Marrick when youth hostelling before the War. I fell in love with the place. It had a Rip Van Winkle air, and more than its share of aged cottagers. There were bearded great-grandfathers smoking pipes at cottage gates, and dear old ladies calling in their cats at the end of day, and loiterers at open doors only too ready to chat. The hostellers brought a welcome breath of outside air, and enlivening comings and goings. Almost all the houses were then occupied, roses arched over the porches, gardens were gay, and all the tiny walled-in crofts which partitioned the green were full of fat lambs or young calves, or were grazed by tethered goats, and agile kids ran along wall tops and frisked where they would.

The youth hostel was the old post office. For meals we went to a farm on the fringe where the wife was always kneading dough, or bringing crusty loaves out of the great oven. "Fifty pounds of flour I make into bread every week—and I've been doing it for forty year", she used to say.

Marrick is not what it was. Last year I could find none of the familiar picture-book characters, only one or two of the chimneys were smoking, buildings were empty, derelict or gone. Its splendid isolation and aerial height, more than 500 feet above the dale, have proved too much. Is it now awaiting 1970s 'conversions'?

But the landscape is unchanged. Lambs still run races round the pastures, curlews still wail over the Eller Beck and Nun Cote fields, and cuckoos shout. Even more pronounced is the stillness over the evening landscape. Lingering above Nuns Steps on a June night all was so hushed it truly seemed

> As if the whole world knelt at prayer
> Save me, and me alone.

A path descends to the priory fields and makes for Grinton Bridge. The coach road also leaves the tops to roll down to Fremington, a lovely spot below scars and trees just short of Reeth, gazing across the Swale at Grinton.

GRINTON—AND MOTHER CHURCH

Centuries ago, whilst the nuns were at Marrick and Ellerton, and the earls at Richmond, Grinton was most important of all Swaledale communities, with the mother church of Swaledale and a bridge arched across the river. Many roads converged upon it; the corpse road from the upper dale 'outback' along which corteges wound their slow way bringing the dead for burial, voices intoning a dolorous chant, the Swaledale Dirge, fell ways tumbling down from Harkerside and Robin Cross, tracks wandering in from Fremington Edge and Arkengarthdale. Wayfarers benighted listened for Grinton's curfew bell; one traveller lost on the moors reached the dale in safety thanks to its sound carried on the storm wind, and in gratitude willed that money should be given so that it should be rung fifteen minutes longer every night to aid others in like plight.

Everything clusters close against the churchyard wall, and very pleasant is the picture, completely unruffled. 'I have been here for a thousand years. I have had my day, I have seen that upstart Reeth rise—and come down in the world. I am still here, and shall continue to hold my ground till the end of time. To me time matters not at all'. That is how Grinton looks at life.

The fine old church, the Cathedral of the Dale, rose by Swale soon after the Breton earls came to Richmond. A daughter of Stephen, one of the brother earls, was richly dowered when she wed Walter de Gant; her husband became lord of Swaledale, their descendants taking Swale for their name. She founded the church and much her builders worked upon remains, especially beautiful the fine west-end arch with a Norman window inset, and an eleventh century font, carved with chevron design, below. The original chancel arch is intact, complete with stone steps twisting up to the rood loft, though cross and loft are gone.

West of the church is a lost lane, the last stretch of the Corpse Road, once worn smooth by mourners' feet, now choked with a tangle of nettles, brambles and midsummer flowers—meadowsweet, ragged robin and canterbury bells, campions and ragwort, foxgloves and St. John's wort. West again, on the slopes stood Swale Hall, for five centuries home of that once noble family which disappeared in the seventeenth century. Sir Solomon, the staunchest of Royalists, only partly recouped his Civil War losses at the Restoration. He was eloquent in support of Charles II's return to England, and the Merry Monarch rewarded him with title of Baronet and an easy repayment loan of £2,000. Sad to say, Sir Solomon was not able to surmount his financial difficulties and soon the family suffered its final eclipse.

Think of Grinton's heyday before crossing the dale to Reeth. Once well-attended cattle markets were held here, and twice a year folk celebrated feasts or fairs. The young folk had their own amusements, including a football game played by Grinton girls versus Fremington lads; the ball was kicked energetically over the bridge and returned with vigour by the opposing forces. Why no one knows, unless it had its origin in local wedding customs; after old time weddings bride and groom stood against the church wall whilst footballs were kicked over their heads! And why this was done is also a mystery. Unless this went back to the days when native tribes had their own marriage rites at their nearby sites below Harkerside.

ANCIENT SITES—FOR ANTIQUARIANS

Anyone with the least interest in antiquity must range Harkerside, the high fell south-west of Grinton, before going on to Reeth. Walkers may carry on from the fell tracks to Swale levels at Low Whita Bridge. What a day-out for an archaeologist, amateur or otherwise! The map shows two miles of fell covering lines of entrenchments, round barrows, and dikes which may form part of an ancient defensive system called Scots Dike running from Swale to Tees—and Maiden Castle. We climb up tilted meadows to a track which joins many farms, some derelict, then make our way to higher level intakes and finally to the open, unenclosed heather-clad slopes. Here tracks become sheep trods, peter out altogether, and we take stock, finding suitable turfy banks to sit on—these may well be earthworks raised by prehistoric hill men—as we survey hill and dale, field and fell. The sun picks out scores of ledges and terraces on the slopes across the river; these are the strip lynchets which Anglian and later dalesmen laboriously ploughed outside their villages at Reeth, Healaugh and Feetham. If the wind is boisterous we find welcome shelter in rock-walled hollows where the grass has been close nibbled by centuries of sheep—surely known to the men who laboured to raise at higher level the formidable defences of the castle.

Just who made Maiden Castle, and why, no one knows. A stone avenue led to it, circular earthworks with deep dug outer ditches enclosed a large site, big enough to be used as gathering place for tribesmen met for worship, or stock counting, or for law-making, or as lookout when enemies were many. It is said the Celts designed it, Roman troops made good use of it as it was in direct line with forts at Bainbridge and Stainmore, and local tribesmen, possibly Brigantian, when organizing resistance against the invaders, held it as strong point and citadel, or as a retreat and backs-to-the-wall, last stand.

REETH—AND ROUND ABOUT

Back to Grinton Bridge and the road to Reeth. The handsome mansion at Fremington, serene within high-walled gardens, its façade a study of Georgian elegance and symmetry, is Draycott House where formerly lived the Dennis family, important mine owners whose fortunes were founded in local lead. The famous Old Gang mines were theirs, and many Victorian workings where new levels were each named after Dennis's sons and daughters.

Reeth starts near Fremington Bridge, haphazardly, and takes shape
at higher level, flung upon the cold hillside, encircling a spacious
green. Until the seventeenth century it was of little account but when
the powerful Wharton family took over control in the dale—the
Swales then in decline—and obtained a market charter Reeth looked
up. Lead mining prospered, Reeth expanded and its site allowed room
for it. Old cottages string along narrow back lanes but it was round a
vast cobbled market square the seventeenth century building began
and continued through the eighteenth.

The new Reeth provided many new inns to cater for market traders,
and fine tall Georgian houses in the gaps between them. Lead was
all important; whilst the mines prospered so did Reeth, drawing in
the entire neighbourhood to its fairs, markets and the September
'Barney' Feast. Grinton looked on the way to becoming a disused
backwater—apart from the mother church, and there were times
when Reeth threatened to build a new one, nearer home. Reeth was,
with support of the nonconformist Whartons, active in dissent. But it
never made a clean break with Grinton Church; the church path, a
short cut across the fields, was well-used.

Fresh breezes rake the green; folk huddle together as they wait
for the bus, and children home from Richmond schools emptied from
the buses raced away mad as blown autumn leaves. The green which
gives the winds free play is excellent for games, and local junketings,
and on November 5th for careering round a giant among bonfires.
The grass is a thick carpet over the cobbles of the old market place.
The wide circle of buildings has dwindled. The 'Black Bull', 'King's
Arms' and 'Buck' look on, but you will not find the 'Half Moon',
'Red Lion', 'Farmers' or 'King's Head'; they have long been out of
business. When the lead mines closed and population shrank, they
fell on bad times too.

Now, Reeth is a pleasant healthy spot which looks quieter than
it really is. Try to find a room for the night during the season without booking in advance! Countrygoing folk find it to their liking,
an excellent centre and half way house in Swaledale.

Mount Calva, an exciting hill, shelters Reeth from the north. East
of it Arkle Beck waters a leadmining valley and brings down the
long grey road from Arkengarthdale and a vast barren region wherein
the earls of Richmond gave chase to wolf and wild boar. New Forest
and Arkengarthdale Chase were valued preserves, a wild hinterland
which remained so long after the earls had gone from Richmond and
their proud fortress had become a ruin. Their tenants living rough
in lonely places were prey to superstitions, and so were the lead-
miners whose homes were at Arkletown, Langthwaite, Booze and
Hurst equally prone to belief in the evil eye, in second sight, augurs,
omens. Miners imported from Cornwall found just as many 'ghoulies,
ghosties and long leggetty beasties' lurking in these fells as on west
country moors.

In the 1830s Arkengarthdale and the whole of Swaledale were
caught up in a period of acute distress; low wages, semi-starvation

were the accepted state of things and most of the cottagers were
reduced to paupery. With little hope of the mines recovering, scores
of families were helped to emigrate. Many found work in the coal-
mines of Durham, some went south to the Lancashire cotton mills.
Some clung to their homes in the hills, until the 1890s when the bottom
finally fell out of English lead markets. Very few mines remained
open after that. Very few cottages by Arkle Beck or on Calva slopes
remained tenanted.

If you take the road from Reeth north to Stainmore you must
sense the melancholy which always hangs over places 'where men
have been and are not'. Can you picture it as a busy highway, lively
with shouting drovers and lowing of slow moving herds of Scots
cattle, with shepherds and dogs urging tight flocks of sheep along
to market, and long processions of laden packponies, the 'bell horse's'
bells tinkling, and yapping heeler dogs behind, all moving over the
hills towards Reeth? The 'C.B.' inn—named after the mine-owning
Charles, Lord Bathurst, lord of the manor—was once the most
frequented wayside inn. It used to be the 'Lilly Jock', night halt for
drovers, with extensive areas of common where the cattle could be left
till morning.

'From time immemorial'—that was how long the Swaledale rock,
the limestones and cherts, were worked for lead. It is still there, as
any dalesman will tell you; the workings are in good heart and could
be re-opened. But the market is gone, imported lead is cheaper and
contains more silver. Reeth and all the neighbouring communities
which rose and fell with lead are back where they all began, the land
their chief concern, sheep and cattle.

Every morning there is a great exodus from Reeth. Buses leave
carrying not only all the 'over elevens' but those whose daily bread
is earned in Richmond town or at Catterick camp.

5. Reeth to Muker

The road swings merrily updale, low by Swale edge, looping
wooded banks where squirrels are busy garnering October hazelnuts,
rising high above the dale floor, and in and out of Healaugh, Feetham
and Low Row, wayside villages which seem to have in common a
desire to face into the sun, and a plan which followed the amblings
of kine and homeward-plodding husbandmen.

HEALAUGH—AND PARK OF HELEY

Healaugh is an old-fashioned place which local pride once insisted
was built by Romans, and according to Speight who appreciated its
antique air sixty odd years ago 'might well have been built by the
ancient Britons'. Place names—Park Hall, Birk Park—recall the
medieval Park of Heley and the days of Walter de Gant, lord of
Swaledale, and Matilda, his wife of noble lineage whose dowry raised
him in the world. His hall at Healaugh became seat of Gants who
gave many rights within their hunting preserves to the abbots of

Rievaulx. Here was splendid hunting to be had. The sporting abbots used their right to keep 'hounds and horn' in the dale. Distinguished visitors came to enjoy the wolf and wild boar hunting.

When John o' Gaunt was possessed, through Edward III, of many royal lands in the north, lord of the castle and barony of Knaresborough, lord of the Swale Marches, he once brought a party to the hunting lodge of Heley to indulge his favourite sport. With him came his new constable of Knaresborough, no less than Chaucer's son who was nephew of the beloved Katherine Swynford. This is a Healaugh tradition onto which one might build a colourful story.

To recapture the flavour of the hunting days leave the high road and the dale to follow Barney Beck with its chuckling falls, fairy pools and dark depths into the uplands around Kearton and Blades, and up higher still to skyline pastures and Melbecks Moor which is lonelier now than when the royal and noble took their pleasure here.

WHARTON LANDLORDS

A time came when Gants were no more, Bigods—later landowners —were 'out' and Whartons out of Eden dale had wheedled themselves into the favour of kings. From the sixteenth century they owned most of the dale including lands formerly held by Rievaulx abbey. Whartons were staunch church and state men. Honours poured on them so that lords, earls, viscounts succeeded each other and in 1718 the second marquis was created duke of Wharton.

Healaugh long remembered this first duke and many of the wisest endorsed what the poet Pope wrote of him, 'poor Wharton, nipped in Folly's broadest bloom'. Unlike his forbears, Whigs and puritanical all, as a young man he shocked Swaledale by a complete somersault in both religion and politics. Local comment was that his doings were enough to make his father, the bible-distributing Philip, Lord Wharton, and forbears who had encouraged dissenting ministers and held nonconformist meetings at Smarber Hall and given Low Row its first chapel, all turn over in their marble tombs.

One day young Wharton came riding over from Wharton Hall with a neighbour from another Eden bank castle, young Christopher Musgrave. He summoned all his tenants to assemble. Flushed and excited, he raised his glass, urged all to do the same, drinking to the health of James Edward Stuart, the Pretender. The dalesfolk could not believe their ears—a Wharton drinking to a Jacobite Stuart! When the incident was duly reported the local J.P.s laughed it off as a youthful escapade and took no action. But his later doings could not be silenced. He became ardent Tory, fervid Jacobite, and later took arms against his own country. A confessed Roman Catholic, he died in 1731, at an early age, in a Spanish convent.

In Swaledale it is said that many a Scots fir, tall and dark by a farm gate, was planted after the '45, with a purpose. Two brothers from Westmorland who had fought for the Young Pretender later bought land in Melbecks. They planted firs as a sign to any wanderers of Jacobite leanings that here friends would help them.

You cannot miss Feetham, the long drawn out village with the handsome inn sign of Punch in the Bowl. Wander to the river—an old ford was here—and there is an ancient mill site and old cottages. An unassuming place it soon passes us on updale, to Low Row.

DISSENTERS—AND MIDSUMMER FEASTS

In the seventeenth and eighteenth centuries with the strong encouragement of the Whartons of Smarber, Low Row became particularly active in dissent and continued so, with meetings at the hall, open air gatherings to hear travelling preachers—a tree sheltering the 'pulpit', when the weather was kind, and services in humble cottages when the rain came down. Low Row knew Wesley well. They watched him riding over the fells, horse and rider weary; they watched him drop, dead-tired, at a welcoming cottage door. Then silence would fall upon the household. The minister was fast asleep, stretched out on the kitchen table—for sixty minutes exactly. An hour later folk were gathering outside, and up he would sit, completely refreshed and ready to conduct the eagerly awaited service. They remember many a tale hereabouts. Up at the hamlet of Blades I have heard of the Spenceleys who gave him hospitality; a brass porridge pan used for his breakfast is a treasured heirloom.

I think the best of the dale is found in terrace-high hamlets like Blades and Kearton, each a knot of greystone cottages, which until the lead mines closed down were well populated and important each in its own way. Lead miners produced large families, homes were almost fit to burst with the teeming life within them. A century ago thirty or forty youngsters descended upon Low Row school from the breezy heights.

Come updale in June and you will see shop windows and bill boards giving notice of Midsummer Feasts. Gunnerside celebrates on a Sunday and Low Row on the following Tuesday, not in 'profane' feasting such as we associated with Reeth's and West Witton's 'Bartle' fairs and many feasts up and down the dales, but, as befitting communities professing a simple piety and puritanical restraint, in a round of preaching, singing, choral music, a Love Feast, and a Grand Tea, after which families and friends gathered in from faraway places for the annual occasion exchange news of native dale and places of exile. It is amazing how they roll in, from other dales, out of Lancashire and Durham towns to which grandparents emigrated in the bad days, and even from overseas where local mining families sought their fortunes generations ago. And each year the visiting preachers, the imported tenors and sopranos, are the best yet, and the tea and the social event exceed all others.

GUNNERSIDE AND LEAD MINES

You might pass through Healaugh, Feetham and Low Row without recognizing them as distinct places, but not Gunnerside. Gunnerside is a village with something about it which holds you back. Gunnar, a Viking hankering after settlement, chose this site where a beck tumbling out of a deep gill runs more slowly over level pastures to the Swale. The sheltering fells are like a high wall behind, almost sheer and broken into crazy patterns by dark stone walls. All dwellings turn their backs to deep gill and high fell, sun worshippers every one. Farms and out-laithes alone in quiet pastures, cottages by the beck, inn, literary institute, chapel and smithy make up a Gunnerside which is, as we see it, but a shadow of its old self.

Stand across the valley, near Springs End below Crackpot, and the village is seen as a whole, and the land from which it drew its livelihood for so many centuries. Up the dark ravine, straggling out to

Gunnar's Sett, Gunnerside

Melbecks Moor by farms with odd names like Barf and Winterings, Bents and Potting, Whaw and Wham, by Wetshaw and Blakethwaite, miners' paths and tracks used by packponies lead to a desolate upland riddled with abandoned mine workings. Up there are the Old Gang Mines—old as Roman times, traditions say—and Surrender Mines, which in full production late in the eighteenth century sent out 6,000 tons of lead a year to ready buyers. The mines are still there, in some workings adits and shafts in sound condition and lead easy for the getting—if native lead should be required.

The men who gather at the bridge are the sources of information about the old days of their grandfathers. They tell of the sad decline of the 1830s, of men who sought work elsewhere, and those who stayed to use their skills on new labour. They rebuilt the Swale bridge when floods destroyed it. Many were glad to work from dawn to dusk raising those miles of stone walls which parcel up the fells into long enclosures, their pay 1s. 2d. a day. One recalls a Sunter who long after the mines were shut down took a cart to get lead from Old Gang but his pony bolted and he was killed. Another tells you to take a look at the smithy which has an anvil which was brought down from the Old Gang mine shop.

And because Gunnerside belongs to modern times we find the new-style farming gear at the smithy door fascinating, sleek and shining hay sleds made of metal, and a fine array of wrought iron rails and gates.

When a bus draws up and young folk pile in, all bound for Richmond, we are suddenly aware that Swaledale has many faces. Towns seem remote, far behind us is the gentle, cradled valley floor of Downholme and Marrick. Here we are gripped between the hills; the deep dale is about to draw us in.

6.   Dale Head—Muker and farther up Swale

Muker looks a last outpost but must give way to Keld which, much farther updale and much nearer the clouds, is the closer to World's End.

As a place Victorian writers thought little of Muker, but as a centre 'for pedestrian pursuits' it was admirable. We like it for its own sake as well as for what lies about it. I have known Muker from the 1930s. It has changed less than any place I know.

VILLAGE LIFE AND THE DAILY ROUND

Mornings in Muker follow the same pattern. The first time I wakened to a new day when quiet was shattered by a stampede of fell ponies playing the 'Last Round Up' down the main highway. I looked out to see a slow procession of cows filing in to morning milking and heard a flow of highly coloured invective from farmer giving chase to runaway and very skittish heifers. Silence returned; I was conscious of the beck's chatter, of a curlew calling, of a rattle of milk kits and rumble of wheels. I dressed and was out walking through the meadows to the Swale footbridge before the dew had gone and my footprints still showed green on the hoary grass.

The last time I wakened to morning life in Muker—twenty-five years after—the reveille was little changed. Robins trilled, starlings wheezed on chimney stacks from which the first plumes of smoke rose, a man going out to feed his hens called time of day and was answered from a cottage door by a remark, "Nice bit o' sun", to which another voice added prophetic comment, "Too glishy! Too bright, too early!" Dogs barked after cows, farmers shouted after sheep, milk kits rattled and footsteps echoed across cobbles.

Later, the school bus carried away the 'eleven plus' boys and girls, and much later in came the under-elevens, all with bright morning faces, none like snails or unwilling, converging with satchels and slipper bags on the roadside school. The bell rang out, a scampering of feet, silence, and all were safely gathered in. Soon a low hum of voices was heard through open windows. That same school knew the brothers Kearton, Richard and Cherry, young lads destined to become world famous naturalists.

The country silence wraps me quite.
Silence and song and pure delight.

That is Muker on most days, 'a place where it seemeth always Sunday afternoon'—but *never* on a Sunday!

Sundays in summer see large scale invasion of the dale, streams of cars, even coaches, attack the hazards of the once-formidable Buttertubs Pass, every patch of roadside grass is sardine-packed with parked cars, on all hands voices, laughter and strains of music. The villagers endure it stoically. They bide their time in crossing the highway between cars slowing down by the bridge. They smile with tolerance when hearing 'townies' ask "What on earth do you find to do in a one-horse place like this?"

Come between September and Easter and you will soon know how Muker fills its winter evenings. Always something going on! There are church and chapel occasions, the evening classes, Women's Institute meetings, Brass Band practices (Muker's Brass Band is something, old established and much sought after at fairs, carnivals, shows, sports days and such dales' events, producing gay, melodious or martial music, with the most junior member resplendent in green and gold braided uniform), whist drives, dances and preparations for the annual Christmas festivities which culminate in the Twelfth Night Concert. This last event is a much toned down continuation of the 'Muker Old Roy' of a century and more ago, when local miners chose a king to preside over the three days—and nights—of revelling, play acting, masking and good humour.

Television is conspicuous by its absence. Here is a place where few folk have as yet become square-eyed, glued to the 'goggle-box'. Reception in the hemmed-in-by-fells dale bottom is bad, and 'Who wants to pay to see snowstorms on the screen when we get enough snow without?' It is refreshing to find a community not dependent on canned or organized amusements to keep its sanity in the dark months of the year.

One November just before the war we stayed at a Swale side farm. We joined a quilting party round the kitchen fire and watched busy fingers assemble gay coloured prints into what was to be a wedding present for one of the girls, a patchwork quilt. They talked of the traditional quilting patterns, of which each dale adhered to its own, used for the stitched and padded bed covers. Swaledale has always incorporated the fern leaf, stars and bellows, plait and twist motifs. The mother was industriously prodding 'ashen cloth', producing a peg rug.

The assortment of rag rugs under our feet in Swaledale homes! Flagged floors are covered by them, heavy feet on stone passages deadened by them. But when a foot is put out of bed it steps softly into sheepskin.

WHEN IT RAINS!

Of course it rains in Swaledale. Seventy inches have to be dropped in an average year. Sometimes it drizzles with a persistence that is maddening; there seems no end to it and cloudwrack lies low. Often rain descends in icy rods, without pity, and we crouch against walls and linger in laithes, and feel very sorry for ourselves. As we wait small runnels become frothing becks, innocent babbling becks turn into foaming torrents, and we know soon that these, and countless others, will be gathered up in one galloping roll-back flood and Swale, brim full, will be bursting its banks and green holms be turned into dale wide lakes. Indeed 'Swale's wondrous holy flood' has done a great deal of damage in its time.

Rainy days need not be wasted days. Then is the time to get to know the dalesfolk also marooned indoors. And when the rain is over? Out we go to see the swollen galloping river, and staircase waterfalls now lost in single shining waterslides. The clouds roll upwards and show hundreds of nameless rills, white waterbreaks seaming the fells.

'To see them all in flood with their white tails galloping over the mist-screened hills and craggy steeps, and the amber foamed cataracts leaping madly in the valley below is a scene truly Alpine in its wild and forbidding character,' wrote Speight who knew how to enjoy all Swaledale's moods.

If you have not seen the dale after rain, smiling and repentant, you have not seen it at all.

The Victorian guide, dismissing Muker as small and uninteresting but praising it as 'touring centre for the good pedestrian who loves Nature in her wildness and solitude', warned intending walkers they must 'endure fatigue and philosophically content themselves with such accommodation as the somewhat primitive people can afford'. There is still much of the rough stuff of mountain and fell walking for those who range the tops; the solitude is complete, the wildness untamed. Accommodation is homely rather than primitive, just as country-lovers best like it.

AND WHEN THE SUN SHINES !

When the sun shines no spot is more welcoming, no paths more inviting than those by the river banks across flower-filled meadows, through green and shadowy woods in deep gorges, rounding the slopes of lovely hills like Kisdon. Even the confirmed motorist who stays in Muker becomes enthralled and discovers there is more in this 'countrygoing lark' than just passing up and down dales in cars.

A spring morning, sun chasing across fell and dale, breezes tossing green boughs and scattering blossom in showers white and pink: this is a day for Kisdon, for mounting its rounded shoulders, birds blown screaming across our path, mountain pansies and purple orchises in our way, and as we stop to look around every upward yard raises up more heavenly ridges and ranges, each changing from blue to gold as sungleams and cloud shadows race over them. Or when the dale floor paths please me best, across the flower-filled June or early July meadows before the hay cutter mows down swathes of dark-headed burnet, creamy pignut, meadowsweet and campions, pale

pink bistort and dark crimson clover heads, and drifts of blue and
purple, deep cerise and red cranesbill. Only Tyrolean slopes are more
thickly set with flowers than those above Swale in midsummer, or in
late spring when the low pastures are awash with bluebells, the tide
of colour flowing into the hazel copses and invading the very sides
of Kisdon and Swinnergill.

A THOUSAND YEARS OF HISTORY

Muker which began as Mewaker, a small plot of mowing ground
by beck and river, was always a small, cramped place, cottages
crowded round church, stony paths insinuating themselves between
churchyard, inns, farms and houses, playing a child's hide and seek
game in and out the buildings. It was cosier that way. That was how
the Norse settlers knew it, and the tenants of Rievaulx Abbey who
owned the manor prior to the Dissolution. Later Whartons became
landlords of these 'backwoodsmen'.

You see the track running half-way up the slopes between river
and fellside, making for Gunnerside? That was the Corpse Road taken
as direct route to Mother Church at Grinton, until Muker was given
its own place of worship in 1580. It had a grammar school too, thanks
to income provided by a Metcalfe who gave them land on Whitaside
in the year 1678. It was known as market town, with its annual
fair held on the Wednesday before Old Christmas Day, coinciding
with the 'Old Roy' Rant.

Of course it had a chapel, its building a labour of love, men working in their spare time from fields and mines, bringing down costs to
no more than £96. The chapelgoers were great ones for Sunday evening
hymn-singings—on the patch of grass near the Literary Institute—
and as for their Tea Festival, it was a highlight of the year.

The institute was 'literary' in that it dispensed learning in the form
of a collection of six hundred volumes assembled in 1867 for the use
of villagers who could read; Reeth's Mechanics' Institute possessed
a library of one thousand books.

The inns? The 'Farmers' has a welcoming look at the roadside but
the 'Queen's'—the ancient stopping place for mourners and church-
goers, much patronized by miners who frequented its bar and
measured out weekly pay in a pint pot borrowed from the landlord—
has a retiring position in a quiet corner behind the church. It is a
guest house now.

In the churchyard are ranks of lettered tombstones—Aldersons,
Metcalfes, Fawcetts and Peacocks, Harkers and Rukins, generations
of them, and many unnamed graves of folk

> Of whose life and death is none
> Report or lamentation.

The names lettered boldly were the 'Sunday names' of local dalesmen,
whereas among their own kind these were almost unfamiliar. Nick-
names were the rule, descriptive, genealogical, occupational, the classic
example a century ago being that of Matty John Ned, innkeeper of

Thwaite. Refer to him as Edward Alderson and blank unrecognition followed!

In the 1890s it seemed possible that Swaledale, always isolated, was to be brought into the world of railways. Plans were made to tunnel through dale head fells to Hawes, linking this with the Northallerton-Garsdale line. Landowners were ready to agree. Opposers of change became apprehensive. Speight prophesied a grand exodus of Swaledalians. As soon as 'train whistles rouse the echoes on Shunner Fells—away will go Aldersons, Metcalfes and the rest'.

Nothing came of it.

Dalesfolk always plan for a winter of isolation and blocked roads. When thaws arrive they expect floods, but not so devastating as that which tore hamlets from their mooring in the 1890s. That one left little of Thwaite standing by its beck.

NORSE 'SAETERS'

Thwaite, where Norsemen settled in the water edge clearing, where south-facing cottages watch all who descend from the wreathing mists of the Buttertubs, is a pleasant huddle. Cottages borrow shelter one from another, flowering creepers on the walls and flowers by the doors blooming late and early. I like it for its nooks and odd corners—in one the Pennine Way sign points through a gate into a farm yard —and for delicious peeps between walls. The babbling beck which once wrought such havoc, on most days is a merry prattler with trout in pools and young anglers intent with their rods practising casts which experienced fishermen have taught them. Anglers' paradise with choice of many streams; walkers' element where Great Shunner beckons and Lovely Seat, once 'Luniset', throws down a challenge, and scores of minor dales all watered by little Swale-lings are waiting to be explored.

The road which leaps upwards out of Thwaite, taking the occasional Percival's bus to still remoter places, at higher level passes places named by hardy Norsemen and settled by them a thousand years ago. Angram is one, 'homesteads among meadows', holding on like grim death to almost sheer fellside, and Thorns, set one step higher, also with its feet dug well in to prevent it slipping downhill— just like Alpine chalets on tilted slopes. As for Keld, 'no place in England except Clovelly where you almost require the use of ropes to let yourself down the principal street . . . is more singularly or astonishingly placed'; so wrote Speight. As White noted in 1858, the buildings are rugged as the rocky landscape. 'With unlimited supplies of stone to draw on, houses are rough and solid as if built by druids. Every door has its porch for protection against storms. . . .'

BY 'KELD'S COLD STREAM'

Muker villagers number around seventy, the parishioners total five hundred to which Keld contributes a few more than twenty—about the same number which made up one of its four 'native' families of a century ago. They were the Harkers, Rukins, Aldersons and Peacocks, who 'they say' came in with the Norse settlers and remained firmly attached to Keld until modern times.

What did the Norsemen find so attractive about this dalehead? It was over 1,100 feet above sea level, a wide, wind-raked valley, 'a majesty of nothingness' westwards to the Pennine watershed, a land riven by raging torrents, full of the mighty roaring of many waterfalls, and without doubt haunted by trolls and demons, yawning and fearsome below, enough to give any Anglian farmers downdale the 'horrors'.

The gorges and forces reminded some of home. 'Keld's cold stream' was to their liking; their shielings were clustered on the platform below Kisdon and above the Swale ravine, which glaciers had gouged so deep, and their flocks and herds found pasturage in the many dales from which becks tumbled their waters to the river. Every fell and gill, beck and foss, hamlet and farm is of their naming.

Norman earls took over this 'outback' as hunting country, the folk became their servants or were herdsmen when Rievaulx Abbey was given sheep pastures in the high dale. Centuries later Keld was the first community the Whartons, the new landlords, rode into when they came over by Tailbrigg and Birkdale to their manors by Swale. The men worked the Wharton lead mines in the neighbouring hills. Whartons fostered the local dissenters; the ancient Keld chapel fell into disuse and 1695 records state 'Walling up the chapel door— 1s.' Calvinists, then Independents, took over, rebuilding it in 1789 after a most successful money-raising trip of their minister to London and back. He walked both ways, collected £700, and put down his out-of-pocket expenses as a modest—sixpence!

No head of the dale community is quite like Keld. Take a look round,

By Keld's cold stream : Swaledale Head

starting from the highway and bus terminus. The Cat Hole Inn so thronged with miners before 1890 when the bottom finally fell out of the lead market—it was called 'Miners Arms' then—has no longer a licence. That gaunt building—you can buy stamps there, and sweets —was Lord Rochdale's shooting box, bringing many visitors and much activity to the sleepy village after 'the twelfth' each year. I remember seeing the late lord being taken out to the grouse shoots in a pony-drawn sledge. Another flow of all-the-year-round visitors, their average age considerably lower, now pours in and out of the house; it is a youth hostel, one I found fine for cross-Pennine route-making. Inn and hostel, cottages and a silent Wesley chapel (1841) make up the top side of Keld.

Wander down the twisty, walled-in lane to low Keld and you find that its twenty-odd folk have more public buildings than many a place ten times its size.

Round the square all is 'laid on'. On the left, the public hall with reading room—remember the literary institutes?—billiards, and many warning public notices telling of shows, sports, concerts, sheep sales and regarding Keld's November 'Stir'. Across the square—chapel and graveyard, village school and county library, and a ring of stone cottages with flagstone roofs, stone sheds, all sited for shelter rather than for the sun.

You will think twenty an over estimate of the population, it is so still and deserted. But when school 'looses', when the little ones romp out of doors, when the older ones come home from Richmond, when parents appear—then life flows and ringing voices echo through the land. They have strong lungs and powerful voices in these parts, after generations of competing with raging of wind and roaring of waters.

Odd corner collectors will be satisfied to have discovered Keld, but what we have seen is not the reason why country-lovers have for a century or more, encouraged by the praises of White, Speight and Bogg and the Victorian guides, converged here.

Walter White saw 'how much Swaledale has in common with the Alps', and around him found everything to be desired in a mountain holiday.

Speight declared that the deep gorge below Keld held in it one of the 'grandest combinations of rock and water scenery in the kingdom'. He was describing Kisdon Foss, most dramatic of Swale waterfalls and most difficult of access, shrouded in mystery in the deepest, loneliest reaches of the gorge, far below Kisdon and hidden by its dark woods.

Also below Kisdon foot and reached by a staircase of a path from the rim of Keld are Catrakes Falls, catlike creepings in dry weather but tigrish after heavy rains. Higher upriver and doing their stuff in the broad light of day, quite uninhibited, are Rainby Foss near the Swale bridge, and near the Kirkby Stephen road Wain Wath—that is 'cart ford'—Force and Huggarts Leaps, and in Stonesdale, Currack Falls. Each one would be a tourist attraction in any other place.

Greedy for more? Then wander up the two Stonesdales, or up Easter-
gill and Swinnergill, where tradition says a 'cave' was used for secret
worship by early dissenters, or strike out by the banks of becks
frolicking through Whitsundale or Great Sleddale and Birkdale. The
waters of the last two combined become the Swale below their
meeting place.

Walter White was intrigued by the ingenuity of a man at Keld
who lived near the spot where sightseers descended the path to Catrakes. With the trunk of a hazel, two horizontal branches and a
score of old clock bells (chromatically tuned) he made his Bell Tree,
attaching his instrument to a harmonium. He played the keys, the
bells he tapped with a thin stick, and the result was 'extremely
musical', and very popular with the Victorian tourists. The old man
had a Rock Band too, rather like the one we know at Keswick, this
made of local stone whereas the other was made from Skiddaw slates.

Two roads leave Keld for wild places. The Kirkby Stephen road
follows the Swale as far as Hogarths where it forges ahead, alone, into
a region soon empty of habitation, treeless and beyond the last farm,
Birkdale, desolate. I always feel like a traveller leaving the last oasis
and all Sahara ahead. Like a whiplash the road loops Birkdale
Common, making for the county boundary at Hollow Mill Cross,
a long lonely road for the walker but the motorist is soon at the
watershed, the boundary stone boldly marking 'Township of Birkdale. County of York' though for centuries all this was debateable
land, the exact borderline long disputed.

Westwards, Tailbrigg, Nateby Common—and Eden.

TAN HILL—AND THE EDGE O' TH' WORLD

The second road from Keld is shorter, sharper. Over Park Bridge,
sudden bends, fierce unexpected hills and up we go to the edge of
the world, Tan Hill inn. Everyone knows of it as one of England's
highest, a welcome halt for travellers now but far, far more so in the
past. Eight centuries of stormwinds have battered the walls of the
inn, eight hundred winters and each prepared for as for a seven
months' siege.

They buy in two months' supplies at once at Tan Hill; for fuel they
can always 'make out' with coal dug from a good yard thick seam
not far from the door. You will not see a cow for miles but there are
a few goats, the household's milk providers. In spite of rigorous
climate, "it's healthy enough. My children only missed two weeks'
schooling in the three years we were up there," a former landlord
told me.

Long ago the inn beckoned wayfarers—and Scots raiders and moss
troopers—on what was the high, very high, main route from Scotland by Eden, Appleby to York. Open doors, open house, day and
night, and there was food, warmth and shelter, dry clothes if necessary
and a guide to hire in proceeding into lonely places and over pitiless
wastes.

In 1880 Speight found the landscape patched with snow in June, skylines snow-powdered in August, and pools frozen and ground white with rime by the inn door in September. But welcome was warm and food ample—'good bread and butter—bread baked with water for milk had to be carried some miles—and excellent Appleby ale.'

In 1858 White was offered 'oaten bread, cheese and passable beer,' and a chance of hobnobbing with many miners and colliers gathered at the door. Not far away the fell top was spiked by timbers of coal pits. Pits and lead mines were in use then and the tracks busy with pitmen and buyers of pit head coal. Tan Hill coal? An old man down in Kirkby Stephen told me that his father paid 7s. 6d. for a load of ten or twelve hundredweights—'Good coal too, best kept for lighting fires and small coal for backing up'.

Changes come. Since the mines closed Tan Hill has depended for trade on passing travellers, and in more recent times on countrygoers and motorists who take the fearsome hill roads in their stride. Livelihood has to be earned while 'the sun shines', in July and August. Then, for eight weeks, it is the good smell of ham and eggs day in day out, and knots of visitors working up an appetite on windy vantage points, surveying enormous vistas.

You will hear a lot about Pennine Way walking at Tan Hill—and maybe about another marathon indulged in on August bank holidays. Stalwarts, after adequate refreshment here, set out to cover the long miles to the other 'highest' Pennine inn, the 'Cat and Fiddle' on the Buxton–Macclesfield road.

7. Ways north: very high ways and byroads

Road routes north of Swale:

Into the Eden valley: leave Keld on the Kirkby Stephen road, leaving Birkdale farm for the lonely wastes of Hollow Mill Cross and Tailbrigg Hill. The highest point is 1,698 feet; it strides the Yorkshire-Westmorland boundary and one time 'debateable land'. Distance: 13 miles. Once a well used shepherds' and cattle drovers' route, especially in October for the Kirkby Luke Fair, it is now reasonably surfaced with posts to mark the unfenced verge over Birkdale Common. A bare outline for a magnificent fell crossing!

From Keld to Brough and the Eden valley: from Keld to Tan Hill is a climb to 1,732 feet in 4 miles; the drop from the inn is even more formidable. Wild mosses and moors intervene between the Swaledale rampart and the Stainmore highway, reached by quiet routes to Barras—station closed—and Bowes. A byroad making west reaches Kaber—place of the Plotters of 1663—and Augill which is not far from Brough.

From Reeth through Arkengarthdale to Stainmore: beyond the lonely haunts of leadmining the road heads north over the barren lands of Stang and Hope, crossing the Greta to reach A66 and roads off to Barnard Castle and Tees. Reeth to Barney: 14 miles.

Richmond to Greta Bridge and Barnard Castle: a wide highway,

Watling Street and A66, makes this interesting journey, but I enjoy the off-lanes which local buses squeeze through with traffic jams, backings, manœuvrings and general good humour. We tap the sources of much Swale and Tees history, Gilling, a quiet roadside village, was head place of an Anglian 'shire', home of great thanes and earls, known to kings both English and Danish. Aske Hall has memories of Robin Aske, leader of the Commons in the Pilgrimage of Grace, and Kirkby Hill church is a place of old traditions. Ravensworth has meagre ruins of the castle of Fitz Henrys and Fitz Hughs, and their mark is clear on Tees country. Whashton and Barningham, Newsham and Dalton—these are just as comfortable as their old English names. Clear breezes rake their fields. Gipsy types bound for Brough Hill or Appleby New Fair park caravans and tether ponies by the wayside.

8. Walkers' ways through Swaledale

Remember, pedestrians were having the best of it long before the first internal combustion engines were heard in the dale. Nowadays those confined to cars look enviously after walkers striding free away along Swale side paths, over the heather slopes.

The dales' highways are pleasant walking at quiet times—not weekends. The byways are rarely busy, but the parallel paths are the highlights, those at water level, others half way between dale floor and skyline like the old lanes linking Richmond, High Park and Marrick, or Reeth with Riddings and Thirns, or Healaugh with Kearton, Blades and Gunnerside, and on (high level) above Calvert Houses and Ivelet, the Swale below, to Swinnergill, Stonesdale and so across to Keld. Routes such as these, sometimes walled-in, sometimes running unfenced along moor edges, or short-cutting across pastures—stile to stile—by-passing farm or lead mining hamlet, or passing through farm yard and open 'goose greens', offer a tantalizing choice. Climb higher above the dale, and green paths trail over the close-bitten limestone pastures—only sheep or cows for company now. Walls are left far below; the sky is the limit. Peeps into far dales are enchanting.

So, choose north or south side of the river and with a one-inch map to help direction-finding the walker has two or three alternatives, high, middle and low.

Warning: cow pastures with the bull at large May to October; and also at lowest level, the Swale floods frequently and water edge paths become waterlogged and impassable unless you are prepared to paddle.

Treat any reference to local bus services warily. In ten years many have been curtailed, many axed. Any survivors could suffer the same fate before reprinting.

Baliol's Tower, Barnard Castle

Six

TEESDALE

1. Pattern of History

THE PATTERN OF history woven in Teesdale's tapestry rivals all others in richness and variety. Kings and queens, powerful thanes, Norman barons, lesser lords, (though no less proud); royal palaces, battlemented castles, castellated halls and an abbey in grey ruin; forest and chase, wild treeless mountains and deep woodland glades—what a picture!

EARLY DAYS

Men of prehistory crossed the landscape making for the crossing of Stainmore; so did the Romans. All halted at the fords of Tees' feeder, the Greta. After the Dark Ages, the Anglian settlements, many below the Greta and Tees waters' meeting, and when the Danish boats pushed up the rivers as far as their flat bottoms could float, and the sea-rovers became land-seekers, they found many a suitable site where their Bys are neighbours of English Hams and Tons. Canute had his royal palace at Staindrop near Raby, the thanes and earls of Mercia at Gilling, Viking warriors were lords of Ravensworth, Romaldkirk is named from a Norse prince and hero, and Eric Blood Axe, last of Northumbria's Norse kings, fell to a traitor's axe on the heights of Stainmore. Plenty of history before William came and conquered!

LORDS OF TEESDALE

Guy de Ballieul, friend of William, built the first motte and bailey castle above Tees; his son with less haste and urgency erected the first tower of stone, and gave Barnard's Tower and 'Barney' town his name. Later generations of the same family finally enclosed no less than seven acres with formidable curtain walls and high towers watching the fords of Tees, protecting spacious wards or courtyards. Though Barnard Castle was a world of Norman aliens shut off from the natives who began to erect dwellings close to its outer defences for comfort and safety, the Ballieuls opened the outer ward gate to all when beacons blazed and Scots were rumoured on the rampage; then it was everyone to the castle, driving stock, carrying valuables, until danger was over. Here one Ballieul entertained Alexander, king of Scotland—and was witness of the killing of a Magna Carta baron by a bolt from a crossbow—and here dwelt John Baliol and his wife, Devorgilla of Galloway, their son 'Barney' born destined to be chosen king of Scotland.

Baliols lost Barnard Castle by later 'disloyalty' to the Edwards in the terrible Scots v. English wars which followed. The Nevilles came on the scene, and Richard of Gloucester who as husband of Anne Neville claimed the castle for his own and often lived here. Nevilles lost Barney by disloyalty to Elizabeth, plotting the Rising of the North to put Mary queen of Scots on her throne.

Baliols, and Nevilles—here and at Raby where we must follow their rise and fall, as we have already done at Middleham—the Bowes family of Streatlam, and other noble names are in Teesdale history. The Fitz Hughs descended from the Viking warriors of Ravensworth, with a castle there and above Tees at Cotherstone, and with tombs and mailed effigies in the churches of Romaldkirk and West Tanfield —because of Marmion alliances—and within the walls of Jervaulx Abbey and Egglestone, their name is written boldly too. So was that of the Rokebys who as high ranking landowners under the Earls of Richmond came to Rokeby, dwelt there for generations until the Scots destroyed their hall; they built Mortham Tower in its stead, formidably fortified against further attacks, a typical north country pele with barmkyn wall and gatehouse.

All ranged Tees side on pleasure bent, their horns sounding loud and clear over Marwood Chase or Forest and Frith, across New Forest or Stainmore, in company with royal princes and, occasionally, Scottish kings! Where they had the privilege of hunting, solitudinarians today have all the space and loneliness which their hearts desire.

Now the land on Durham side of Tees is owned by Lord Barnard whose forbears have been long 'of Raby', whilst the successors of the Bowes of Streathlam, the earls of Strathmore, owned estates on the Yorkshire side. No longer haunts of wild boars and wolves but moorland grouse shoots have brought distinguished sportsmen to the old forest lands. For instance, before the 1914 war, Lord Lonsdale with his Lowther huntsmen in red escorted to Wemmergill Lodge his guest Kaiser Wilhelm with his Bavarian Chasseurs, a long procession of vehicles with armed guards coming over from Brough to Lunesdale in upper Teesdale. Record 'bags' have been made at Wemmergill, one was inscribed on a stone at Barningham, 190 grouse brought down in 25 minutes!

I have named the great, but who were the good, or given to good works? The earls of Richmond sited an abbey of their foundation on land south of Tees at Egglestone, in Yorkshire, so the religious house nearest Barnard Castle, which was in Durham and had the prince bishops of Durham as overlords, had very little link with the castle. In fact animosity flared frequently between abbey and town. Town was out of bounds to the brethren. On occasions they were compelled to hide daggers in their gowns for their own protection when braving the townsfolk on their own ground.

Barnard Baliol founded 'Barney's' parish church, and John Baliol a hospital for the infirm. His good works, in association with the royal Devorgilla, are better known: Balliol College in Oxford and a new abbey on Solway shore, Dulce Cor, Sweetheart Abbey, where his heart lies entombed.

Ancestors of the Ravensworth Fitz Hughs were founders of Fors

abbey by Ure, later translated by the earls of Richmond to Jervaulx.
The lords of Rokeby were benefactors of the Greyfriars at Richmond, as who does not know who has heard of that felon sow,
though their gift was a mixed blessing, 'a fiend in likeness of a swine'.

> She was more than other three,
> The grisliest beast that e'er might be—
> She was bred in Rokeby wood.
> There were few that thither gaed
> That came on live away.

BARNARD CASTLE AND BARNEY TOWN

Now to Barnard Castle which is to Tees as Richmond to Swale,
Knaresborough to Nidd, Skipton to Aire. The stronghold still 'stands
stately upon Tees', tottering towers poised over cliffs in the most
dramatic manner. And the town has its own atmosphere. A walk-
around is fascinating. We begin at the beginning, by the bridge and
the riverside.

The bridge, splendid fifteenth century work, parapets breached by
a Bren gun carrier, traffic lights to send single streams across, looks
as impressive as all engravings and paintings have shown it. Above
rise high castle walls and Mortham's Tower head in air above 80-
feet cliffs considered impregnable. Bridgegate turns right into the
town, opened out by the heavy hand of progress, tall Georgian houses
swept away, and cottages which clung like limpets to the castle walls
torn away from their holdings; instead, water-edge gardens, seats,
and council houses of synthetic stone. Bridgegate leads into Thorngate with memories of carpet weaving, spinning, worsted weaving,
shoe thread making, hempen rope walks and the like, from the last
century when the tall ranks of old factories by the river were in their
way as impressive as the castle walls above. Now, on either side the
tree lined street are gracious Georgian houses, older houses with
bowed rooflines, pointed gables and mullioned windows, some with
dormers or bow windows. Between them dark archways and alleys
go creeping into ancient yards, once close and cramped, escape routes
from high street to the Mains, but now demolished; sun shines on
rubble and broken walls.

Thorngate rises to the Bank, with old inns, more yards off, and
that picturesque house called Blaygroves after its owner in 1672,
where they gave Cromwell 'burnt ale and shortcakes' in 1648. Old
houses, all with great variety in roofline and chimney stacks, and the
parish church tower rising above them, make a fine picture of Old
Barney on the right hand as far as Amen Corner where Newgate
goes off.

Equally interesting is the street frontage on the left hand where
close fitting houses, side by side, hide castle curtain wall, their sites
covering castle ditch, clinging to the outer bailey defences. Inns too,
the most imposing the 'King's Head' where you might miss a small
pointer—THE CASTLE—directing you through its gate and stable yard

to the ruins. Charles Dickens and Phiz stayed here in 1838. The
writer set his watch from the clockmaker's time piece across the
road; he also struck up acquaintance with the owner—and that led
to *Master Humphrey's Clock*—and he also was helped in search for
information about the disgraceful boarding-school racket—which led
to *Nicholas Nickleby*. You remember Mr. Newman Noggs? 'Name
my name', said he, 'and at the "King's Head" you'll get a glass of
good ale for nothing'.

From another inn, the 'Turk's Head', higher 'up town' two marksmen once, after a wager, took aim at the Market Hall's weathervane
on its turret; look for the bullet holes!

What a handsome pillared and arcaded Market Hall. It replaced
the ancient Tolbooth in 1749; Thomas Breaks built it. It is centre of
local life now as in the past though no longer do farmwives set out
their eggs, butter and special Cotherstone and Romaldkirk cheeses
on market day under the sheltering portico. Old folk and foot-weary
tourists sit there instead, on the stone benches. Inside the hall town
archives are housed, whilst the old lock-up above is likely to be used
for a local art exhibition or some kindred show.

Northwards Market Place and Horsemarket, busy thoroughfares
for all the traffic of the Barney to Durham and South Shields highway—A688—comes this way. These are eighteenth century streets,
their houses backed upon Town Ward and Brackenbury's Tower,
their gardens and orchards acually within the castle walls; that was
how the town developed two centuries ago, by leaping the walls.
Newgate is a wide street; some of its houses, narrow-fronted, have
garden several hundred yards long, sloping downhill to the edge of
the Mains. Galgate which is parallel gets its name from the medieval
gallows; this is a busy and thronged shopping street; buses pull up
and we hear the jolly ringing voices of Northumbrian folk and all
County Durham.

A century ago Galgate was packed with countryfolk and their
conveyances on market days. As a writer saw them, 'Darby and Joan
came in to Barney seated on a grey pony, jogging lovingly together,
whilst families and parties of grown-up folk, some seated on chairs,
travelled in merrily in ordinary heavy country carts'. Now—buses!

Barney has its quiet places. At the top of Horsemarket turn left
to the garden on The Motte—where Guy Ballieul's first earthen and
stockaded motte and bailey were—for exciting views over dale and
serried green and blue hills. Through the gateway in the curtain wall,
in part of the castle's Town Ward, is an unsuspected garden which
was once tended by a doctor whose house hugged the defences; a
public garden now, it has all the charm of one lovingly cared for
down the centuries. The high medieval walls are foil for herbacious
borders, benches in tower recesses are sheltered from the winds, roses
ramble over battlements—and old Barney folk sun themselves and
grow garrulous of the old days.

Then, not far away, paths run away into Flatt Woods wherein a
century ago Lord Barnard's forbears set the workless and workhouse

inmates to create miles of paths through enchanted glades and ferny dells for the delight of Barney burgesses; a place of faery, especially on spring mornings and summer evenings.

Almost everyone familiar with old castle towns knows of short cuts round rock and bastion whereby they can race motorists held up in the jams of narrow streets. From the Motte—my favourite; it curves under the great round tower (Bernard Ballieul's foundations) leaps down the steeps below Richard III's Great Chamber—looking up you may see under the sofit of the lovely oriel window his boar badge carved on stone—descends rapidly leaving buttressed curtain walls and Mortham's dizzy tower behind; and we are at the bridge and Tees bank.

The 'King's Head' entry, through its garage—once stable—yard, and we are within the vast Outer Ward which occupied almost half of the seven-acre site; on our right a wide dry moat and high inner walls divided this from the less accessible Middle and Town Wards. Here, when Scots were raiding, townfolk, dalesfolk and cattle were one jostling, shouting, milling mass. A century ago horses were stabled in a medieval tower, cows were stalled in a ruined chapel and the rest was gardens or orchards 'their trees, sheltered by grey walls, giving generous fruit'.

The gatekeeper lives in a cottage without the walls but enters by a door within the thickness of it. We are admitted into the inner defences, that part of the castle occupying the highest ground with the 80-feet drop to the river where the Ballieuls felt most secure. First we come to the Middle Ward, where retainers milled around and was all the activity which followed the comings and goings of lords and barons, kings and queens. Again a massive wall running from Bernard Ballieul's round tower to another, and another deep dry moat adds further security to the core, the Inner Ward, where the most important remains are still to be seen. Here dwelt Ballieuls and later Baliols, here their banquetting halls where kings were feted and entertained, chambers where deliberations led to peace or war, and airy chambers high in tower and turret where sad-eyed their ladies watched, 'their gold combs in their hair', waiting for their true loves who often did not return—from fighting back the Scots, from wars in France, from all those campaigns when men of Tees side went forth behind their lords, Ballieuls, Baliols, Nevilles, and Richard of Gloucester.

A pity there is no bearded hermit now to act as guide as a century ago. He was one who had quarrelled with the world and 'took possession of a vault and wall cavity in Baliol's Round Tower and has lived there ever since', wrote Walter White, 'making and selling rustic furniture. When the Duke of Cleveland, the owner, gives him hint to quit he pretends not to understand'.

Since 1962 when this visit was made the castle has been given full treatment as a very ancient monument, with custodian, information kiosk, guide books. The men at work are busy digging up the past and keeping venerable ruins upstanding.

Climb the winding stairs inside Baliol's Tower; magnificent views which none omits who has read *Rokeby*. Scott catalogued in verse each of the streams which are tributaries to Tees, and according to Victorian guide books—assuming every tourist carried his poems in their valises—'Scott's word pictures may be appropriately quoted from here'.

The named streams are very lovely within their green woods. Downdale is Greta, by Egglestone abbey ruins is 'Thorsgill's murmuring child' and higher is 'Deepdale's slender rill' very romantic. Poetic fancy gave Balder dale the name of Odin's son. The river out of Stainmore is 'silver Lune' and the rural brook of Egglestone—the village not the abbey—hides in wooded ravines north of Tees. You will find them all—just as Scott knew them.

Barnard Castle possesses a building reminiscent of a great château on banks of Loire, the Bowes Museum which is a good reason for travelling far for its sake alone. No gallery or museum in England is quite like it. A century ago John Bowes and his wife, Countess of Montalbo, brought together in France a private collection of art treasures unexcelled; they intended to house it in France but the revolution made them trans-ship the treasures to England, to John Bowes' home country, Teesdale. Their museum may be alien in style and out of scale—but what a possession ! Pray for a wet day when in the dale. You may well need more than one day to get an *idea* of the many treasures. Countrygoers will enjoy the collection of Teesdale bygones.

Of the Bowes family many Victorian street names in Barnard Castle are reminders. Their hall at Streatlam is no more, though the earls of Strathmore—remember, the Queen Mother was a Bowes-Lyon —are as large landowners as their ancestors in Tees country.

One mighty pile no one should miss whilst in Teesdale is Raby Castle, for generations stronghold of the Nevilles. Lord Barnard opens his house to the public on Saturdays and Wednesday afternoons in the summer. In the nearby village of Staindrop are many of their family tombs also Not To Be Missed.

THE NEVILLES OF RABY

We have met Nevilles at Middleham, earls of Salisbury and Warwick, king maker and throne shakers, top dogs from the fourteenth century. Before they came into Wensleydale it was Raby Castle not far north of Tees which was 'cradle, ancestral home and heritage' of their family.

Raby came to them through the marriage of Isabella, the heiress of Brancepath and Sheriff Hutton, with the lord of Raby. His ancestors had Raby from the monks of St. Cuthbert to whom it had been given after pilgrimage to the saint's shrine at Durham by none other than King Canute; probably the king had a 'palace' near by, at Staindrop. As County Durham had bishops of Durham for overlords, to the bishop did John Neville apply in 1379 for permit to fortify Raby. He must have made a completely 'new' castle preserving little or nothing of the early dwelling on the site; so, look carefully at Raby, considered a perfect example of a fourteenth century stronghold which was primarily a residence, 'the largest castle of lodgings in all the north country', said Leland.

You would expect a great soldier like John Neville, who had crushed the defenders and won back no less than eighty-three walled towns, castles and forts in Aquitaine and France, to see his castle had strong defences. Here is a castle within a castle, central towers linked by strong curtain walls, impregnable in themselves, within a surrounding, open platform and an outer ring of many jutting bastions rising from the base of an embattled wall; outside this, the moat encircling all and flooding towards the south into a large lake.

After a visit to the castle carry on to Staindrop church. The Neville tombs are, as one would expect, splendid. Look for Lady

Raby : castle of the Nevilles

Isabella's tomb, she who brought the Neville name to Raby, and the effigy of an infant Neville. Euphemia, wife of an early Ralph Neville, has a winged angel at her shoulder; her son built this south aisle in 1343. At the west end is the magnificent alabaster tomb with three effigies; John o' Gaunt owned the Tutbury quarries from which the marble came. A later Ralph Neville was his son-in-law, his first wife Margaret Stafford, the second Joan, who became a Beaufort when young Richard II pronounced Katharine Swynford's children legitimate. Ralph, created first earl of Westmorland, builder of the later 'outer castle' at Middleham, wears chain mail and vizor : Joan has a long cloak over her rich gown.

Having the closest links with the royal family, Ralph Neville's children were to be deeply concerned in the troubles involving half-cousin Richard II and half-uncle Henry IV. When the fair Cicily, Rose of Raby, a twenty-first child, married the Duke of York, Nevilles were destined to play major roles in the York-Lancaster wars about to break upon England. By then Middleham, not Raby, was their chief northern residence. But when the House of York fell and the Nevilles with it, Wensleydale lands forfeit, the survivors of the family were at Raby again; and there was plotted the rising which was the final downfall—the abortive attempt to put Mary Queen of Scots on the throne, and down with the Protestant Elizabeth. Many others have owned estates once theirs: Vanes, dukes of Cleveland, now Lord Barnard whose residence is at Raby.

2. *Teesdale Approaches*

Teesdale is my kind of country, stern and wild in the mountains and fells near its source, a compact of smaller delights, pastoral pleasaunces, flowery meadows and sylvan glades in its middle reaches, and saturated in history from Barnard Castle and Waters Meeting to the end; infinite variety, something to satisfy every mood.

Yorkshire claims its south bank, Durham the north, whilst Westmorland looks in at the birth. To Lancastrians it is virtually unknown country—unless they be students, geological and botanical—which is a pity. The voices which made the welkin ring by Greta Woods and Brignall Banks a century ago were from Tees and Tyne and Wear mouth; the waggonettes which met the trains in Victorian times filled up with trippers from Darlington, Middlesbrough and Stockton, and occasionally from the more northerly Yorkshire towns, never from Lancashire. Of cars and coaches today the same applies.

FROM LANCASHIRE AND WEST OF THE PENNINES

Teesdale is easy of access, even from Lancashire and west of the Pennines. From A6 is a choice of roads over the Great Barrier heading for Barnard Castle. Take A684 from Kendal to Sedbergh, or A683 from Lancaster and Kirkby Lonsdale to Sedbergh; both combine to follow the Rawthey river over the watershed into Ravenstonedale and Kirkby Stephen and Brough. Here A683 is joined by A66 which has come east from Lakeland and A6, from Penrith by Appleby and the Eden valley. From Brough to Bowes and Barnard Castle the streams of traffic combined cross Stainmore. This ancient cross-Pennine route into Tees country, recently much widened, is so exciting, its history so interwoven with that of our northern dales, the borderlands and Scotland, I am giving the pass of Stainmore a section to itself.

From this great highway lesser roads into upper Teesdale strike away from Brough to Middleton, from Bowes to Cotherstone. From Swaledale even lonelier routes come into the Stainmore road from Reeth and Arkengarthdale, from Keld and Tan Hill, each to the liking of 'let's get off the highways' motorists with pioneering spirit and loads of experience.

The highest route and the wildest, and most liable to complete blocking by snowdrifts—how we listened to the weather reports of winter '63—is the one which takes in Teesdale from dale head to the estuary. A6277—from Carlisle to Alston in 18 miles, then from the highest market town in England, which we feel is quite true, climbing to 1,962 feet above the upper reaches of the South Tyne, over the watershed and county boundary to roll down to Langden Beck and the Tees. 'Barney' is 32 miles from Alston.

STAINMORE AND BORDER HISTORY

The Pass of Stainmore was made easy for cross-Pennine travel in that remote period when combined ice flows from the Irish Sea crawling round Cumberland, forcing a way down the Eden, with others from Ravenstonedale and the Lune valley and Shap fells were pushed eastwards, grinding and graving their way over the watershed, scooping out a groove which the Greta was to use, leaving the Pennine mountain-caps inviolate. When glaciers were no more and prehistoric peoples turned towards the Pennines, Stainmore and the

Memories of coaching days: 'Unicorn', Bowes

Aire Gap were their earliest inroads. From 1000 B.C. it must have been something of a Yukon Trail, with laden traders of the Bronze Age returning from Ireland, their Eldorado; those were the days of the gold seekers. Some careless merchant or smith left behind a handful of gold rings at Bowes.

The men who named Stainmore a thousand years ago knew the landscape as a stony moorland; men described it as a 'howling wilderness', as 'nothing all round but a wild desert', and adjectives most often used were 'dree, dismal, inhospitable'. Doubtless the Scots homeward bound for Hogmanay a few years ago added a few more epithets; they were marooned in their long distance coaches in fierce blizzards on Bowes Moor. Some staggered to shelter—one died, Brough villagers opened doors to the distressed—and they sat out the storms, not for the first time in its long history.

Roman road makers with great tenacity engineered a military route over the Pass, building two forts, Lavatrae at Bowes, Veterae at Brough as guardians. A string of camps and signal points between sent out beacon lights by night and smoke plumes by day. Look for them near Bowes and New Spital hotel, at Rey Cross where the twenty-acre site could house a legion—and now accommodates a car park! Maiden Castle, a half way mark between forts, is not so named from maidens recruited from among the natives acting as builders' mates, carrying laboriously—as popular tradition likes to believe— 'earth in leather aprons'.

REY CROSS AND THE SUMMIT

Rey Cross, that battered stump within enclosing fence—so often hidden by cars and crowds around the snack bar—is, some think, almost as old as the Romans, and it looks older! Possibly it was a first century boundary mark setting limits for Celtic Cumbria and Strathclyde where it came up against the power of Rome. When borders ran along watersheds 'as heaven the water deals' this was an undisputed mark at the edge of a debateable land.

A pity if jolly trippers from Tyneside with 'Kiss Me Kate' and 'Chase Me Charlie' on their fancy hats, decide to take a breather from coaches just when we arrive at Rey Cross. My first sight of the stump silhouetted on the rugged skyline, with stormy clouds scudding behind it, was just right. It was Brough Hill fair and along the road cantered a cavalcade of horse-drawn caravans, all gaily painted, no two alike, with brown-faced women and tow-haired children gazing out. Frisky piebalds and skewbalds and leggy foals trotted behind with boys rounding them up if they strayed, sticks in hand.

When they had trailed away—an exciting and stirring picture they made—the highway was quiet for a while. I looked westwards after them and saw England rolling away to the Eden, a fair land mellowed in the golden sun, to the serried Lakeland fringe sunlit too though dark clouds were gathering over the high mountains. South, the glacial trough, a brown and sere wasteland beyond Barras across miles of desolation to the Swaledale rampart, and Tan Hill inn like a toy on top. There were tiny walled intakes too—and broken-down sheep bields, and distant farmhouses which have such thought-provoking names, like Stainmore's Blue Grass and Light Trees, Upman Howe, Mouthlock and Palliard.

The close-up and intimate view of that landscape was from the most exciting of all Pennine railways, the Kirkby Stephen-Barnard Castle line, alas, no more!

At Rey Cross are gathered up many threads in the tapestry of border history. Scotland is far enough to the north but here was once the border and that meant a share of the rapine, bloodshed, raids and backwash of many wars.

The Angles who named Stainmore, stony moorland, were seventh century invaders who found in the rich floor of the Eden valley the land they needed, amenable to cultivation and plenty for everyone. They took their names from the moors; we are the Westmoringas; they declared, the folk who dwell west of Stainmore. When centuries later a new county was formed from the combined baronies of Appleby and Kendal this was the name given to it—as Westmorland.

In their days Stainmore was infested by wild men and wild beasts. The Normans were later to protect the wild life for their own sport; the deer were plentiful, so were wild boars, and wolves. Hands off the wolves, they ordered their tenants, the brethren of Jervaulx who had grazing rights. Lune Forest which ranged from Stainmore to Mickle Fell, New Forest south from the Greta to the Swaledale ramparts, and the Chase of Arkengarthdale were jealously guarded by the Norman earls.

In the tenth century when one wide Scandinavian kingdom bridged the north with rival capitals at York and Dublin, Stainmore was a main link. Across the barrier had come Danish invaders sweeping from the eastern daleheads to win lands to the west and the Eden. Later came Norsemen up the Eden on the same tack, land-seeking and meeting the Danish settlers around Stainmore. The pass also witnessed in A.D 954 the tragic end of the last Norse king of Northumbria, Eric Haraldson 'Blood Axe', making a desperate last stand against treacherous attack 'in a lonely place called Steinmore', falling before Earl Oswolf's hireling, Maccus.

Never a dull moment. Times were even more hectic following the Conquest. North country Englishmen fled over the pass, heading for Scotland before the Conqueror's devouring hand, seeking protection at Malcolm Canmore's court and welcome from his English queen. The Scots king was glad of their help; he wished to hold the border land, his richest source of cattle and slaves. He invaded England; according to local tradition a remote spot in Balderdale—between Stainmore and Tees—was scene of deadly struggle. After this—again tradition—the king of Scotland met William the Norman and became 'his man'; the meeting place—Roi Cross of the Kings. They came with arms but wisely decided to settle disputes amicably 'thereupon setting up a cross with images of both kings, William's south and Malcolm's north to signify one is to march to England, the other to Scotland'. An uneasy truce. A pact broken when William Rufus, opposed by his eldest brother, Robert of Normandy, who did not see why England's crown should not be his, forced men to take sides.

Now began centuries of 'unease' for north-country folk. We do not realize how closely linked are our two histories, Scots and English, and how they affected the lives of all who lived around Stainmore.

Skip the next page if history is not your line.

ROYAL FAMILIES

Malcolm and Robert were close friends for the best of reasons. Robert was godfather to a Scottish princess and threw up the New Castle on Tyne on his way south after the christening. William

Rufus to force Malcolm's hand marched his armies north and threw up a border fortress at Carlisle, and his supporters, the earls of Richmond, rushed up a castle on the Roman site at Bowes; another watchdog for Stainmore was thrown up at Brough. These castles were in turn to be battered, stormed, beseiged, replaced in stone, lost and won in centuries to follow.

Did Stainmore folk ever know which side to shout for? Even Scottish royalties were Norman in upbringing. Donalbain on Malcolm's death chased out his nephews and nieces, the little princes being brought up in the Norman court and the princesses in Romsey Abbey near the capital of Winchester. The princes became in turn kings of Scotland, David lasting longest and happy to honour boyhood friends, Brus, Ballieul and De Morville. Edith Matilda became Henry I's queen and their daughter, the hapless Matilda, on taking the crown plunged both countries into long and bitter war. So many princes and lords had friends on both sides, for Matilda, for Stephen.

How was the north affected? King David was for his niece Matilda, but his son, Prince Henry, supported Stephen and therefore received from him debateable lands his father's support of Matilda would have lost. All Stainmore was involved at that time, and dalesmen were at the battle of Northallerton where David, looking for his friends, found Brus and Ballieul with the English forces: David wept.

With every new king there were new troubles in spite of more attempts to use sons and daughters as pawns. David's grandson, William the Lion, fought strenuously to keep the land from Stainmore northwards in Scotland—the edge of the Glasgow diocese reached the Pass—but he was overcome and became prisoner of the earls of Richmond in their castle above Swale. His daughter, Princess Margaret, married Conan, fourth earl of Richmond and their only offspring, Constance, became bride of the English king's son, Geoffrey Plantagenet.

Royal cavalcades were no unusual sight crossing Stainmore then, when Ballieuls at Barnard Castle, the earls at Richmond Castle and the lords of Appleby too entertained kings of both countries at their tables and rode out with them to hunt.

The matchmaking which followed! Unfortunately the one royal union which might have brought peace for all time was fated not to be. William's grandson, the third Alexander, wed Henry III's daughter Margaret, sister of Edward I who in his turn built his highest hopes on winning for the first Prince of Wales—you remember, Welsh born, not English!—the heiress to the throne of Scotland. Alexander III's sons died tragically, his daughter—named after her English mother—who married King Eric of Norway died young too, leaving one infant princess, sole heiress. She was only three when Edward made plans to secure her—and Scotland; a ship laden with good things to please a small girl took her on board and set sail to carry her to her betrothal in England. She died before the ship came to port—some say of too many rich foods.

Ever since 1067 there had been ding-dong fighting from Stainmore to the Cheviots, between kings, north-country lords, and barons interested in their own accounts, and the rank and file anxious to share the pickings. There was two way raiding whenever crops failed, cattle had the murrain, or life became tedious. "Let's go a reiving", was a battle cry north and south of the movable border. At one period only were the two countries officially at peace, when Richard Coeur de Lion to raise money for Crusading equipment and supply, 'sold' northern lands and castles to Scotland.

Far worse troubles followed the death of the little Maid of Norway. Shoals of claimants were whittled down to a short list of two—Bruce whose forbears had once been Yorkshire Normans, Baliol whose ancestors had built Barnard Castle. Edward I was called in as arbiter. John Baliol, born at 'Barney', was chosen as king of Scotland. We all learnt at school about the Wallace share in Scotland's fight for independence, Robert the Bruce, his defeats and ultimate come-back, the successes and overwhelming defeats of the Edwardian wars—especially bitter the reversals during Edward II's unhappy reign with the disgrace of defeat and annihilation of England's chivalry at Bannockburn.

DARKEST DAYS

What the north suffered then—as we have seen as far south as Ribble country—villages fired, halls razed, cattle driven north and the most furious Scots attacks on lands owned by knightly families in the forefront in the invasions of Edward I wars, fierce reprisals.

All through the fourteenth century northern Englishmen fortified their homes, walled in their possessions—scores of peles remaining as witness along every route which led from Scotland through the plains and the dales.

After Bannockburn; a sad time long remembered in the north. After Otterburn; a period as troubled, reprisals, men said, for the death of Scotland's hero, Douglas. The bloodiest battles then raged along the Eden, around the storied walls of Appleby, at Burrills where 3,000 dalesmen were slaughtered by Scots, fighting mad, and around the castle of Brough where—as a burly Westmerian once described to me with great gusto, tilt, thrust and gurgle—"It was never fighting wi' bows and arrows but ripping 'em up, slicing through skulls wi' pikes and daggers". I could almost hear the yells, bloodcurdling screams and combat in Brough's back lanes and dark alleys; and looked to see if the innocent waters of Eden showed the red of spilled blood.

The backwash of reiving, raiding, war and invasion always flowed through Stainmore.

Enough of fighting and bad times. During the intervals the lords of Richmond, of Ravensworth and Barnard Castle hunted the wild creatures of forest and chase, the brethren of the abbeys saw to their pasturage, and the nuns of Marrick carried out the good work of providing for wayfarers at their hospice or 'spittal' on Stainmore.

STAGE COACH TRAVELLERS

Time passed. Costumes and weapons changed, modes of travel changed, but Stainmore still carried most traffic. Whenever times were 'out of joint' fighting men poured through—especially during the Civil War when every town east or west of the mountain barrier was held for king or Parliament.

Eighteenth century. After the second Jacobite rebellion, with roads improved, over came the London-Carlisle-Edinburgh coach advertised as 'post coaches with 4 horses and armed guards' to protect passengers against robbery on the highway. Scheduled stops? Greta Bridge, 'Unicorn' at Bowes, Spital on Stainmore. Fare? £3 10s. through fare, but 3d. a mile if taken up on the road.

All coaches had recognized stops. The Lancaster-Sedbergh-Barnard Castle coach had one halt at the 'Cross Keys' inn at Cautley, once with near disastrous results.

In 1830 on a bitter winter night, the crew lingered long in the 'Cross Keys' kitchen. The 'Lord Exmouth', patient passengers and impatient horses were out in the cold. Growing restive the horses decided 'for off' and away they went, only one young man having his doubts about a missing driver and guard. His suspicions proving all too true he decided to slip unseen from the coach and go back for help. Not easy with dangerous road, ice-clad and perilously near deep rivers. He slithered his way to 'Cross Bank' inn at Ravenstonedale, the coach careering northwards. He hired a horse, gave chase and caught up at Kirkby where the horses had drawn up at a familiar stop in mid-street. The passengers were only just realizing what had happened. The noble young man was still 'game'; he took the reins and drove the coach over Stainmore as far as the 'Spital' where new team and driver were always waiting to take over.

Plenty of macabre! A headless woman, they say, haunts the Bowes highway, a fair Norman maiden whose lover, unrequited, grasped her flowing locks and off with her head! Also there was the Hand of Glory. One dark night in 1789 a heavily cloaked woman was admitted to the 'Spital' inn by George Alderson's maid servant. The traveller's feet sounded heavily on the flagged floor; under the cloak—a man's boots! Hidden in the folds—the Hand! It was firmly believed that a malefactor's hand severed at the gallows, its fingers grasping a candle made from the fat of the dead man, had power to paralyse any who beheld its light; it was much prized by thieves and housebreakers. Imagine the horror of the girl when the Hand of Glory was brandished before her eyes and a deep male voice intoned,

> Let those who rest more deeply sleep,
> Let those who wake their vigils keep.
> O, hand of Glory shed thy light
> Direct us to thy spoil tonight.

What happened next, how the girl quenched the light, the scattering of the lurking robbers in league with the intruder, and the inevitable

Do-the-Boys Hall: yard and pump

'tourist' attraction of the Hand he left behind, that is the old Spital's own story.

The large Bowes Hotel is successor of the ancient hostelry; on the highway near by, but one valiant wind-twisted tree, sole survivor of wild winters.

BOWES—HISTORIC

Ahead, the grim dark tower of Bowes Castle, blank eyes fixed on pass and Greta valley; stringing out by the highway the village of Bowes, its story that of Stainmore.

The first house on the right; look carefully, this is Do-the-Boys

Hall of ill fame, Wackford Squeers' Academy, straight from the pages of *Nicholas Nickleby*. Dickens and his illustrator, Phiz, came north on the London Coach, their intentions to investigate the boarding schools to which the same coach service had carried many a boy who was never required to take a return ticket. Just as baby-farming of unwanted infants many a north country academy, advertised in glowing terms in south country papers, was no more than a dump for equally unwanted children.

Dickens in 1838 looked through the same archway, into the same yard with the same water pump and stone trough. The place looked bleak and cheerless on the bitter February day; the head of the Bowes Academy gave them an equally cold reception, which was to be expected.

Not long afterwards the novel exposed the 'racket'. This school and others like it in the dales closed down. Walter White in 1858 described this 'the original of Do-the-Boys Hall as doorless, windowless, dilapidated. The exposure was too much for it and it ceased to be a den of hopeless childhood, a place to which heartless parents condemned their children because it was cheap.'

As I was sketching and thinking about poor Smike and other hapless lads, two strangers came up, turbanned Indians hawking nylons! Later walking down the road to the 'Unicorn', the famous coaching inn, I saw a large limousine draw up and out stepped, in silken saris and glint of gold, brown-skinned ladies from the Orient.

The world and his wife have long been familiar with Stainmore. Remember the Beaker men and Bronze Age traders, the Roman legionaries; goodness only know where they hailed from.

Relics of ancient history; behind the castle and the church the site of Lavatrae, king pin in defence of the Stainmore military road; in the castle built on the Roman camp, masonry taken from the Roman ruins; in the church a carved stone commissioned by the Thracian cavalry corps to honour their 'Emperors Caesars Lucius Septimus Severus Pius Pertinax the great conqueror of Arabia etc. and of Marcus Aurelius Antoninus', and also Caesar Optimus Geta but his name is erased—by the order of his twin brother who murdered him.

The castle was never residential with great chambers, halls and solars, but purely a military post rushed up by the earl of Richmond for William Rufus in his struggle to hang on to the northern borderland, and later replaced by a permanent castle in stone during Henry II's reign. There are steps to climb to the upper cavities in the hollow keep, and deep embrasures into which cold winds blow through gaping holes which were the 'winds' eyes' and out of which are wide and exhilariting views over Greta to the far Swaledale tops.

Victorian tourists always made a bee-line for a certain grave near the bell turret at the west end of the old church. It is shared by star-crossed lovers, Roger Wrightson and Martha Railton, local sweethearts. 'He died in a fever and upon tolling his passing bell she cried out, "My heart is broke," and in a few hours expired, purely through love'. This happened in March 1714. A ballad kept their story green; 'Edwin and Emma', sentimental tear raiser!

Bowes has a varied collection of old houses and some which were obviously inns and taverns, like the 'Rose and Crown' and the low-browed 'Club' facing the 'Unicorn'. As for the 'Unicorn'—put back the pump and well into the large 'forecourt', replace the mounting block to its old place, and return the garage in the triple-arched coach houses to the coaches, and the petrol station in the harness room to the ostlers—and it would be the old time hostelry, perfect in all its eighteenth century detail. Of course it had to move with the times and has done so with admirable good taste.

3. Near the Banks of Tees

UPRIVER: FROM GRETA BRIDGE
TO BARNARD CASTLE

From Durham and the North the approach to Tees country is by A688 from Bishop Auckland. From the river mouth and Darlington the 16 miles to Barnard Castle on A67 is pleasant and a link with many historic villages—Piercebridge and Gainford, Winston, and along byways crossing the Tees to Barford, Ovington, and Wycliffe which claims the great reformer as its son.

Most country goers from Yorkshire and from the south travelling on the Great North Road leave A1 for A66 at Scotch Corner, thereafter arrow-straight following Watling Street to Greta Bridge.

Here for a number of reasons, all excellent, we stop. Where else is such a concentrate of history, beauty, drama, romance? Greta, renowned in song and story; known to all the V.I.P.s of the past.

Victorian topographical and guide writers got over their problem of concentrating a gallon in an egg cup by giving up the task and borrowing from Scott. Sir Walter was a godsend; he had said everything in *Rokeby* so they borrowed stanza after stanza.

'No description can be perfect or bring home to the mind the beauties of Teesdale unless it is embodied in the language of that master of romantic poetry, as in Scott's *Rokeby*,' said a writer of 1870. Which was his excuse for borrowing, as for scores before him. Before Scott and *Rokeby*, tourists did no more than change coaches at the Greta Bridge inns, or rest and refresh themselves as men had been doing for more than two thousand years. Yes, prehistoric Beaker men used the Greta fords on their way to the copper mines of Cumberland; they lit their fires and slept by them whilst wild creatures prowled around. We met later Bronze Age gold seekers on Stainmore; here was a shelter for them, and maybe a trading centre for bartering metals, hearths for smiths who had the secrets of metalwork and could repair weapons and design bracelets and ornaments. One bracelet was left here and never called for. Roman soldiers also 'fell out' and sought the road-side tavern for that drink to help them on the next long miles. Near by is a Roman camp.

The chief inn, 'Morritt Arms', was called after the family which played host to Walter Scott at Rokeby in 1809. Colonel Morritt fell over himself to please his guest and aid the Muse. He turned a small cave overlooking the Greta ravine into a study. The visit over, Scott wrote to the Colonel, 'Rokeby is one of the most enviable spots I have ever seen,' and was soon enlisting his help in rooting out legends 'truth or fiction I care not if it be picturesque,' to work into a romance in verse. *Rokeby* was the result.

When the colonel read the poem he declared, "I shall raise the rent of my inn at Greta Bridge on the first notice of your book." His hunch was right. The best-selling poem turned a tourist trickle into a flood. And the 'Morritt Arms' raked the benefit.

'Guides conduct visitors to the scenes of the poem in Rokeby grounds every day but Sunday,' was a notice soon on view. The railway era brought even more excursionists to Greta Bridge—but the inn fell on bad days. White in 1858 noted how the inn, once so famous, so noisy when coaches with their four panting horses drew up day and night on their London-Edinburgh run, had deteriorated into a 'not happy looking farmhouse'. Where now 'the unscrupulous profits'? he wondered.

The waggonettes rollicked by, their loads were emptied at Rokeby gates, and guides at the ready shepherded them 'through the glens which Scott had described . . . where seats are placed in judicious positions on the romantic paths . . . where the lover of solitude tiring of gladsome voices and merry laughter of numerous detachments of trippers may lose himself in lonely recesses where the manifold combinations of rock, water and wood fascinate the eye at every step in solitude profound'.

After a century, many changes. The glens are no longer open to tourists. But one perfect June evening with friends of the 'Barney' Art Group, the owner allowing us the freedom of his grounds, we discovered the enchanting ravine which so delighted the poet—and the picnickers. The romantic paths are now deserted, overgrown; we picked our way through flowers and high grasses, startling the birds. Few ever invade their hidden sanctuaries; they sing undisturbed below Scott's Study and carol away to the accompaniment of the singing river. No wonder the poet was in his element.

Devote all the time you can to the Greta and Tees. I felt so sorry one perfect June morning when a coach party of American tourists were emptied at Abbey Bridge and allowed by their courier, who waited watch in hand, exactly three minutes to point their cameras and ciné cameras this way and that. Paradise so near—and opportunity gone for ever. Lunch waited at the 'Morritt Arms'!

Take time to explore Greta woods and Brignall Banks, and little Scargill too. Follow the river to Waters Meet, a heavenly spot, where Tees, rippling, glancing bright over its stony bed, released from its deep graven 'trench of marble' waits impatiently for the Greta to join her. Greta has come down through secret places, in a deep gorge, Rokeby on one hand, Mortham Hall on the other, under creeper mantled Dairy Bridge—where you can look down into sinister depths and dark swirling currents—before being allowed to leap into the sunlight. Mortham Tower is waiting, 'round the corner'.

Lanes come roundabout to this enchanting cul-de-sac, close to the outer limits of Rokeby Park. Paths follow Tees edge all the way from Barney.

If you love water-edge wandering then from Waters Meeting walk Tees, right bank, through the glades called Paradise Walk, where beeches dapple the ferny floor, and it is flowers all the way to Abbey Bridge. Here we cross the river, after taking a closer look at the ruined abbey so near.

Egglestone Abbey with its grey soaring arches, window tracery of diverse periods, and ancient tombs on greensward where once were

Mortham: fortified tower of the Rokebys

pavements of chancel and transepts, where Premonstratensian canons lived under the protection of the earls of Richmond, is a ruin dreaming amid all the pleasant sounds of farm and field. The site above Scargill and Tees is a beautiful one. No wonder many families held it in great respect and chose it for their last resting place. Few tombs remain;

> Peasant hands the tombs o'er threw
> Of Bowes, of Rokeby and Fitz Hugh.

Back to Abbey Bridge. No tolls or tollkeeper's lodges now, the drum tower foundations being turned into giant 'flower pots'. Impressive rock and water scenery below, where Tees is

> Condemned to mine a channelled way
> O'er solid sheets of marble grey.

The left bank path goes on, through woodland and pasture, all the way to Oldmill, the weirs, the Mesnes—and Barney.

'BARNEY' TO TEESDALE HEAD—BY COTHERSTONE, ROMALDKIRK AND MIDDLETON

Two roads go up the valley from Barney to the secondary 'capital', Middleton-in-Teesdale, that on the north side climbing up and over the bare slopes of Marwood Chase, the other—B6277 and the Maud's bus route—linking charming villages.

From Startforth we come to Lartington, a seventeenth century hall amid wonderful trees, and run through open country passing one of two plague stones of 1644. This is the Butter Stone, and across the dale a Bacon Stone, used, we are told, for leaving stores of food for villagers cut off from their neighbours whilst pestilence raged.

At Cotherstone, a smiling hamlet with never a wrinkle on its brow, on a high bank above Tees is a small park called The Hagg. We have already met Fitz Hughs at Ravensworth Castle and seen their tombs at West Tanfield, and Jervaulx and Egglestone abbeys. Here are but scanty ruins of their Tees-side stronghold telling so little of the noble Fitz Hughs who rode out so proudly. One, according to local tradition, returning from the hunt on the steeps of Marwood Chase fell hundreds of feet to the river and horse and rider were dashed to pieces. Fitz Hughs and the Fitz Henrys led Teesdale's men, armed with bills and bows, to war. In Romaldkirk's aisles we shall see where the brave Hugh Fitz Henry, slain in the early Edwardian battles, has his last resting place.

So proud the lords of Ravensworth and Cotherstone once, their memories so fragile now. Five centuries ago, a different story.

> The Baron of Ravensworth prances in pride
> And he views his domains on Arkindale side,
> The mere for his net, and the land for his game,
> The chase for the wild, and the park for the tame;
> Yet the fish of the lake and the deer of the vale
> Are less free to Lord Dacre than Allen-a-Dale.

High hills with bold, rounded heads rise above Balderdale; wander south from Cotherstone and Romaldkirk along deeply cut lanes with primroses and violets in May and bright gold carpets of cowslips on green banks overhanging them, and you are in Hunderthwaite and ready to be wheedled updale nearer and nearer to Goldsborough and Shackleborough. With names like that their tops should be Brigantian hillforts like Addleborough and Ingleborough. Ahead, beyond long reservoirs, the wild bounds of Stainmore!

Over the distant tops 'which raise their solid bastions to the sky' imagine stragglers from skirmishes on Stainmore sweeping down the rough Balderdale tracks. Scott embroidering on the Norse theme visualized Vikings roaring in from the west, fixing on each spot where they settled 'a runic name'. In fact the countryside hereabouts is salted with pithy Norse names, apt, descriptive and very provocative. What of Slack, Wham and How, Rotten Rigg, Nettlepot, Swinket Meas, Wool Ingles* and Nichol Hopple? The Balder river and Wodin Croft intrigued Scott.

A battle in Balderdale; men of Teesdale fighting the forces of Malcolm Canmore of Scotland, the year 1070, the site somewhere near Hunderthwaite, or so tradition says. This tiny hamlet has the last relics of the last ancient thatched farms, though for how long the roof timbers will hold I do not know. The only clamour—barking dogs!

Romaldkirk I think loveliest of Teesdale villages, equal to any of the prettiest and best kept in the dales. Charming houses, side by side, in friendly groups, are disposed around a large green where hay was being baled when I was last there. Old lanes wriggle round its outer edges, and one tumbles down to bridge and river and one to an ancient 'ore ford'. Iron smelting was an early industry around Egglestone which looks at Romaldkirk from across river and county boundary. At the bridge end (they say) was once a chantry where priests offered prayers for wayfarers setting out into dangerous places.

Romaldkirk with Norse name was here long before the Conquest. Malcolm Canmore destroyed it. Again Scots wrought destruction leaving the fine old church to be rebuilt in the thirteenth century. The largest parish—and one of the most sparsely peopled— its boundaries ran with Dufton's far up the Pennine watershed and along all Tees skyline. Once its rector was lord of the manor too.

Inside the church, Hugh Fitz Henry the brave warrior lies quietly in effigy, clad in chain mail. Right of the chancel arch is a splayed hagioscope or squint, left of it the worn steps winding ladderlike to a rood loft no longer there. In the churchyard; gravestones with names of boys who died, unmourned by relatives, in schools like Do-the-Boys Hall. Outside, consecrated ground; in communal graves the dead struck down by 'Almighty God the Plague' three centuries ago. The miller of Egglestone brought home and displayed with pride a bundle of fine clothes he had bought cheap. The dread pestilence was in them. The local villages were stricken; hence the Butter and Bacon Stones where food was left and money disinfected in lime water or vinegar.

Just beyond Romaldkirk we come to Mickleton, crossing into County Durham, and there, flung out on the windy slope, is Middleton. It is a rather bleak hard-bitten village, not unlike Reeth also 'built on lead', its houses of dark gritstone, angular, grouped around open squares. Its rapid growth dates from lead mining in the eighteenth century; its decline, like Reeth's and Grassington's from the last century and cheaper imported ores.

The hunting preserves of the Nevilles of Raby, the land from which the earls of Derwentwater had drawn wealth in minerals, both came eventually to Greenwich Hospital and a newly-formed London Lead Mining Company. They brought prosperity to the dalesfolk, and scarred the face of the lonely fells. Walking over the hills we see relics of mine shops, gaping adits, rifts in the slopes, roofless huts and on the map scores of names all dating from the lead-working period.

A network of roads was flung over the dale head. The mining company needed ways to transport the ore; over from Middleton to Egglestone and Stanhope, up to Langden Beck and over to the barytes mines near Alston, the Lune Forest road by Grains O'Beck to Brough —all were mine roads, all busy with packhorses and waggons.

Being Quakers, the company had a restraining hand; they put up the public buildings, encouraged learning and sobriety, kept down the 'drunks'. There is a solid, respectable look about all they built.

Above Middleton—a landscape change. Trees are fewer, those of Park End wood the last survivors of what was the Forest of Teesdale, the dale floor being long ago heavily timbered though the heights

Teesdale farms: English Hill near Langden Beck

were typical open hunting country. South rises Holwick's dark whinstone cliff and bared quarry walls.

Northwards the sunny slopes are dotted with many smiling farms, the houses dazzlingly white walled though stone-flagged roofs and long ranges of gritstone outbuildings are dark. All these Durham white farms anyone will tell a stranger are 'Lord Barnard's', that supplies of whitewash are doled out at regular intervals to tenants, that such has been the case ever since an ancestor, a duke of Cleveland, was humiliated when lost hereabouts being refused hospitality when he knocked at a farm door and a farmer, not one of his tenants, turned him away. "Never again", he swore. "All my properties will be clearly distinguished from the rest. Whitewashed!" And a practical tenant of today will add, "And so all the farms have been well preserved."

Cheerful they look, very well cared for amid their green pastures and enclosed meadows, some with provocative names like Hard Struggle, a neighbour of Brockersgill where we once stayed. At close quarters they are even pleasanter, porches festooned with roses and clematis, old fashioned flowers, especially the scented kind under their windows. Every window frames a heart raising picture. "And I never get tired of looking at it", says the farmer's wife.

Walking the older and higher level road parallel with the highway from Middleton to Newbiggin, we have the same wide views. The Tees loops its valley holms, the margin white pebbles; beyond is a long hollow, the line of a glacial trough. One summer day we saw the river margined in pure gold and wondered what flowers were growing there; too late for sallow willow flowers, too high for mimulus, too bright a yellow for the golden globe flower. Dropping to river level the bloom we discovered was the yellow shrubby cinquefoil, a rare plant. But Teesdale is full of precious rarities. A land of flowers! I remember rounded knolls low in Balderdale carpetted with cowslips, and pastures above Holwick gold-washed with acres of troilus—and a suitable habitat if this was indeed the 'trolls' flower' named by Norse settlers.

In the Victorian heyday for trippers high waggonettes carried hundreds every summer day from Middleton to High Force. Later a little local bus served the same purpose, dropping us by the High Force Hotel, near the gate to the gorge and the falls.

STONES AND WATER: ROCK SCENERY
AND ROARING FORCES

Being a Must for every seeker after the grand in scenery, High Force draws the crowds; for two centuries it has been Teesdale Number One Scenic Beauty Spot. But do not let that be off-putting; it is worth seeing, and coming many miles to see, though it is 'nothing but rocks and water'.

School children are brought by the coachload to gaze on the mighty spectacle. First awe soon over they scramble up and over rocks, leap across pools; mixed parties 'show off', that is the boys perform monkey tricks and the girls squeal with real or simulated alarm. My first visit coincided with such an invasion. Some girls shrieked, "Adders!" A stampede for the path followed, screams almost drowning the thunder of the falling waters. My next visit was more to my liking, all deserted, in the quiet of evening. How the force thundered then.

We are all so familiar with pictures of High Force, the channel of stone, the architectural masses of rock, the columnar portals of whinstone, so hard it has withstood the battering of eons of raging water which is hurled 70 feet into a cauldron-like and sinister pool. We look downriver, along the gorge, and wonder just how long the river has been eating its way back from the outlet, the first high ledge over which Tees leapt in the beginning of time.

For walkers only; come from the south side of Middleton bridge by the Tees bank path which conveniently cuts across the horseshoe bends making for Park End—the old forest land—and finally, after 4 miles, allows you to cross at Winch Bridge near Low Force; or, still on the Yorkshire bank for another 1 ¼ miles, by the footbridge below Holwick Head House. An alternative is the pleasant and direct lane three miles uphill from Middleton Bridge, south end, to the great rocky whinsill cliffs of Holwick—it stands high though the name means a dairy farm, Norse style, in a hollow—and, where the surfaced road ends, work down through the greenest of pastures, by smiling farms, to either of the two Tees bridges, the second below Holwick Lodge leaving less main road walking to the Force.

Lost, deserted, forgotten villages; do they intrigue you? There is one off the Holwick lane, its site a tumble of grassy mounds, its name out of the distant past is—Unthank.

Whether you think of High Force as the end of all things or a beginning, it is without doubt a break. The landscape above is a 'majesty of nothingness' a wide, bare bowl rimmed by blue mountains, somewhat akin to the vast open spaces in Mayo or Galway. There is a Paul Henry quality about it, especially on a spring day which turns mountains to deep blue and the herbage of the hollows to pale gold. The road is open to all winds; the motorist does not notice this, but on foot the barren wasteland can strike appalling. This is the geologist's and botanist's paradise; no dale head in Britain is quite like it. Small wonder all Britain protested when I.C.I. planned to flood this area—the protectionists and conservation bodies v. I.C.I. The needs of industry won ! I remember the pride of a Teesdale man (a keen botanist) as his arm swept from Cronkley and Widdybank to the dale head. "No place anywhere like it for flowers. I could show you damp spots over yonder, blue with gentians. . . ." He told us of other rare finds too, as he said, "likelier to be found inside Arctic Circle."

Two centuries ago botanists began to converge upon upper Tees nosing by beck, sike, in rock slit and bog margin, seeking out rare flora found only here. At the end of the last glacial period peat bogs began to accumulate along the edge of the ice field and plants happiest in sub-Arctic conditions continued to grow along the haggs. They still do, after years of despoilers who uproot and carry away 'specimens' to gardens where they cannot possibly survive.

Gentians, vernal gentians ! One blissful morning in early June we searched over the windswept wedge between Tees and Langden Beck. We were down on our knees at the first glimpse of deep blue. It was a discarded scrap of paper, thrown out by some picnicker from a bag of crisps ! Later we were rewarded; a cuckoo shouted, curlews called and wailed in the immensity above and the river laughed over its grey stones—and we sat and rejoiced as we looked on flowers of the purest, richest blue. There were others also, masses of primula farinosa in damp places, butterwort, and dancing mountain pansies.

At Langden Beck, a community with hotel, youth hostel and a

scattering of farms, a last outpost where out goes the very high highway to Alston, B6277, was a point where in lead-mining days processions of packponies, the jaggers laden with panniers of ore, a bell horse leading and a 'heeler' dog bringing up the rear, came to a halt and rested. Now buses and coaches change gears and go upwards with noise and fumes; and how the fells resent their intrusion, getting their own back during the fierce winters.

Here walkers cross bridge and beck, making along the old mine track towards Widdybank and Cauldron Snout, a way once gated but now supplied with grids. It is a desolate and rough way, especially beyond the last sign of man's handiwork at the old derelict mine shop. Half an hour's trudge to the meeting of the Tees with Maize Beck—then be prepared for a spectacle grander than any yet seen, all the more impelling by its isolation. 'Shut out of the world amid scenes of savage beauty, the sense of remoteness begets a profounder admiration of the natural scene,' as a Victorian guide put it. True enough.

High Force has a far higher—or longer—single plunge but here at Cauldron Snout where the Tees changes character with remarkable rapidity, still waters running deep in a long brown pool then—without warning—quickening, go tearing through an imprisoning rift of dark columnar basalt and hurling over the fell rim in perpetual fury and the flurry of white spray. From far off the Snout looks like skeins of white silk, strands of lamb's wool, or, in sunlight, silver threads. At close quarters we see it as a succession of cataracts falling, plunging, recoiling upon itself and continuing to do so for no less than 200 feet.

No swarms of squealing children, no coach parties in cocked hats —probably no one at all to intrude. If you like your waterfall viewing all to yourself Cauldron Snout is for you.

Why does the water come down so? The fell edge shows the native rock—call it whin, whinsill, basalt or dolerite—iron hard, resisting the graving power of water, providing the Tees with a black staircase fit for the halls of a mountain giant of a king. The Whinstone also gave High Force its long trench of shining rock, it is exposed on Cronkley Fell and is worked in the quarries near Middleton.

Bewildering boundaries wander above the Snout and the pool of The Weel. Tees from Snout to its fountain source below the high cap of Cross Fell is the Durham-Westmorland border. West of the young river is the wide-cast parish of Dufton, Birkdale Farm its loneliest outlier. Hardy walkers make for 'Bir'dl' and Maize Beck; they can well believe tales of the long winter sieges the occupiers have to endure, the large food stocks built up for weeks of isolation—and how, desperate with loneliness, the farmwife of the past has downed tools and off on pony back to taste the gay life of Middleton or Barney. They are faced beyond Bir'dl with the most sensational Pennine crossing—the mighty rift called High Cup Nick, where if the good saint really banished the evil spirits and devils from the mountain he must have sentenced them to eternal torment. From the Nick the descent is to Dufton and a delectable land called the Vale of Eden.

Tees rises in a well basin on the reedy, rushy plateau below the summit of Fiends Fell which the saint renamed from the cross set upon it. It is cool, clear water welling up through fine sand; cold strong breezes blow on the hottest days in summer. Then, looking east, we watch the thin trickling of Tees over lower slopes drenched with haze, to disappear in dreamy unreality into a glimmering dale below.

Scott must never have stood at the beginning.

> Tees in tumult leaves his source
> Thund'ring o'er Cauldron and High Force.

There is a melancholy quiet, not tumult, on Cross Fell shoulder. The young Tees bides its time before making a stir in the northern landscape. It is compelled to do some falling and tumbling to lose 2,000 feet in less than 20 miles—as we well know if determined to walk and not stray from the river banks.

Seven

ROUTE-MAKING THROUGH THE DALES

1. Castles and Abbeys Tour

THIS A COMPREHENSIVE tour with nine major castles, as many abbeys, and much more, in 100 miles. A feast for countrygoers. As most castles have busy market towns about them all are linked by bus services. So all may enjoy this 'Grand Historic Tour'.

From Yorkshire—leave the towns by Aire or Wharfe making for Skipton or Bolton Bridge, there to join travellers out of Lancashire. Harewood Castle of the Romillys and Kirkstall Abbey of De Lacy foundation are links with dales' history.

From Lancashire—travellers from Liverpool and Preston on A59, or from Manchester, Bolton and Blackburn on A666, meet near Whalley (Cistercian fourteenth to sixteenth centuries abbey ruins) and go on to Clitheroe Castle (Norman De Lacy's twelfth to seventeenth centuries). North up Ribblesdale to Sawley Abbey (Percys, Cistercian twelfth to sixteenth centuries), to Gisburn and over to Aire and Skipton (castle of Norman Romillys, eleventh to twelfth centuries, Cliffords, fourteenth to seventeenth centuries) and 6 miles beyond to Bolton Priory (Augustinian twelfth to sixteenth centuries). A59 continues by the ancient highway over Blubberhouses into the Forest of Knaresborough through Harrogate to Knaresborough with a ruined castle above Nidd (Norman Serlo and royal princes, eleventh to fourteenth centuries). Northwards on bylanes above the Nidd, or the highway A61, we reach Fountains Abbey (Cistercian, twelfth to sixteenth centuries) with seventeenth century Fountains Hall nearby. Back to A61 and Ripon for the magnificent minster (St. Wilfred's, twelfth to fifteenth centuries. Just out of the area of this book but worth seeing whilst so near, are West Tanfield church and castle of the Marmions, as we take A6108 up the Ure valley to Masham and Middleham Castle (Breton lords and the Nevilles, twelfth to fifteenth centuries) near which are Jervaulx Abbey (Cistercian, twelfth to sixteenth centuries) and Coverham Abbey (Premonstratensian, thirteenth to sixteenth centuries).

Work up Wensleydale and byways north side to Wensley, Redmire and Castle Bolton for the sake of the splendid fortalice raised by the Scropes (fourteenth to seventeenth centuries). A high level byway due north crosses into Swaledale; not far downriver from Grinton (Mother Church of the Dale) are Marrick Priory (Benedictine nuns), Ellerton Abbey (Cistercian sisters), both in fragmentary ruin and only 5 miles upriver from Richmond.

Richmond Castle (Breton lords, earls of Richmond and Brittany, royal princes and dukes, eleventh to seventeenth centuries) looks down on Easby Abbey (Premonstratensian, twelfth to sixteenth centuries).

To Tees; north through Gilling (once a great hall of noble thanes,

Anglian and Danish earls, and kings) but leave Roman Watling Street, A66, by narrow lanes to discover Ravensworth where Danish thanes and the Norman Fitz Hughs had a castle. Back to A66, descend to Greta Bridge, round the park limits of Rokeby Hall and turn to Dairy Bridge to track down Mortham Hall, another fourteenth-century fortified manor house, most impressive. On the way to 'Barney' is Egglestone Abbey, (Premonstratensian, twelfth to sixteenth centuries). Across the Tees in County Durham is Barnard Castle (Norman Ballieuls, Baloils, Nevilles, Richard III, eleventh to seventeenth centuries). Raby Castle of the Nevilles (fourteenth to eighteenth centuries) is 6 miles east.

ON TO THE BORDER

This string on which so many precious jewels are strung might well be used *en route* for Scotland, east side of the Pennines on A68, the Carter Bar highway, or on the Great North Road. When making for the Lakes or the Border at Carlisle cross from Greta Bridge to the west Pennines and call in at Bowes Castle and Brough Castle each on guard over Stainmoor Pass, gaze at Clifford's feudal pile over-looking Eden at Appleby, and take time off to wander around Brougham Castle (Cliffords' after Veteriponts, twelfth to seventeenth centuries) on Eamont side and Penrith Castle's red sandstone ruins watching over the meeting of many roads.

TO COMPLETE A ROUND TOUR TO LANCASTER

To complete a round tour and back to Lancashire from Barnard Castle, cross to Stainmore Pass and Brough, travel down Eden to Kirkby Stephen and by way of A683, the Lancaster road, link up Wharton Hall (Whartons, Pele and Tudor manor house) with historic places in the Lune valley. There is Middleton Hall (Middletons, fourteenth-century pele with later hall within barmkyn walls), Kirkby Lonsdale, and southwards, Thurland Castle (demolished by Crom-well's troops, within a moat) and Hornby Castle (twelfth to eighteenth centuries, Harringtons after the early lords Stanley and lords Monteagle and the 'infamous Colonel Charteris').

Lancaster has grown up about the castle (Roman site, Norman lords, John o' Gaunt, earls and dukes of Lancaster, the Crown, span-ning every century from the twelfth to the twentieth), with the priory adjoining now the parish church. Away across the Lune deeps where the Cocker flows out to the sea, are the lonely ruins of Cocker-sand Abbey where only the chapter house remains of St. Mary-in-the-Marsh (Premonstratensian, twelfth to sixteenth centuries). Barnard Castle—Lancaster : 59 miles.

2. Hitting the High Spots: Along the Pennine Roof Top

The Pennine Way for hillwalkers strides north through sunshine, strong winds and cloudwrack from Derbyshire to the Border. At many points on the highways heading for Skipton, Malham, Hawes,

Muker, Tan Hill, Stainmore and the northern giants, the neatly carved Pennine Way sign points the 'followers' over the roads, their nailed boots striking sparks, and away they are off, like greyhounds unleashed, across heather, bracken and peat mosses where their feet sink deep and make no sound.

If the motorist so minds he can abandon his car and away after them at a score of points. Or he may dream of unattainable summits, sigh, and proceed as near as maybe.

This route demands good driving, steady passengers. In part it takes in good B and classified roads; the rest rides high on the many adequately surfaced 'unclassifieds' which were until 1950 rough fell roads, but the Milk Marketing Board and farmers' inclination to cars has changed all that.

Leaving the south-east Lancashire towns for the Calder Valley and Colne, and the West Riding towns for their East Calder and West Calder route crossing the Cliviger watershed for Burnley and Colne, the high spots are soon attained. From Bradford and Leeds strike west for Haworth and the high level Trawden moor road to Colne. From Wakefield, Dewsbury, Huddersfield, Halifax, make for Hebden Bridge, there to climb into the sky-ey places on the Long Causeway, by Slack, Widdop Moors and on to Colne, in the heart of the Lancashire Pennines.

From 'bonny Colne in the hills' use the Old Skipton Road, the coaching way of the past, north to Lothersdale, beyond which turn to Elslack from the crossroads. Dropping swiftly to the green low country strike out for A56 (Manchester and south Lancashire traffic) and bridge the short gap into A59 (Liverpool, Preston and west Lancashire traffic) and much road widening.

By the 'Bull' at Broughton a short hill road makes north for Gargrave on the Aire. Prospects of England's backbone, rocky and knobbly, ahead; tremendous mental and spiritual uplift I hope! The best of the north lies before us.

Follow the signposts to Kirkby Malham, Malham village and the staggering scenic impact of the Craven Fault at close quarters.

Zigzagging byways strain up from The Cove to The Tarn. To reach Littondale: the Arncliffe road by Darnbrook, or go west towards Penighent which broods head in clouds, and turn north for Penighent Gill, and Halton Gill lying low below great swart fells near dale head. Walkers and travellers of the past, took that fearsome packway over Horse Head to Raisgill by young Wharfe. Cars must go downdale by Litton and Hawskwick into the Kettlewell Road, B6160, strike away up Wharfedale to Kettlewell and Buckden where to reach the rooftops it is bowling along the length of Langstrothdale and the summit on Fleet Moss at 1,852 feet. What bald beasts lie in wait, great leonine mountain giants, head on paws.

A slow, low-gear crawl down Sleddale to Gayle and Hawes. A breather, a glance at the Ure river, then we are hurled upwards to Buttertubs Pass, 1,726 feet, and thrown down as steeply to Thwaite very near Muker and the Swale.

A choice: by lone Birkdale and Tailbrigg Hill, 1,698 feet, to Kirkby Stephen and north by Eden to Brough; or from Keld the exciting road up to sky-high Tan Hill inn, 1,732 feet, and down the fell wall to Barras and Brough.

A mile or so out of Brough on the Stainmore highway A66, a road forks across to Lune Forest, the wild land where is all the 'majesty of nothingness', at the foot of the highest mountains. The stark horse-shoe of Mickle Fell crags is very near, and Cross Fell, the highest Pennine summit, behind it. This fell road, B6276, runs by Grains o' Beck to Lune Dale and Middleton-in-Teesdale.

B6277, the mountain highway from Barnard Castle to Alston, proceeds innocently enough updale—above the gorge of High Force—to Langden Beck, where explorers strike away to Widdybank to find the ultra-sensational Cauldron Snout. The next 22 miles are the highest riding on northern highroads, at Yad Moss reaching 1,962 feet. In winter it does not reach this point; snowdrifts bar the way. Alston, the highest market town, seems to ride the watershed though a thousand feet below; five wild roads converge upon it, the most exhilarating our way out to the plains, or the Lakes, over Hartside—where at almost 1,900 feet we stop on the brink. Others too; surprised.

And there we take stock. With the garden of Eden valley far below and the magic mountains before and behind us we ought to give thanks that, being northern, all this is ours.

3. Walkers Only; Grass Underfoot

Walkers' special; where wheels cannot go. Walkers cross the tracks of car-users at many points in the 'Castle and Abbey Tour' and when 'Hitting the Highspots' on the roof of England. This route is one with variations; it is possible to walk from dale to dale with hardly ever doing more than cross over a surfaced road, with grass and turf beneath the feet for day after day, which is what the fell walker needs to be perfectly happy.

STRIDING NORTH; FROM SKIPTON TO KELD: 50 MILES

Maps needed. Sheets 96, 90 and 84 of the Ordnance Survey. From Skipton and Airedale to Embsay (frequent buses), path from church to Easby, fieldpath to Halton East and unfenced byway to Bolton Priory. On Wharfe banks, east or west, to Strid, and Barden Bridge; path on east bank to Burnsall—with a digression to Appletreewick *en route*. From Burnsall hug the wateredge to Grassington; or—over pastures to discover Thorpe, over the lynchets to Linton, and church path to stepping stones by Linton church, and over to Grassington.

Upriver again, by Ghaistrills or through Grass Woods, and on to Conistone. Lane walking if on east side of river, but from west bank footpaths to Kettlewell bridge. Water-edge, west side, updale to lane near Hubberholme or cut east to Buckden. Follow the Rake (Roman road) above Cray hamlet to Kidstones Pass. Wharfedale is left behind on the rough stony track climbing to The Stake.

Now towards Wensleydale: many paths down towards Stalling Busk and enchanted Semerwater, and river Bain leads to Bainbridge. Short cut church paths head across Ure to Askrigg. North of Askrigg find paths into the fell road which goes over to Swaledale, to Reeth or Gunnerside. Cars cannot go your way if you chose the right fork to Reeth and the first left fork into Summerlodge Gill—very rough—and down to Crackpot, and Gunnerside bridge.

Swaledale: upriver from Gunnerside, either low level by Ivelet or high level by the old 'Corpse Road', each keeping parallel with the Swale. Curve with the river to Swinnergill and so to Keld.

To Eden: by the stripling Swale to Birkdale and over the watershed to Nateby Common and Kirkby Stephen.

To Tees: follow the beck in Stonesdale to Tan Hill—then choose your course to Greta and Stainmore and the valley beyond.

WALKING ON THE WATERSHEDS; NOT THE
PENNINE WAY, BUT PARALLEL

From Lancashire and A59 or A56, walkers make for Gargrave on the Aire. From East Marton (A59) or Thornton (A56) walk north by the canal towpath and/or the accompanying bylanes as far as the Aire. North from Gargrave an old lane makes for Bell Busk, and from this paths cross low hill ridges to the Malham road—the blue pool, Eshton Tarn, being a waymark near this highway. Follow the east side of the young Aire—Pennine Way signs—to Airton, Kirkby and Malham village. So by The Cove paths, climb above to The Tarn and Malham Moor; choice of many paths.

Over to Littondale; by paths to Stangill and down to Darnbrook, and follow Cowside Beck to Arncliffe. Or, keep high from Tarn and Middle House on limestone pastures between Parsons Pulpit and the precipitous cliffs of Yew Cogar Scar; look out for wandering bulls. Or strike from Street Gate north-eastwards for Great Close and High Mark, a lonely crossing to Cote Gill between Arncliffe and Hawkswick Clowders to the Skirfare.

Over to Wharfedale: from Arncliffe and Hawkswick steep paths climb to Old Cote Moor, and descents are either to Starbotton, or down The Slit—a crack in the limestone ramparts—to Kettlewell Bridge.

To Coverdale and Wensleydale: take the uphill Cam road and with a climb over the shoulder of Buckden Pike make for Cover Head and Coverdale, paths and tracks farm to farm, or drop down Walden Beck from Walden Head to West Burton. Wensleydale stretches across the feet of both dales. Make for Wensley village; paths through the park and near the Ure lead to Redmire, others go up to Castle Bolton and here high-level fellroads cross to Swale. Old tracks led to mines; many may be followed, or the surfaced fellways taken instead to Grinton.

Alternative route from Malham Tarn: cross Fountains Fell and drop to Penighent Gill head, walk down to Halton Gill there to climb the Horse Head Pass to Raisgill high up the Wharfe; over to Fleet Moss and by Cam Houses near Wharfe and Ribble sources to Ribblehead; or Wether Fell to Bainbridge; or forward down Sleddale to Hawes. There take the ancient route from Cotterdale to Hell Gill Bridge, to Ure springs and Eden source.

Books to Read

The following I have found invaluable in helping to reconstruct the past. They are in all reference libraries, in most lending libraries and often to be bought in second hand bookshops.

The journals of George Fox and John Wesley; both were tireless travellers, preaching and teaching in the dales.

Both Wordsworth and Sir Walter Scott knew the dales. In his notes on the poems 'The White Doe of Rylstone' and the 'Force of Prayer' Wordsworth has much to say about Wharfedale as he knew it. Read the poems too. Scott put Teesdale and 'Greta banks' firmly on the tourist maps with Rokeby; poem and notes about his correspondence with the owner of Rokeby Hall are valuable if you are Teesdale bound.

Dorothy Wordsworth's Journal has some pleasant descriptive passages on journeys with her brother and sister-in-law through Wensleydale.

Dr. Whitaker delved deep into the past when compiling his histories of Craven and Richmondshire; he includes detailed family and parish histories with occasional passages on the dales as he knew them in the late eighteenth century. He goes great guns about the encroaching hand of industry.

Scores of minor writers inflicted dairies or journals of their Tours to the Lakes or The Dales on their friends at home. Thomas Gray— by no means a minor writer—sent letters to his friend who had been unable to share his visit to the Lakes. Returning south through Craven, he left for us clear pictures of the countryside in the 1760s. I read another account of dales travels in *Gleanings in Craven*, written by Frederic Montague in 1839. Highly diverting! His dangerous journeys required a guide and he carried a pistol!

William Cobbett's *Rural Rides* brought him into Wensleydale in the 1840s; Charles Kingsley as guest at Malham Tarn House gathered background material for *Water Babies*, and John Ruskin later for his *Proserpina*; both delightful in different ways to lovers of Malhamdale.

Walter White's *Month in Yorkshire* (in 1858) is my favourite. He is lucid in his writing, clear sighted, not given to over-praise, not too concerned about histories out of books—probably he had none to consult—and far more modern in his language and outlook than the indefatigable Speight and Bogg who followed some decades after.

These two Yorkshire wanderers who belonged to the great walking and cycling age read all the existing histories, they rambled in all weathers, and with friends who were artists, geologists, botanists, and bird-lovers to collaborate produced dozens of volumes. They must have chased each other round the dales, Harry Speight collecting material for *Complete Accounts of History, Antiquities and Scenery in Picturesque Valleys* and Edmund Bogg ten years behind him concentrating on *Description of Picturesque Features, History, Antiquities, Rare Architecture, Tradition, Old World Story and Also the Flora*. Their photographs give a dark and gloomy picture of the dales, the highspots in each being little girls' white starched 'pinnys' and small boys' high white collars; their dalesfolk, male and female, all look very fierce or very melancholy.

They must have had endless enjoyment. We must envy them the empty roads—but not the clouds of white dust—and the pioneering zeal which sent them wheeling. Their illustrators, too, went about with sketch book, paint box and camera, equally zealous. They were quite early in the field of 'fully illustrated' topographical works. Their book titles show they left not one corner of the dales unseen, from Eden, Lune and Ribble to the six rivers slowing down in the Plains of York.

Among more localized books are Harker's *Grassington*, Crowther's *Silver Gars*, Bishop's *My Moorland Patients*—about the Mashamshire backwoods. In fact some local antiquarian or historian has written up something about every aspect of his own special part of the dales.

For geology I find H.M.S.O. publication, the *Pennines and Adjacent Areas*, invaluable.

Library shelves are lined with books written by twentieth century livers-in, and lovers-of, the dales, and by those who feel they belong to the dales and the dales belong to them. With me, being a daleswoman, I had to share with others my love of the land which bred my forbears.

In *Three Rivers* and *Off to the Dales*, in the Craven half of *West Pennine Highway*, in the Yorkshire half of *Lancashire Countrygoer* I was able to express much of what I felt for the Pennine Country. This is a concentrate of what I appreciate most in the dales—my personal pleasures.

Four years after this book was first published its western companion, *Countrygoers' North*, appeared. *Countrygoer in the Dales* follows the east-running Pennine dales; the second book follows those westwards: the Eden and Lune valleys, Garsdale, Ravenstonedale, Dentdale, Lyvennet and Eamont, and takes in the exciting fell country from Stainmore and Cross Fell to Shap, to the mountain masses of east Cumberland and Westmorland.

The two books taken together encompass what is for me the best of the North.

Index

A

Addleborough, 101, 118, 137
Airedale, 20, 29, 35f., 211, 214, 215
Aire Gap, 20, 35, 51, 191
Airton, 19, 35, 37, 215
Aisgill, 141
Alexander III, King of Scotland, 194
Alston, 190, 204, 207, 217
Angles, 19, 20, 35, 38, 60, 84, 101,
    114, 146, 149, 150, 183
Angram, 83, 95, 97
Appersett, 140
Appleby, 27, 28, 212
Appletreewick, 50, 58f., 214
Aram, Eugene, 88, 96
Arkengarthdale, 147, 167, 166f., 179
Arncliffe, 44, 68-72, 76, 213, 215
Arthur, King, 154
Aske family, 108, 145, 160, 180
Askrigg, 129f., 132, 155
Attermire, 43, 46
Augustinians, 50, 147, 211
Aysgarth, 132, 137f.

B

Bainbridge, 112-15, 132, 215, 216
Bain river, 111, 215
Balderdale, 202f.
Baldwin apples, 30
Baliols (Ballieuls), 183, 194, 212
Bank Newton, 30
Bannockburn, Battle of, 24, 51, 195
Barden Bridge, 57, 214
Barden Tower, 25, 27, 57, 58
Barnard, Lords, 184, 186, 188, 190,
    204
Barnard Castle, 101, 104, 179, 183,
    185-8, 212, 214
Barnet, Battle of, 104
Barnoldswick, 31, 85
Barras, 192, 214
Bastow Wood, 73

Beamsley, 50, 53, 55, 90
Beckermonds, 79, 80
Bedale, 105, 133
Bell Busk, 36
Bellerby, 158
Benedictines, 211
Bensons, 34
Bewerley, 91
Birkdale (Swale), 155, 178
Birkdale (Tees), 207, 214, 215
Bishopdale, 110, 116f., 118
Bland family, 50, 60
Blore Heath, Battle of, 103
Blubberhouses, 53, 54, 90, 211
Bolton Bridge, 53, 54f., 55, 90, 211
Bolton Hall, 123, 124
Bolton on Swale, 159
Bolton Priory, 19, 25, 37, 40, 50-53,
    75, 149, 211, 214
Bordley, 40, 45
Bosworth Field, Battle of, 104
Bowes, 190, 197f., 212
Bowes Museum, 187
Bracewell, 31
Brandon, Lady Eleanor, 25, 26
Breton earls, 146, 148, 150, 164, 211
Brigantes, 101, 113, 159, 165
Brompton on Swale, 165
Bronze Age, 35, 45, 66, 80, 191
Brough, 179, 190, 195, 212, 214
Brougham, 27, 28, 29, 212
Broughton, 31f., 32, 35
Bruce, Robert, 85, 88, 92
Buckden, 54, 67, 76-7, 117, 213
Burn river, 98, 152f.
Burnsall, 54, 60f., 214
Burtersett, 138
Buttertubs Pass, 55, 172, 213
Byland Abbey, 94, 96, 106, 131

C

Caldbergh, 120, 134
Calton, 38

Penhill, 117, 120, 136
Penrith, 211
Penighent, 44, 213
Penighent Gill, 44, 71, 213, 216
Percys, 21, 49, 77, 80, 84, 85, 104, 121, 126, 211
Pilgrimage of Grace, 26, 50, 108, 126, 160
Premonstratensians, 105, 211
Preston family, 50, 59
Preston-under-Scar, 122, 158
Prior Moon, 40, 52

R

Raby Castle, 103, 104, 184, 188
Raisgill, 77, 216
Ramsgill, 84, 96
Ravenstonedale, 190, 191, 196
Ravensworth, 101, 180, 184
Raydale, 112, 116
Redmire, 123f., 155, 158, 215
Reetih, 122, 145, 155, 157, 158, 164f., 165f., 169, 215
Rey Cross, 192f.
Ribblesdale, 46, 53, 210
Richard I, King of England, 84, 195
Richard II, King of England, 86, 117, 124, 128, 129
Richard III, King of England, 25, 103, 126, 128, 184, 187
Richmond, 101, 145, 148-55, 211
Earls of, 148-55, 185, 212
Ripley, 92f., 109
Ripon, 101, 132, 211
Rising of the North, 50, 104
Robin Hood, 95
Rokeby Hall, 184, 199f., 212
Romaldkirk, 202f.
Romans, 19, 33, 46, 74, 75, 91, 101, 113, 115, 146, 159, 165, 193
Romillys, 19, 22-4, 32, 50, 61, 148, 211
Rupert, Prince, 32, 55
Ruskin, John, 19, 42, 53, 110, 137
Rylstone, 46, 50, 53

S

St. Alban's, Battle of, 25
St. Helen's Well, 36
St. Mary le Gill, 31, 33
St. Robert's Cave, 84, 86
St. Simon's Chapel, 119

St. Wilfred, 60, 101, 123, 211
Sawley Abbey, 29, 46, 211
Scaleber, 46
Scargill, 75
Scar House, 78
Scots raids, 21, 23, 24, 35, 51, 75, 86, 92, 106, 159, 178, 187, 195
Scott, Walter, 188, 199f.
Scotton, 92
Scriven Hall, 92
Scropes, 102, 123-6, 133, 147, 159, 211
Sedbusk, 138
Semerdale, 111-16
Semerwater, 27, 111, 113, 116
Sheep breeding, 127, 139
Shepherd Lord, 25, 57
Shipton, Mother, 86f.
Skipton, 20-29, 46, 53, 89, 101, 113, 148, 211, 212
Skirfare river, 70f., 215
Skyrakes, 36
Skyreholm, 59
Skyrethorns, 65
Sleddale, 110f., 213, 216
Slingsbys, 84, 89, 92
Snaizeholm, 111
Snape Castle, 133
Spital inns, 196
Staindrop, 188, 189
Stainforth, 44
Stainmoor, 165, 167, 179, 183, 191-7, 212, 213, 214, 215
Stake, the, 27, 110, 116, 215
Stalling Busk, 116, 215
Starbotton, 27, 76f.
Stockdale, 46
Stone Gappe, 34
Stone Raise, 113
Stonesdale, 215
Streatlam Castle, 184
Strid, 56, 214
Stump Cross cavern, 91
Summerlodge Gill, 92, 215
Swainby Abbey, 105
Swaledale, 145-80, 211, 213, 215
Swales family, 145, 147, 164, 166
Swinithwaite, 132
Swinnergill, 92, 215

T

Tailbrigg Hill, 155, 178, 214, 215
Tan Hill inn, 155, 178f., 190, 213, 214